Renegotiating Postmemory

Dialogue and Disjunction:
Studies in Jewish German Literature, Culture, and Thought

Series Editors:
Erin McGlothlin (*Washington University in St. Louis*)
Brad Prager (*University of Missouri*)

Renegotiating Postmemory

The Holocaust in Contemporary German-Language Jewish Literature

Maria Roca Lizarazu

CAMDEN HOUSE
Rochester, New York

First published 2020
by Camden House

Camden House is an imprint of Boydell & Brewer Inc.
668 Mt. Hope Avenue, Rochester, NY 14620, USA
www.camden-house.com
and of Boydell & Brewer Limited
PO Box 9, Woodbridge, Suffolk IP12 3DF, UK
www.boydellandbrewer.com

ISBN-13: 978-1-64014-045-5
ISBN-10: 1-64014-045-X

Library of Congress Cataloging-in-Publication Data

Names: Roca Lizarazu, Maria, 1985– author.
Title: Renegotiating postmemory : the Holocaust in contemporary German-
   language Jewish literature / Maria Roca Lizarazu.
Description: Rochester, New York : Camden House, 2020. | Series: Dialogue and
   disjunction : studies in Jewish German literature, culture & thought | Includes
   bibliographical references and index.
Identifiers: LCCN 2019051200 | ISBN 9781640140455 (hardback) | ISBN
   9781787446731 (pdf)
Subjects: LCSH: German literature—Jewish authors—History and criticism. |
   Holocaust, Jewish (1939–1945), in literature. | German literature—21st cen-
   tury—History and criticism.
Classification: LCC PT169 .R63 2020 | DDC 830.9/8921296—dc23
LC record available at https://lccn.loc.gov/2019051200

This publication is printed on acid-free paper.

Printed and bound in Great Britain by TJ International Ltd, Padstow, Cornwall

Contents

Acknowledgments

THIS BOOK DEVELOPED from doctoral research that I undertook at the University of Warwick's German department from 2013 to 2017. It was thanks to the Early Career Fellowship scheme at the Institute of Advanced Study, University of Warwick, as well as the Sylvia Naish Postdoctoral Fellowship scheme at the Institute of Modern Languages Research, London, that I had the time and resources to develop the initial project further and write this book. It was during an Early Career Fellowship at the University of Birmingham, funded by the Leverhulme Trust, that I was able to dedicate myself fully to the completion of this manuscript. I would like to also acknowledge both the Association for Jewish Studies (AJS) and the Association for German Studies in Great Britain and Ireland (AGS), each of which awarded me a generous publication subsidy for this book.

This research and I have benefited enormously from the advice and support of many colleagues in and outside of Warwick; first and foremost Anne Fuchs, who has accompanied, inspired, and encouraged the development of this book from its earliest stages. I am also very grateful to my former colleagues Christine Achinger and Helmut Schmitz, who read through and helpfully commented on earlier drafts of this project. Mary Cosgrove, James Hodkinson, Jim Jordan, and Linda Shortt have also all contributed to the growth and success of my research. Mark Philp from the History Department at Warwick and Alison Ribeiro de Menezes from Warwick's Hispanic Department also deserve my warmest thanks, not least for providing such a vibrant forum for me to think through many aspects of this study in the shape of the Warwick Memory Group. I would furthermore like to express my sincere thanks to Godela Weiss-Sussex and Sara Jones, who have also engaged with this manuscript at various stages and have accompanied, mentored, and encouraged me throughout my postdoctoral career.

I am grateful to Teresa Ludden and the anonymous peer reviewers at *German Life and Letters* who supplied helpful feedback for parts of chapters 1 and 4, which have appeared as "Beyond Unspeakability—Configurations of 'Travelling Trauma' in Contemporary German-Language Literature about the Holocaust," *German Life and Letters* 72, no.4 (October 2019): 499–521, Copyright © 2019, John Wiley and Sons. Permission to reprint this material has been granted by John Wiley and

Sons. The same goes for editors Peter Davies and Helmut Schmitz and the anonymous peer reviewers at Camden House who read an earlier version of parts of chapter 2, which appeared as "Thomas Mann in Furs: Remediations of Sadomasochism in Maxim Biller's *Im Kopf von Bruno Schulz* and *Harlem Holocaust*," *Edinburgh German Yearbook* 11 (2017): 113–31.

Last but not least I would like to extend my gratitude and appreciation to the editorial team at Camden House, specifically the editorial director, Jim Walker; the series editors, Brad Prager and Erin McGlothlin; and the anonymous peer reviewers for the time and effort they have all invested in this book.

I could not have written this book without a support network of friends and family, both in Germany and the UK. I would specifically like to thank my good friend and former Warwick colleague Hanna Schumacher, who has been such an integral part of this project and my life in the UK. I am also indebted to my friend and former colleague Rebekah Vince for innumerable enriching discussions involving this research. Further heart-felt thanks go to Valentina Abbatelli, Cathrin Bengesser, Adelheid Heuwieser, Stephan Ehrig, Irene Dal Poz, Ira Ischebeck, Katharina Karcher, Anahita Keyhani, Sebastian Kirsch, Annika May, Jennifer Lander, Sofia Mercader, Pedro Monteiro, Ken Searle, Uta Caroline Sommer, Sarah Träger, Joseph Twist, and Elisabeth Wallmann, who have all helped out in so many ways.

I dedicate this book to my immediate and extended family: to my mother, Barbara; to my sister, Anna, and my stepfather, Antonio; and to Jochanan, who was always so supportive of my academic work and then sadly could not see me finish this project.

Finally, Fred, even though you were a little late to the party that is this project, your presence in my life has made this process and everything else so much better.

Abbreviations

BS   Binjamin Wilkomirski, *Bruchstücke*

DbG   Vladimir Vertlib, *Das besondere Gedächtnis der Rosa Masur*

DgJ   Maxim Biller, *Der gebrauchte Jude*

DL   Benjamin Stein, *Die Leinwand*

DZ   Bruno Schulz, *Die Zimtläden*

HH   Maxim Biller, *Harlem Holocaust*

IKvBS   Maxim Biller, *Im Kopf von Bruno Schulz*

Q   Eva Menasse, *Quasikristalle*

V   Eva Menasse, *Vienna*

Introduction: Holocaust Memory in the New Millennium—Between Continuity and Change

New Ecologies of Holocaust Memory?
Hypermediation, Overrepresentation, Discursivation

IN A SURVEY COMMISSIONED on the occasion of 2018 Holocaust Memorial Day, the Jewish Claims Conference found substantial gaps in Holocaust knowledge among the adult US population. The subgroup with the least knowledge comprises so-called millennials, that is, people in their early twenties and thirties, among whom 66 percent did not know what Auschwitz was. The situation appears no different in the former perpetrator societies, as has been shown for both Germany and Austria.[2] Interestingly, 89 percent of those consulted in the 2018 study say that they have "definitely heard about the Holocaust";[3] while the knowledge of historical details is thus shrinking, the influence of the Holocaust as a cultural icon and reference point seems undiminished. This suggestion is confirmed by the abundance of Holocaust analogies, comparisons, and images in contemporary culture, which range from frequent Nazi comparisons in the political arena to Holocaust allusions in the context of a number of hotly contested yet widely disparate issues such as animal rights, abortion rights, climate change, or migrants' rights.

This paradoxical mélange of an abundance of images, analogies, and references, on the one hand, and a dwindling factual knowledge of the events, on the other hand, might well be typical of Holocaust memory in the new millennium. The time period since 2000, marked by the dying out of the eyewitness and survivor generation, the hypermediated dynamics of the internet age, and the increasing globalization of memory cultures, has brought about major shifts in Holocaust remembrance and representation that both connect to and differ from earlier, postunification discourses. Some of these changes are mostly quantitative, such as the disappearance of the survivor and eyewitness generation that marks the transition from embodied forms of Holocaust remembrance, based on firsthand accounts, face-to-face encounters, and intrafamilial transmission, to an increasingly mediatized, institutionalized, and globalized cultural memory of the events.[4] As Kirstin Frieden has pointed out, the media and other institutions of cultural memory play a crucial role in this process: "Durch den Wegfall von persönlichen, familiären Tradierungen und einer zugleich nicht unwesentlichen zeitlichen und emotionalen Distanz zu den historischen Ereignissen werden die kulturellen Medien und ihre Deutungen diskursbestimmend."[5] The transformation of personal into cultural memories depends on various media, whose purpose increasingly transcends mere conservation. As the emergence of the so-called Holocaust holograms demonstrates,[6] these cultural media are meant to keep alive, connect, and transmit these memories to future generations, thus expanding and replacing the memorial framework of the family and the face-to-face encounter and aiding the creation of what Sara Jones has termed "mediated remembering communities."[7]

Other changes might indeed be qualitative and cannot be separated from the broader cultural logic of the internet age. As recent criticism in the field of media studies has shown,[8] these new media and "memory ecologies" force us to reconsider common conceptions of experience,[9] memory, and collective identity, since they give rise to a new set of cultural paradigms, governed by the cult(ure) of immediacy, the "connective" turn, or the dynamics of "remediation." In his book *The Culture of Speed* sociologist John Tomlinson traces the emergence of a new condition in the twenty-first century, which differs fundamentally from the machine speed of classical and late modernity. This new culture of "immediacy" is essentially marked by "the apparent 'closure of the gap' separating human desire from its attainment."[10] With the disappearance of this gap, the spaces and temporalities that shape our experiences, subjectivities, and agency will change, along with our ways of thinking about them. Andrew Hoskins calls for a similar recalibration in the realm of collective memory, as a concept that is still too closely modeled on the communicative and distributive patterns of mass media and "broadcast-age thinking."[11] Against this institutionalized idea of collective remembrance, Hoskins proposes a more diffused, "connective" notion of memory,[12] based on the functioning principles of digital media. For Hoskins, the connective turn in the Western world is governed by the incessant production and stream of data as well as the permanent accessibility of internet-capable devices. "Connective" memory is inherently more fluid than its mass-mediated predecessor, and so are the collectives shaped by it. The steady production, tracking, and storage of data produces memory traces that are tied not so much to the agency of individuals or communities but to "the flux of contacts between people and digital technologies and media,"[13] thus calling into question established notions of collective identity. Hoskins also remarks that the "connective" turn fuels specific "'inter-medial' and 'trans-medial' . . . dynamics of old and new media,"[14] which Jay David Bolter and Richard Grusin have termed "remediation."[15] Astrid Erll usefully reformulated "remediation" in terms of literature and cultural studies research:

With the term "remediation" I refer to the fact that memorable events are usually represented again and again, over decades and centuries, in different media. . . . What is known about a war, a revolution, or any other event which has been turned into a site of memory, therefore, seems to refer not so much to what one might cautiously call the "actual events," but instead to a canon of existent medial constructions, to the narratives and images circulating in a media culture.[16]

These cross-media dynamics shaping a "canon of existent medial constructions" are particularly apparent in recent Holocaust discourse. Holocaust representations have arguably entered a new, hypermediated stage,[17] marked by an abundance of mediatized accounts, which have become entangled in an ever more complicated and globalized web of mutual referencing. The interplay of old and new media has fostered a proliferation of icons, images, and signifiers, whose circulation has become increasingly accelerated, decontextualized, fluid, and uncontrollable. The movement of these images and references is governed by a new set of cultural techniques, such as de- and recontextualization, hypertextuality, copy and paste, and the remixing of materials, which have relevance beyond the realm of the ostensibly digital. The turn in both Holocaust and memory studies toward "connective," "travelling," or "unbounded" forms of remembrance,[18] for example, cannot be isolated from the broader digital episteme that underlies these newly emerged descriptive and analytical categories.

Remediated media ecologies do not only give rise to a new set of cultural dynamics and techniques but also contribute to what Andrew Hoskins calls the "post-scarcity culture" of the digital age,[19] marked by media and memorial abundance. These combined developments raise the important question of whether many of the arguments and keywords that dominated German, and, to a lesser extent, global Holocaust discourse in the 1990s and early 2000s, that is, the postunification phase,[20] have been supplanted—or at least supplemented—by new concerns. The prominent catchphrases of "normalization" and "historicization" now appear as a mere prelude to the current issues of representational and memorial routinization and overrepresentation. Have we thus continued the push or even made the leap "beyond normalization" that was implied in Paul Cooke and Stuart Taberner's early 2000s volume on the topic?[21] And how do these developments affect the cornerstones of Holocaust discourse, particularly idea(l)s of authenticity, empathy, and unspeakability?

Whereas debates throughout the 1990s were still very much shaped by "memory contests" that tried to differentiate between appropriate and inappropriate, normal and abnormal forms of remembering and dealing with the past,[22] today's cultures of memory seem to be shaped by a more generous and pluralistic attitude, as has also been noted by Katja Garloff and Agnes Mueller: "instead of 'normalization,' however that might be defined, diversification and heterogeneity became the 'new normal.'"[23] The flip side of this pluralization might, however, be apathy, fueled by a cultural climate in which former contests have been settled via the canonization of a globalized Holocaust memory. The survey quoted above illustrates the paradoxical dynamic resulting from these processes: on the one hand, there is by now a widely shared awareness and consensus (at least in the Western world) that the Holocaust was the major catastrophe of the twentieth century and should "never again" repeat itself. Most people taking part in the survey had "definitely heard" of the Holocaust, and 80 percent agreed that "it is important to continue teaching people about the Holocaust, in part, so it doesn't happen again."[24] At the same time, the canonization of this particular memory narrative seems to hinder deeper engagement with the event, as evidenced by the curious gaps in knowledge of even basic historical details. This might be so precisely because the Holocaust is no longer a controversial or contested but a musealized and thus somehow distant memory. Hence, the fluidity and plurality of unbounded Holocaust memories seems to correspond to an ossification of the images and modes of expression that are available. This has also been observed by Jennifer M. Kapczynski, who denounces the "formulaic quality to contemporary debate, in which current events that seem to echo the Nazi era are processed by means of a predictable set of discursive manoeuvres."[25] This routinization also pertains to media depictions of the event, which have become increasingly clichéd in their reliance on an established iconography of destruction. Arguably, the memory of the Holocaust has become normalized, historicized, and canonized to the extent that the event as such has disappeared in the thicket of representations, routines, and rules. The shift from normalization to overrepresentation has various consequences: what Frieden calls the "Übermacht sprachlich 'dogmatischer' Diskurse und 'festgezurrter' Holocaust-Narrative" provokes feelings of frustration and fatigue—what can we still say about the event that is truly new?[26] Why do we have to learn and talk about the past yet again—can we not simply move on? These sentiments seem to have sparked a crisis of empathy, as has also recently been noted, in a rather provocative manner, by the German-Jewish writer and journalist Mirna Funk:

> Am 27.1 ist der Internationale Gedenktag der Opfer des Nationalsozialismus. Die allgemeine Reaktion auf einen solchen Tag, auf Mahnmäler und bedeutungsschwangere Reden, ist in etwa dieselbe, als sähe man auf Tinder das Selfie eines Typen mit einer Hantel in der Hand. Man swipt eiskalt nach links [swiping left means turning down a potential match on the dating app Tinder].[27]

The process of overrepresentation and -routinization can also have a different outcome, however, sparking a renewed search for and commitment to authenticity and immediacy. This longing arguably pervades Shahak Shapira's controversial *Yolocaust* project, which employed shock tactics to violently shake off people's apathy: on a website entitled *yolocaust.de* (a play on words with "YOLO" = "You only live once," a contemporary reformulation of the old "Carpe Diem"), Shapira collected images from social media accounts, where people were featured in all sorts of "inappropriate" activities (posing for selfies, performing acrobatics, jumping around) during a visit to Berlin's Holocaust Memorial. Movement by the cursor revealed a second photoshopped image that transplanted the same visitors in the same poses inside a concentration camp. Shapira's project was meant to expose and shame the lack of piety and empathy among the general public.[28]

Both Funk's and Shapira's interventions point to an important new development, which could be described as a metamemorial shift in Holocaust discourse. Rather than engaging the past as such, it concerns itself with the cultural conventions, discourses, and tropes that shape our access to the events, increasingly scrutinizing the by now established culture of memorialization. While debates in the era of "memory contests" were still very much driven by the perceived need to remember, and by questions of *who* was allowed to remember *what*, recent concerns seem to focus much more on *how* we remember, particularly in relation to the ubiquity and formulaic nature of the memory templates that have been created. While the move from normalization to overrepresentation, which is embedded in the wider culture of hypermediation, thus urges us to reconsider questions of canonization, discursivation, and empathy, Holocaust memory in the new millennium also calls for a metadiscursive reexamination of what Leslie Morris has recently referred to as the "exhausted tropes of testimony, witnessing, belatedness, trauma, postmemory."[29] This is so not least because, alongside empathy, the powerful tropes of authenticity and unspeakability are also being challenged in an age of re- and hypermediation.

Discussions about (un)representability are an integral part of Holocaust discourse and can be traced back to Theodor W. Adorno's famous statement on poetry after Auschwitz and its subsequent reception: "Nach Auschwitz ein Gedicht zu schreiben, ist barbarisch, und das frißt auch die Erkenntnis an, die ausspricht, warum es unmöglich ward, heute Gedichte zu schreiben."[30] While this statement has often been read as a ban on all representations of the Nazi genocide, Adorno's wider argument in "Kulturkritik und Gesellschaft" is more complex: for Adorno, culture is implicated in capitalist exchange and consumption, and therefore in its commodifying logic. This notion of complicity is central for Adorno, who addresses the vexed question of how Auschwitz could have happened in the German *Kulturnation*. Adorno's essay articulates a critique of the bourgeois notions of "Kunstautonomie," which seek to catapult art and culture outside the broader political and social sphere, thereby supposedly shielding it from the dangers of instrumentalization and complicity. Adorno does not, however, simply embrace the opposite position, which denies the possibility of transcending the status quo via art. Instead he argues for a dialectical approach, based on the insight that the notions of culture and criticism cannot possibly be separated from the processes of objectification ("Verdinglichung") that penetrate capitalist society as a whole.[31] They are thus bound to replicate and perpetuate the societal structures in which they emerge, meaning that there is no superior and innocent position from which one can speak. This also explains why it is not only barbaric to write poetry after Auschwitz but even impossible to say so—every word uttered about the event necessarily reproduces the logic and crime of objectification.[32]

Adorno's philosophical analysis of complicity and commodification differs from influential notions of the unspeakable as they have been popularized throughout the 1990s by poststructuralist trauma theorists such as Cathy Caruth, Shoshana Felman, and Dori Laub.[33] These scholars do not necessarily understand trauma in terms of the Holocaust but conceptualize it as a violently disruptive, external event that shatters the ego's coherency and cognitive abilities, making the experience categorically unavailable for conscious processing and representation. Because every conscious representation of this experience is necessarily and irrevocably inadequate, the event can only be accessed obliquely, through the failure of representation. Felman, Laub, and Caruth read the Holocaust in a deconstructivist fashion, as an extreme example of the necessary failure of all modes of referential representation. It is built on the assumption that, because the traumatic event cannot be integrated into the subject's experience and is not available for representation, it can only be accessed through traumatic repetition, which Caruth understands as "the literal return of the past."[34] This unrepresentable, and ultimately unmediated, experience of trauma is then passed on contagiously in the process of witnessing.

While critical theory in the tradition of Adorno thus debates the appropriateness of certain kinds of representation, the poststructuralists use the Holocaust to problematize and query the very notion of representability and referentiality as such. Literary scholar Naomi Mandel has highlighted the irony behind the fact that a discourse predicated on the impossibility of (all or some forms of) representation has produced an unending string of comments, resulting in an entire "rhetoric of the unspeakable": "The more we speak about Auschwitz, it seems, the more prevalent and compelling our gestures toward the limits of our speech, our knowledge, and our world."[35]

Mandel's paradox points to a crucial problem: the ongoing recourse to the trope of unspeakability is somehow at odds with recent developments in Holocaust discourse. Since the turn of the millennium, we have witnessed a paradigm shift—the disappearance of the survivor and eyewitness generation entails a transition from firsthand memories of the war period to an increasingly ritualized cultural memory of the events. This transformation intersects with the above-mentioned larger changes that encompass the hypermediation and globalization of Holocaust memory. The Holocaust has thus emerged as a highly discursivized "floating signifier,"[36] which has crossed cultural, generational, media, national, and representational boundaries. Whereas Holocaust memory—like any form of memory—has always been mobile and mediated to an extent,[37] the recent developments have accelerated these processes and created a new set of issues: not only will media depictions increasingly supplement and substitute personal memories of the event; in the age of remediation, these representations have also become entangled in an ever more complicated and globalized web of mutual referencing. The steady stream of Holocaust-related works of fiction has furthermore contributed to the establishment of fixed genre conventions and narrative patterns, as they shape, for example, the so-called family or multigenerational novel, which has seen a surge in popularity since the late 1990s, both in the German-language context and internationally.[38] This boundless circulation of images and tropes is complemented by the above-mentioned proliferation of Holocaust analogies and references in a range of historical or political contexts. While some scholars posit that the emergence of the Holocaust as a "global narrative template" has enriched the ways in which we discuss and perceive other traumatic events around the globe,[39] the ethical productivity of ubiquitous Holocaust comparisons has been increasingly questioned in recent times.[40] Hence, what we are confronted with nowadays is not so much the unspeakability of the Holocaust as its hyperspeakability, understood as its ubiquitous presence as a "floating" or "master signifier" and/or media cliché.[41]

Holocaust representation as re- and hypermediation, that is, the notion of the Holocaust as a heavily mediatized, "floating" signifier, seems to have supplanted questions of representational accuracy or appropriateness with the problem of representational oversaturation, caused by the speed and boundlessness of trauma's travels. This also affects the notion of authenticity, which has been an integral component of the unspeakability discourse, be it in the form of the alleged authenticity of the eyewitness testimony and/or the authenticity of unmediated trauma that can never be accurately represented, only embodied and/or experienced. One might assume that these idea(l)s of authenticity become somewhat irrelevant in these new media and memory ecologies; the problem, however, is more complicated: certain implementations of the unspeakability paradigm in the wake of Adorno have tended to conceptualize the relationship between (traumatic) events and their mediatization or remediation in terms of an ineluctable distortion or manipulation of the event and a loss of authenticity. As Bolter and Grusin have demonstrated in their deliberations on remediation, however, the dichotomy between immediacy, authenticity, and unmediatedness, on the one hand, and hypermediacy, artificiality, and mediatization, on the other hand, needs to be reassessed, particularly in an age of hypermediation. Authenticity is at the very heart of what they call "the double logic of remediation."[42] The constant replacement and evolution of media technologies has one overriding aim: "experience without mediation."[43] This ultimately means that media are expected to transmit not a representation of the thing but the thing itself, for which they need to be as transparent as possible, virtually nonexistent: "In all these cases, the logic of immediacy dictates that the medium itself should disappear and leave us in the presence of the things presented."[44] Bolter and Grusin, however, illustrate that this passion for immediacy actually leads to the reverse effect. For in order to achieve ever greater immediacy, a growing number of increasingly refined and interactive media technologies is necessary—a phenomenon that Bolter and Grusin refer to as "hypermediacy"[45]—which run the risk of pointing to their own mediality, thus revealing their status as manufacturers of immediacy. Bolter and Grusin conceptualize authenticity and remediation not as opposites but as parts of a "double logic" or dialectics, pointing to the fact that, in our remediated age, authenticity can actually and paradoxically be a media effect.[46] As Allen Meek, Ann Kaplan, and Slavoj Žižek have shown in relation to 9/11 or Abu Ghraib,[47] the emotional impact of these events was essentially generated and maintained through repetition in and across different media formats. It was only through the cycle of remediation that these events achieved iconicity and thereby the familiarity necessary for fostering the illusion of immediacy as well as affect and identification. More specifically in relation to (Holocaust) testimonies, Sara Jones has stressed that these accounts need to be approached as a form of "mediated immediacy,"[48] in which the supposed authenticity of the face-to-face encounter is being technologically re-created in ever more sophisticated ways. In a culture of hypermediation, the perceived "reality" of events and encounters thus increasingly depends on the fact that they meet media-generated expectations and fantasies and are transmitted through ever more immersive media technologies.

How then does the notion of manufactured authenticity or "mediated immediacy" change the perspective? A more dialectical approach to the question of authenticity and mediatization in Holocaust discourse shifts the focus away from the normative approach, which posits that media depictions always distort and manipulate the event. Instead, one could take a closer look at how exactly these media depictions function, how they might actually generate authenticity, which conventions and tropes they recycle to do so, what the implicit and explicit politics of their form are, and how they foster self- and metareflexivity (or not). Focusing on what

Jones calls "the particular cultural form or script" in which these depictions are embedded also implies finding new ways of judging the ethical viability of certain media depictions.[49] As Astrid Erll has noted, the prevalent arguments of authenticity and veracity do not necessarily hold, as the media of cultural memory cannot be judged by the same standards as history books:

> A fictional film, even if it is a "history film," cannot be judged by using criteria which are derived from "history" as an academic discipline, because movies function according to a different symbolic system. This does not mean, however, that the production of cultural memory through literature, movies and the arts cannot be criticized. What is needed is a different methodology, one which allows us to address . . . the "ideology of memorial form," through, for example, an analysis of narrative voice, perspective structures, character constellations, the use of imagery or . . . intermedial structures and references.[50]

Joining together the various changes and concerns outlined so far is the question of how we can still meaningfully relate to the Holocaust, now that the immediate biological and experiential connections are vanishing, and cultural and media representations are not only about to take over but have also developed a life of their own. This implies new modes of authentication alongside a changed understanding of the very concept of authenticity, as well as new challenges for how we relate to the past. Tied to these shifts is the question of how we can transmit memories to future generations, which already seem to struggle to make a connection. While these debates in many ways continue earlier discussions around normalization, historicization, as well as the commodification or "Americanization" of Holocaust memory,[51] they also seem to be grappling with a changed climate of Holocaust remembrance and representation that is, in some senses, more pluralistic and less prescriptive but in turn struggles with newly emerging problems around hypermediation, discursivation, and overrepresentation as well as saturation, disengagement, and fatigue.

Shifting Scales of Holocaust Memory? National, Transnational, and Jewish

Arguably, the border-crossing dynamics of the internet age have provided the conditions for the emergence of the so-called transnational and/or transcultural turn in Holocaust and memory studies.[52] Memories of the Nazi past and the Holocaust are no longer discussed within an exclusively national framework but on a "transnational" or "transcultural" scale. While comparative approaches to the Holocaust were still treated with caution in the immediate postunification period, the "multidirectional" perspective seems to have become the norm,[53] as is also evidenced by the emergence of comparative genocide studies as an academic subject. This new perspective includes examinations of the ways in which memories of the Nazi past intersect with the memories and histories of various minority groups,[54] but the majority of the so-called transnational or transcultural approaches investigate the transformation of the Holocaust into a universalized and traveling memory emblem that interacts with other, for example, (post)colonial, histories and memories of violence.[55] Whereas some adopt a descriptive approach, the majority of scholars in the field evaluate the shift toward transnationalism/-culturalism, albeit with differing results. Early (pre-9/11) accounts of globalized and transnational Holocaust memory—for example, by Daniel Levy and Natan Sznaider[56]—were staunchly optimistic and celebratory, but recent research has adopted a more skeptical tone. Rather than prematurely ringing in a new and cosmopolitan memory culture, these theorists point out that a comparative approach to Holocaust memory also entails issues such as the instrumentalization of Holocaust memory, the possibility of memorial competition, and the obstructions caused by the ubiquity of Holocaust references and analogies.[57]

These developments imply an important question for this particular study, which examines how contemporary German-language Jewish authors from or based in Germany and Austria reflect on the changes in Holocaust memory discussed here. This question concerns the relationship between the particular national contexts from which these authors and their works emerge and the broader transnational trends outlined above. The authors whose texts are featured in this study, such as Maxim Biller, Eva Menasse, Benjamin Stein, and Vladimir Vertlib, are particularly interesting in this regard, as they all intersect national and transnational discourses and no longer discuss Holocaust memory in an exclusively German and/or Austrian national framework. Biller's family is partly from Russia; he grew up in the Czech Republic but now lives in Germany; and his texts tend to be set in Germany and Eastern Europe, sometimes Israel. Menasse grew up in Austria but has lived in Germany for a long time, and her novel *Quasikristalle* (2013) spans both Germany and Austria. Vertlib was born in the Soviet Union but lived in various countries before settling down in Austria; his text *Das besondere Gedächtnis der Rosa Masur* (2001) stages a clash between German, (post-)Soviet, and Jewish memorial cultures. Stein was born and raised in Germany, yet his novel *Die Leinwand* (2010; translated as *The Canvas*, 2012) offers a transnational Holocaust narrative encompassing Germany, Switzerland, Israel, and the US. On the one hand, all of the selected works involve Germany and Austria as countries of perpetration and complicity, taking into account the complexities of postwar German- and Austrian-Jewish identities, relations, and memories, as I will outline in the respective chapters; on the other hand, they also showcase what Jennifer Kapczynski and Erin McGlothlin call "the very geographical, *multi*cultural, and *multi*linguistic diversity of the Holocaust itself [italics in the original]"[58] and of its memory. While McGlothlin and Kapczynski rightly suggest that Holocaust studies might have to rethink its privileging of "German language sources and perspectives"[59] and, in response, supplement them with materials from other cultures and languages, I would also argue that the existing German-language materials need to be read in a more transnational framework, which is what this study attempts. All of the texts assembled in this study approach contemporary Holocaust memory as a phenomenon that crosses cultural and national as well as generational and media boundaries, tracing the dialogues as well as the disjunctions between these different settings. Bringing together these German-language source materials with wider, transnational debates thus achieves a number of things: echoing recent trends in the realm of German and Modern Languages studies more broadly,[60] it enables us to connect German (Jewish) literature more firmly to contemporary discussions on transnational and "world literatures"[61] by investigating how the particularities of German and Austrian literary and memory culture as well as specific cultural and national debates around *Vergangenheitsbewältigung* and normalization might be recalibrated in light of the concerns of a globalized and multidirectional culture of Holocaust remembrance. At the same time, my engagement with these authors and their works aims to illustrate how some of the universalizing and celebratory claims underpinning transnational memory debates can be usefully qualified in light of specific cultural, national, and linguistic contexts such as the German-language one. Vladimir Vertlib's novel *Das besondere Gedächtnis der Rosa Masur*, for example, demonstrates that the intersection of various national histories of violence does not automatically create "multidirectional," cosmopolitan memories. Eva Menasse's *Quasikristalle* critically explores the above-mentioned canonization and universalization of the Holocaust by investigating the—not always productive—influence that Holocaust analogies, comparisons, and references have had on a range of issues such as reproductive medicine, postgenocidal transitional justice, or the Israeli-Palestinian conflict.

In the context of this particular book, an emphasis on transnational literary and memorial frameworks also suggests a reexamination of our understanding of German-Jewish culture and writing. Efforts to redefine these terms are currently being undertaken in a range of other publications and go beyond the remit of this study.[62] While concurring with Andreas Kilcher's notion of an "irreduzible . . . Mehrdeutigkeit dessen, was als deutsch-jüdische Literatur, als jüdische Identität überhaupt . . . gelten kann,"[63] I define the authors examined in this study as "Jewish." Their Jewishness derives from the fact that they have all engaged continuously with questions of (post-)Holocaust Jewish identity, memory, and writing in and outside of their literary works, thus partaking in the project of "selbstreflexive [jüdische] Standortbestimmung."[64] Maxim Biller's work as a journalist, writer, and media personality has built his reputation as a Jewish enfant terrible. Menasse and Vertlib are far less scandalous, but they too have positioned themselves as public Jewish intellectuals. Benjamin Stein discusses various aspects of modern-day Jewish existence in his books and his blog, *Turmsegler*. Their works thus represent a Jewish perspective on the issues discussed throughout this study, which is still underrepresented in the German-language context. Publications particularly on transgenerational Holocaust memory and on the so-called family and multigenerational novel tend to focus on non-Jewish authors and the perpetrator perspective. Although recent accounts by, for example, Davies and Hammel; Fischer, Hammermeister, and Kramer; Kapczynski and McGlothlin; as well as Frieden offer a more nuanced picture,[65] a comprehensive study, dedicated exclusively to German-language Jewish Holocaust fiction, is still lacking. The Jewish perspective on the Holocaust, understood as a victim perspective in the broadest sense, is necessarily different from that of non-Jewish authors or descendants of perpetrators. One defining feature of all the texts under consideration is their particular concern with the ethics and transmission of (post-)Holocaust memory.[66] Preserving these memories for the future is presented as one way to counter the erasure of Jewish life and culture under National Socialism, and the act of writing is implicated in these dynamics in specific ways.

While I therefore suggest reading the body of literature analyzed in this study as examples of Jewish writing, I would like to complicate the notion of "German" or "Austrian" Jewish literature to describe the authors assembled here, as some of them are translingual (Biller, Vertlib) and all of them champion a decidedly transnational angle. They also write from what Andreas Kilcher has described as a position of "Exterritorialität" vis-à-vis the German and Austrian majority cultures that surround them.[67] For these reasons, I have decided to use the term "German-language" as a descriptor, as it captures these writers' special connection to the respective cultures of Germany and Austria but does not reduce them to it. This is also why I do not read their texts exclusively in the settings of German and Austrian memory debates, even though these do inform my analysis to an extent. I thus agree with Leslie Morris's recent call "to unmoor the category of German Jewish text from the strictures of a national literature that has, of necessity, needed to delineate its borders."[68] Inspired by Morris, I would like to suggest that we read the authors and texts in question as situated in translation, travel, and transformation, perched between the national, the transnational, and the Jewish. I therefore perceive the underlying tension between national and transnational literary and memory cultures as deeply productive for this study, not least because it cannot be fully resolved.

New Frameworks of Holocaust Memory?
From Postmemory to "Travelling Trauma"

This book seeks to investigate how contemporary German-language Jewish writers respond to the shifts outlined above and develop aesthetically and ethically novel approaches to Holocaust memory in the age of hypermediation and globalization. It thus poses a range of interconnected questions: how is the shift from living eyewitness memory to increasingly mediatized forms of Holocaust remembrance reflected in second- and third-generation German-language Jewish literature? How are issues of hypermediation, globalization, overrepresentation, and ritualization (re) negotiated in those texts? How are questions of empathy and authenticity reexamined? How, if at all, do the novels under consideration partake in the metadiscursive shift and explore their own implication in these dynamics?

My book therefore engages with various major research trends to broaden the scope of traditional German and literary studies research on the Holocaust. First, it taps into current research on transgenerational Holocaust memories, focusing on Holocaust literature by the so-called second and third generations, that is, by authors who are either the actual (grand)children of survivors or who, owing to their date of birth and Jewish identity, could (have) be(en) the (grand)children of survivors. There are ongoing discussions about whether the differences between the "second" and the "third" generation are of a quantitative or of a qualitative nature. While some, such as Victoria Aarons and Alan Berger,[69] make the case for a distinct third-generation identity, others, such as Esther Jilovsky, Jordana Silverstein, and David Slucki, see the boundaries between these two cohorts as more permeable.[70] For the purposes of this study, I prefer the more open-ended term "generation after," coined by Efraim Sicher,[71] which encompasses both the "second" and the "third" generation and makes historical distance a defining feature, thus also potentially moving us away from a purely biological understanding of Holocaust generations. What unites the authors examined in this book is that they did not experience the events firsthand and can only access them in a mediated and mediatized fashion. My understanding of "generation after" therefore applies equally to authors such as Maxim Biller and Vladimir Vertlib, who are situated somewhere between the "second" and the "third" generations and who have no or very loose familial ties to the Holocaust, and a writer like Eva Menasse who clearly belongs to the "third generation" and a family of survivors.

While there is an established body of research on second-generation Holocaust literature, spearheaded by Erin McGlothlin's influential study,[72] the third generation represents a relatively new field of study with few

publications to date. Furthermore, research on the second and third generation tends to emerge from and focus on the Anglophone research and
literary context, specifically that of the United States, which is shaped by
vibrant second- and third-generation academic and artistic communities.
This in part explains why major recent publications on the second and
third generations by, for example, Victoria Aarons,[73] Alan Berger,[74] Esther
Jilovsky,[75] Jordana Silverstein, and David Slucki,[76] generally do not consider the German-language context. By contrast, a current volume by
Torben Fischer, Philipp Hammermeister, and Sven Kramer focuses exclusively on contemporary responses to the Nazi past and the Holocaust in
contemporary German literature but includes few third-generation examples.[77] The same goes for Erin McGlothlin's and Jennifer Kapczynski's
recent book on the Holocaust and/in German studies,[78] as well as Kirstin
Frieden's study, which engages with contemporary shifts in German-
language Holocaust memory and culture as manifested in literature, performance art, and digital technologies.[79] Katja Garloff and Agnes Mueller's
recent volume, *German-Jewish Literature after 1990*, does feature a range
of prominent second- and third-generation authors, such as Maxim Biller,
Alina Bronsky, Mirna Funk, Olga Grjasnowa, Katja Petrowskaja, and
Benjamin Stein, while also interrogating the shifting position and shape of
Holocaust memory in German-Jewish culture.[80] Their inquiry is very
much driven by the suggestion that the Holocaust, for a number of reasons, is becoming less central for German Jewish discourse and identities
today. While I agree with their contention that Holocaust memory is
undergoing various significant changes, I would argue that it is not becoming less central but, as I have outlined above, potentially less contested and
more canonized, which brings about new sets of problems. This study
therefore charts a relatively new field of inquiry, by seeking to place
German-language literature more firmly on the map of ongoing discussions about second- and third-generation responses to the Holocaust. This
also promises to shed light on the question of if and how German-language
fiction by the "generation after" is connected to and/or different from
contemporary literature about the Holocaust in other languages and
national discourses.[81]

Another central concern of this study relates to the question of if and
how contemporary shifts in Holocaust memory and their reflection in current fiction urge us to recalibrate prevailing frameworks in Holocaust literature and memory research. Much academic inquiry into the second and
third generations after the Holocaust is still dominated by the dynamics of
inter- and transgenerational memory transfer and conceptions of "postmemory." In the realm of cultural production, this has given rise to an
entire genre; namely, the so-called family or multigenerational narrative.[82]
This genre, which has enjoyed unabated popularity since its emergence in
the early 2000s, has produced a steady stream of novels (and, more

recently, films) that explore family memories of the Nazi past through the lens of the children and, more often, grandchildren of victims and perpetrators alike. Instead of a straightforward re-narration of family history and memory, these texts offer investigations into memorial and genealogical gaps alongside the fictions they produce, putting issues of mediation and imagination—and hence the process of remembering and writing itself—at the center. This self-reflexive potential of some (though not all) family novels, emphasized by many scholars in the field,[83] often manifests itself in complex explorations of the relationship between fact and fiction. These often involve—but are not limited to—the strong autobiographical impulses marking the genre. In addition, many of these narratives focus on the overlaps and clashes between the private realm of family memory and the public field of institutionalized historiography, supplementing official discourse with alternative accounts of the past.

Although family narratives and memories continue to shape recent discourse on the Nazi past and the Holocaust, as demonstrated by the success of Katja Petrowskaja's *Vielleicht Esther* (2014) or Per Leo's *Flut und Boden* (2014), my project seeks to complicate the boundaries and conventions of the genre—not least because it might have become home to a number of "exhausted trope(s)."[84] Family memories and novels are undoubtedly still very much part of contemporary Holocaust discourse and enjoy popularity with academic as well as nonacademic audiences. As some critics have noted,[85] however, many of these narratives have become formulaic and might thus no longer offer a resource for critical engagement with the Nazi past. Picking up from Kirstin Frieden's question "Was kommt nach dem Familienroman?,"[86] I have thus chosen texts by Maxim Biller, Eva Menasse, Benjamin Stein, and Vladimir Vertlib that engage with the Holocaust in ways that attempt to recalibrate or even go beyond the family frame. I argue that these writers focus less (exclusively) on the psychology of (transgenerational) Holocaust trauma and memory, which is a prominent preoccupation of the family or multigenerational novel. Instead they highlight processes of cultural hypermediation and discursivation. This approach sets my book apart from other research conducted on the "generation after," which tends to emphasize family stories of the Holocaust and issues of transgenerational traumatization.[87] By contrast, the texts assembled here explore modes of transgenerational, transmedial, and transnational transfer that go beyond living generations or family bonds: they construct intertextual literary genealogies, while also exploring affiliative—that is, nonfamilial—as well as cross-cultural modes of transmission and transgenerational remembrance. In so doing they represent the Holocaust predominantly as a culturally mediated signifier, a "Diskursfiguration and Signifikationsmaschine."[88] These texts thus supplement the ongoing investigation of intrafamilial dynamics with an examination of broader cultural and discursive processes. These texts thus appear as indicative of a postfamilial and metadiscursive shift that might not replace the family narrative but is indeed complicating and complementing it in important ways. These observations are supported by the findings of Torben Fischer, Philipp Hammermeister, and Sven Kramer, who detect "eine Ausdifferenzierung der Erinnerungsliteratur hin zu Formen metahistoriographischen und metafiktionalen, vielleicht sogar 'meta-erinnerungskulturellen' Erzählens" in recent discourse about the German past.[89]

The fact that contemporary Holocaust literature increasingly, although not completely, leaves behind familial-psychological configurations calls into question the broader methodological frameworks that are usually applied in this context. This book therefore also intervenes in current debates in the fields of memory and trauma studies, particularly in the realm of postmemory scholarship. Marianne Hirsch's concept of postmemory underpins much of the academic engagement with belated, indirect, and nonexperiential responses to trauma.[90] Hirsch initially coined the term *postmemory* to describe the ways in which the children of Holocaust survivors relate to and are shaped by their parents' past. She defines postmemory as "the experience of those who grow up dominated by narratives that preceded their birth, whose own belated stories are evacuated by the stories of the previous generation shaped by traumatic events that can be neither understood nor recreated."[91] The children (and grandchildren) of Holocaust survivors have not personally experienced the powerful events of the past, which is why they cannot remember them in the literal sense; instead, they have a "postmemory," which is "mediated not through recollection but through an imaginative investment and creation."[92] What the subsequent generations cannot possibly remember, they must imagine or invent, which puts fiction in the broadest sense at the center of Hirsch's work. In recent years, Hirsch has gradually expanded the circle of those who can have a postmemorial response to a traumatic past. Apart from including the second as well as the third generation of Holocaust survivors, a postmemorial relation can also be formed by those who are not biologically related to the survivor generation but connect to the Holocaust via "affiliative," that is, culturally mediated, channels. This has led to an expansion (and some would say depletion) of the term in Hirsch's own work and other scholarship on the matter. Postmemory now encompasses a range of belated responses to all sorts of traumas that are no longer restricted to the Holocaust.

Hirsch's introduction of the term "affiliative" postmemory is arguably a response to shifts in Holocaust discourse. With the dying out of the survivor generation, the three-generation-paradigm, and the prevalence of biological modes of transmission, are coming to an end. The idea (and foregrounding) of affiliation was thus meant to ensure the survival of the family-centered idea of postmemory in a changed landscape of Holocaust remembrance. The idea of "affiliative" postmemory is, however, fraught with problems, which extend to the concept of postmemory as such. These issues stem from Hirsch's intellectual commitment to poststructuralist trauma theory, particularly the works of Cathy Caruth, Shoshana Felman, and Dori Laub, who promote the idea that traumatic experiences are principally beyond representation: they are intrinsically unspeakable and make themselves felt through contagious symptoms. Drawing on what is arguably a misreading of Sigmund Freud's famous essay "Jenseits des Lustprinzips,"[93] Caruth defines *trauma* as that which cannot be represented (linguistically) but instead needs to be enacted, embodied, and performed. Caruth then fuses this "performative theory of traumatic repetition" with Felman's and Laub's ethics of witnessing,[94] which, according to Ruth Leys, leads her to the idea of transmission as a process of infection or contagion:

> The transmission of the unrepresentable—a transmission imagined by Caruth simultaneously as an ineluctable process of infection and as involving an ethical obligation on the part of the listener—therefore implicates those of us who were not there by making us, as Dori Laub has put it, participants and co-owners of the traumatic event.[95]

Here it is important to note that for Felman, Laub, and Caruth, the ethical response is not so much linked to an active (political) engagement but rather to the act of listening. Listening involves an openness to the enigmatic and abysmal address of the other person and a willingness to let oneself be overwhelmed and hurt by the other's fundamental alterity. Paradoxically, the destructive experience of trauma is thus turned into the site for encounter and nonessentialist types of community, rooted in "the very possibility and surprise of listening to another's wound."[96] While the ideas put forward by Caruth, Felman, and Laub and their various implications have been widely criticized,[97] Hirsch is still very much indebted to what I would call the poststructuralist "contagion paradigm" in her work on postmemory. This has two consequences in particular.

Hirsch builds on Caruth's notions of immediacy and community, combining them with her personal interest in photography and the process of intergenerational transmission. Her indebtedness to Caruth leads to a certain disregard for the material dimension of photography (and any other medium) in her work, which also concerns the cultural-symbolic contexts of its production. The contagious transference of traumatic affect is the central component of her media theory. Allen Meek critically refers to such ideas as the "transmission model" of trauma, "which understands visual media as able to directly convey a traumatic experience to a viewer, and thereby potentially to traumatize him/her."[98] This link between trauma, transmission, and the (photographic) medium ultimately rests on the common misconception that both traumatic experiences and visual media are somehow realms of the immediate and nonrepresentational because they are not accessed verbally in the first place. As Ruth Leys points out, such literalization of trauma is based on the alignment of the traumatic with the visual, which is perceived as "inherently nonsymbolic."[99] As such, the visual image and the experience of trauma are essentialized and naturalized as something that stands outside the dynamics of cultural configuration and symbolic representation.

Hirsch conceptualizes photographs as transparent carriers of (traumatic) affect across time, space, and subjective boundaries. Referring to photographs as "window(s) to the past,"[100] she employs one of the prime metaphors of transparency. The supposed immediacy of photographic images establishes their connection to the realm of the affective (as another alleged residuum of immediacy), which qualifies them as a prime carrier of trauma. As so-called points of memory they "produce touching, piercing insights that traverse temporal, spatial and experiential divides."[101] Through a process of transmission that is first and foremost conceived of as a sensory experience ("touching, piercing insights"), photographs have the ability to contagiously transmit wounding traumatic experiences from one generation to another: "In repeatedly exposing themselves to the same pictures, postmemorial viewers can produce in themselves the effects of traumatic repetition that plague the victims of trauma, even as they attempt to mobilize the protective power of the homoeopathic shield."[102] While it is certainly true that atrocity photographs can move, shock, and deeply affect viewers, it is debatable whether they have the capacity to traumatize the recipient. The implied universalism of Hirsch's claim is also problematic: she simply supposes that atrocity pictures automatically "traumatize" what is imagined as a homogenous group of viewers, completely ignoring that the response to atrocity pictures results from a complex interaction between cultural framing, or even conditioning, and individual and collective psychological identification.[103] The notion of a visually (and vicariously) acquired trauma thus reproduces a problematic universalization of trauma and victimhood that is already detectable in Caruth's writing.[104]

The idea of "touching, piercing insights" produced by photographs reveals another crux of Hirsch's argument: while the adjectives "touching" and "piercing" clearly refer to the realm of the sensory, the bodily, and the visceral, the noun "insight" refers to the sphere of the cognitive. This tension between emotional and cognitive modes of knowing permeates Hirsch's elaborations on postmemory from the beginning. Although she repeatedly stresses the link between postmemory and reflexivity, her writing is imbued with notions of the affective, the visceral, and the bodily, which seem to constitute privileged modes of approaching historical documents and events. Photographs are not appreciated for their evidentiary or informative value but primarily as carriers of emotion and as projection screens for personal desires and fantasies. Hirsch claims that "the index of postmemory (as opposed to memory) is the performative index, shaped more and more by affect, need, and desire as time and distance attenuate the links to authenticity and 'truth.'"[105] In other words, all we can gather from photographs is either the affective immediacy of vicarious traumatization or insights into our own fantasies and desires. In this reading, photographs do not (and are not meant to) aid intellectual reflection or critical engagement with the past.

The idea of a "performative index" of photography points back to Caruth, who presents a similar media theory, this time applied to the realm of literature. The vehicle for Caruth's idea of transmission as contagion is literary language, which becomes a carrier medium via a "shift from language as representation to language as performance."[106] The same shift can be detected in Hirsch's idea of the photographic medium, which is also conceptualized as a (literal) repetition: "And thus, they [Holocaust photographs] *no longer represent* Nazi genocide but, in their very *repetition*, they provoke the traumatic effect that this history has had on all who grew up under its shadow [italics added]."[107]

Both Caruth and Hirsch thus turn language and visual media into transparent carriers of trauma without adequately reflecting the issue of mediality. The Caruthian perception of literary texts as "unmediated reflections of traumatic memory" has been incredibly influential in much research on so-called trauma fiction.[108] This has resulted in a one-dimensional equation of the structure of traumatic experiences and their literary depictions: "An experience that exceeds the possibility of narrative knowledge, so the logic goes, will best be represented by a failure of narrative. Hence, what is called for is the disruption of conventional modes of representation, such as can be found in modernist art."[109] Apart from limiting trauma literature to a rather small, high-brow, and, as Stef Craps and others have noted, Eurocentric canon,[110] this simplistic concept of mimesis also denies the agency of the literary text (and media more generally) in shaping our understanding of particular instances and the broader concept of trauma. Instead of reading literary texts (or photographs) as unmediated expressions of trauma, it therefore seems more productive to focus on the tropes, narratives, genre conventions, intertexts, and iconographies through which trauma is (re)framed, (re)constructed, and (re)produced. From the vantage point of the age of remediation, media like photography and literature are not transparent and negligible containers of literal trauma but, rather, essential incubators, transformers, and enablers of the construction and transmission of historical traumas. These traumas cannot be separated from the cultural, media, perceptive, and political frameworks in which they are embedded and received and thus need to be approached as a "performance through culture," as Jones has suggested.[111] This does not mean that trauma-centered texts (or images) cannot elicit affect and emotion. These emotions are not, however, caused by contagious effects but by specific rhetorical, narrative, and visual framing strategies.

The contagion paradigm also informs Hirsch's model of transgenerational transmission, which, in her writings, is steeped in images of invasion, evacuation, affliction, and contamination:

> To grow up with overwhelming inherited memories, to be dominated by narratives that preceded one's birth or one's consciousness, is to risk having one's own life stories displaced, even evacuated, by our ancestors. It is to be shaped, however indirectly, by traumatic fragments of events that still defy narrative reconstruction and exceed comprehension.[112]

Praising the artist Bracha Lichtenberg-Ettinger, Hirsch remarks that she "allows all these images to invade, inhabit, and haunt her."[113] The influence of Caruth is blatantly obvious in these statements: transmission is imagined as a contagious, overpowering, and exclusively psychological process, in which the subject is implanted with a "knowledge" that remains forever inaccessible. The only possible response requires a paralytic openness to this aporetic, incommensurable knowledge, which underpins an ethics of "listening to another's wound."[114] This concept of transmission is complicated, however, when considering that Hirsch actually works with *two* notions of transgenerational transfer. The one mentioned above involves the transgenerational transmission of trauma in survivor families and is closely tied to the notion of *affliction*. Subsequent generations are regarded as passive receivers of their ancestors' traumas, which befall them through "nonverbal and precognitive acts of transfer."[115] The second notion refers to the cultural transmission of trauma and is linked to the concept of *adoption*. This means that later generations actively identify with a trauma that is not connected to their own experience or familial-biological background. They gain from adopting these memories a heightened sense of historical responsibility. Hirsch hence uses the same term, "postmemory," for two completely different phenomena: while the first designates a psychological process involving survivor families and their offspring, the other can be described as a cultural (and maybe ethical) practice. She tries to solve this problem by differentiating between "familial" (i.e., biological) and "affiliative" (i.e., cultural) postmemory:

> To delineate the border between these respective structures of transmission—between what I would like to refer to as *familial* and as *"affiliative"* postmemory—we would have to account for the difference between an intergenerational vertical identification of child and parent occurring within the family and the intra-generational horizontal identification that makes that child's position more broadly available to other contemporaries. Affiliative postmemory would thus be the result of contemporaneity and generational connection with the literal second generation combined with structures of mediation that would be broadly appropriable, available, and indeed, compelling

enough to encompass a larger collective in an organic web of transmission [italics in the original].[116]

While this quotation appears to provide some clarification, Hirsch, in
the course of her writing, repeatedly conflates "affiliative" postmemory
with the notion of affliction by troping it in terms of contagion, evacuation, and infestation. This tendency becomes all too evident in her analysis
of American Jewish photo-artist Lorie Novak, herself not a descendant of
Holocaust survivors. Although Hirsch reads her work as "a cultural act of
identification and affiliation"[117] and thus as an example of "affiliative"
postmemory, her description of Novak's photographs uses words such as
"crowded out," "haunts" and "bleeds into,"[118] all of which belong to the
vocabulary of "familial" postmemory she has established earlier on. Hirsch
claims that Novak "represents herself as branded by the harrowing memory of the Nazi genocide."[119] While it is certainly possible for audiences
not directly and biologically linked to the victims of the Holocaust to feel
emotionally touched and overwhelmed by their suffering, the vocabulary
of trauma-induced affliction and scarring applied here makes little sense for
those with no familial-biological connection to the events (unless we are
dealing with a case of pathological overidentification).[120] Hirsch thus constantly psychologizes and biologizes a process that, in the case of Novak,
is first and foremost a cultural one, partly because, in the wake of Caruth,
such emotional overidentification can be passed off as an ethical practice.

Going back to the shifts explored at the beginning of this introduction, it becomes clear that the poststructuralist approach outlined here
entails a number of methodological problems in our era of re- and hypermediation. The idea that Holocaust trauma is unspeakable results in fantasies of authenticity, unmediated witnessing, and transmission through
contagion. In Hirsch's work, this is particularly prominent in her handling
of the photographic medium: she ignores its mediality, claiming that it
engenders unmediated traumatic affect in the postmemorial viewer.
Similarly, Caruth's understanding of literary language as a transparent carrier of trauma has contributed to the formation of a Eurocentric canon of
trauma literature and a dismissal of the cultural agency of artistic representations. I also highlighted the psychologizing and biologizing qualities of
Hirsch's conception of transgenerational transmission. These are particularly problematic in an age in which, with the exception of the few remain-
ing survivors and their families, the Holocaust is not so much an
experiential and psychological issue as a question of cultural memory and
politics.

What is thus needed is a new angle that tackles the interplay between
trauma and media(tization), as this is a prominent theme in contemporary
German- and Austrian-Jewish literature written by the so-called generation
after. The prevailing focus on the unspeakability and psychology of trauma

captures neither the increasingly hypermediated nature of Holocaust memory and representation, nor the cultural, material, media, and socio-political contexts in which Holocaust memory, and trauma more generally, are implicated. Jeffrey Alexander's work on cultural trauma provides a productive springboard for formulating a different, less psychologizing, approach to trauma.[121] Alexander approaches the concept of trauma from a sociological and extremely constructivist angle, claiming that, on a collective level, there are no events that are naturally or inherently traumatic. Instead, he argues, traumas are fundamentally and solely social constructs: "Events are not inherently traumatic. Trauma is a socially mediated attribution."[122] He goes on to write that "traumatic status is attributed to real or imagined phenomena, not because of their actual harmfulness or their objective abruptness, but because these phenomena are believed to have abruptly, and harmfully, affected collective identity."[123] To a certain extent, Alexander's position marks the extreme opposite of Caruth's argument: while for Caruth trauma stands outside of the realm of symbolic representation, Alexander claims that trauma can only ever be grasped on a socio-cultural level, implying that there are no objective qualities to any traumatic event, which comes with its own set of issues. The main problem for the purposes of this study, though, is that the "cultural" in Alexander's concept is rather misleading. He is not really interested in the dynamics that shape cultural mediations of trauma—as they are provided by works of art, the media, or politics—but rather in the ways in which trauma, as an initially individualized psychological phenomenon, is collectivized. Alexander's interest lies squarely in "collective" trauma, whereas a theory of "cultural" trauma, such as the one I am interested in, takes into account the ways in which trauma travels through and is shaped by various media.[124] While Alexander's concept is therefore helpful to shift the focus away from trauma as a purely psychological phenomenon, it reaches a limit where the relationship between trauma, media, and hyper- or remediation is concerned.

It is here that the idea of "travelling trauma," as it has been coined by Terri Tomsky,[125] and of the Holocaust as a "floating" or "travelling" signifier,[126] comes into play. In an article entitled "From Sarajevo to 9/11: Travelling Memory and the Trauma Economy," Tomsky introduces the term "travelling trauma."[127] Coined in analogy to Astrid Erll's influential concept of "travelling memory,"[128] it is used by Tomsky to capture the darker aspects of a globalized Holocaust memory. She asserts that the transformation of the Holocaust into a mobile and border-crossing memory emblem cannot be separated from the establishment and dynamics of a larger "trauma economy,"[129] in which some experiences of trauma are valued highly, while others "fail to evoke recognition and subsequently, compassion and aid."[130] Tomsky's approach is helpful as it zooms in on the "economic, cultural, discursive and political structures" in which traumas are represented and in which they travel,[131] that is, their material, media, and mediated dimensions. In the context of Holocaust discourse, "travelling trauma" would then designate an approach that focuses not so much on the problem of trauma's (un)representability—for its (over)representation is simply a given in a global media culture—as on the aesthetics, dynamics, and politics of its representation. In the context of the Holocaust, it brings into focus the event's quality as a culturally mediated impact event and "floating"[132] or, as Mandel puts it, "master signifier,"[133] which travels transgenerationally, transmedially, and/or transnationally. As such, the concept of "travelling trauma" complicates the notions of unspeakability and incompatibility, because it understands the Holocaust as fundamentally implicated in representational and discursive networks and puts these entanglements at the center.

Such an approach responds to recent trends in media and memory studies, which increasingly conceive of memory as socially embedded, dynamic, procedural, remediated, "travelling" or "unbound,"[134] while also answering Erin McGlothlin and Jennifer Kapczynski's call for fresh approaches that consider the Holocaust "in a transgenerational, transnational, and transmedial light."[135] It also differs substantially from Caruth's and Hirsch's position, although they too are concerned with issues of mediation and travel. Their notion of travel, however, involves contagious immediacy and thus a disregard for the material, cultural, and political conditions of trauma's mobility. This is also reflected in their conceptualization of media as transparent carriers of a pristine and unalterable meaning. The idea of "travelling trauma" instead stresses that, during its travels, the meaning of the event is not simply passed on from one medium to the next, but actually shaped and (re-)created via these media(tiza)tions. This is due to the frames, tropes, and narratives that media depictions at the same time apply and rely on, which, in turn, depend on the ways in which they are received by their audiences.

Reframing the Holocaust as a "travelling trauma" is meant to solve some of the methodological problems inherent in the notion of traumatic unspeakability, which also affect the concept of postmemory. The dogmatic claim that the Holocaust is unrepresentable and can only be transmitted contagiously, via a language of symptoms, hinders engagement with its global overrepresentation. One is reminded here of Gillian Rose's famous verdict against "Holocaust piety,"[136] which can be usefully reformulated for the twenty-first century. Already in the 1990s, Rose pointed to the problem that the affirmation of the event's "non-representability," although presented as the ethical option, can actually have questionable effects, since it deflects attention from how both the representation and its recipient are always implicated in what is being depicted. "Holocaust piety" is naive to the extent that it makes us believe that there is an inculpable and transcendental point from which we can approach the event. As

Adorno already taught us shortly after the war, however, this is precisely not the case, and to believe so is dangerous. What is therefore needed, in Rose's words, is not only continued yet "always . . . contestable representation"[137] but also "the critique of representation, and the critique of the critique of representation."[138]

This is, arguably, where the more descriptive approach embraced by Tomsky falls short and will be usefully extended by this study. One major aim of poststructuralist trauma theory concerned an ethical program for the transmission of trauma across cultures and generations. While this was an important and valuable project, I have, however, illustrated that some of the core assumptions underpinning Caruth's, Felman's, Laub's, and Hirsch's thinking actually lead to ethically troubling results. Tomsky's approach allows us to circumnavigate some of the pitfalls associated with the poststructuralist models of trauma and transmission; yet it does not provide any tools for ethically evaluating the existing hypermobile depictions of and references to traumas. If we want to hold on to the ethical impetus driving the poststructuralist project, we are thus left with the question of how we can develop an ethical perspective that is sensitive to our particular cultural moment, in which the Holocaust is caught up in various networks of media, transnational, and transgenerational exchange. A purely descriptive approach to "travelling trauma" is certainly legitimate; the task would then be to trace, but not necessarily evaluate, its movements across generational, media, national, and cultural boundaries. Such an approach also appears more manageable in the face of an undeniable pluralization of Holocaust memories and representations that has resulted in an abandonment of key components of "Holocaust etiquette,"[139] such as the event's allegedly sacred nature, its singularity, and its unrepresentability.

At the same time, this introduction has shown that pressing new ethical and political issues—concerning overrepresentation, ritualization, and Holocaust fatigue—have arisen and that the need for discussion and evaluation persists. It is therefore indispensable to continue a critical and ethical evaluation of Holocaust representations, even (or maybe especially) in the age of re- and hypermediation—but on what grounds? I have tried to demonstrate that (de)valuing artistic depictions of the Holocaust purely based on the fact that they are representations and thus violate the event's alleged "unspeakability" has always been problematic and has become even less viable in an age of irrefutable hypermediation. What we can evaluate, however, is "why, how, and, importantly, for what purpose"[140] these representations engage with the issue of hypermediation and the current state of Holocaust memory and discourse. This requires techniques of self- and metareflexivity, which thus emerge as key features of a possible ethics of representation in the age of Holocaust hypermediation. My readings therefore focus on the ways in which the texts under consideration meta-discursively negotiate the routinization and commodification of Holocaust memory, while also probing the extent to which they allow us to critically engage with what have become major buzzwords in Holocaust and memory discourse, such as authenticity, cosmopolitan memory, transnationalism, trauma, witnessing, and postmemory. This also implies an examination of the extent to which they self-reflexively consider their implication in these developments. We must therefore ask: Are these texts critical or affirmative of recent developments in Holocaust discourse? Do they simply observe contemporary shifts, or do they try to intervene in current debates by, for example, stressing repressed or marginalized aspects, by interrogating the usefulness of Holocaust comparisons, or by providing spaces of contemplation that interrupt the ceaseless stream of hypermediated imagery? How do they reflect on their own aesthetics and techniques in relation to older examples of and debates about Holocaust representation? How do they employ established tropes and narrative conventions, such as the genre of the family novel, and do they reflect on their nature as tropes and conventions?

While all of the texts under consideration resort to metadiscursive and self-reflexive strategies, these work differently in the various texts. Although Stein's *Die Leinwand* and Biller's *Im Kopf von Bruno Schulz* (2013; translated as *Inside the Head of Bruno Schulz*, 2015) are (self-)reflexive up to a point, they also demonstrate significant blind spots. Stein's text dissects remediated Holocaust remembrance, but he replaces it with a folkloristic, potentially essentializing notion of post-Holocaust Jewishness. Biller's writing is self-reflexive in its recourse to certain traditions, such as the literary heritage of "ghetto writing," but this does not prevent him from appropriating the figure and works of Bruno Schulz. In contrast to this, the novels by Menasse and Vertlib are steeped in thoroughly metadiscursive irony. Yet what sets them apart is Vertlib's interventionist and Menasse's detached approach. We will see that there are significant differences in genre and style. Stein's and Menasse's novels boldly experiment with multiperspectivity and the subjectivity of viewpoints, presenting the reader with a dozen different perspectives (Menasse) and two strongly contradictory outlooks and narrators (Stein). Vertlib's work, meanwhile, appears as rather conventional in terms of narration and formal arrangement, as is also the case for Biller's novella. While a new, unified genre of "meta-erinnerungskulturelle" novels does therefore not yet exist,[141] these narrative approaches undeniably complicate the framework of the conventional multigenerational or family novel and of postmemorial discourse more generally. They also highlight the importance of certain self- and metareflexive devices such as multiperspectivity, polyphony, unreliable narration, intertextuality, and intermediality, as well as irony, that might be representative of the evolving genre of the metamemorial Holocaust novel.

Since these are all quintessentially literary devices, these works also showcase the unique potential of fictional discourse to critically, in the sense of self- and metareflexively, engage with recent shifts in Holocaust memory and representation. As has been noted by Niklas Luhmann, the medium of literature is characterized by its ability to carry out first- and second-order observations—fictional discourse contains observations (first-order) and is at the same time able to reflect on the process of observation as such (second-order); it is thus fundamentally self- and metareflexive.[142] With a view to the capabilities of fictional discourse, we can thus further develop the concept of "travelling trauma" in an ethical direction, as certain fictional devices may indeed accomplish "the critique of representation, and the critique of the critique of representation" advocated by Rose.[143] Fictional discourse is thus not only a primary "Medium der Gedächtnisbildung und der Gedächtnisreflexion,"[144] as has been noted by Astrid Erll, but also an important incubator for devising and enhancing a memory ethics for the age of hypermediation. I suggest that this program be tentatively described as an ethics of self- and metareflexivity that is also quintessentially an ethics of fictional discourse. It is therefore crucial to emphasize that the novels presented here depict, reflect on, *and* shape the current discourse about authenticity, empathy, and re- and hypermediation, postmemory, trauma, and transgenerational transmission. They thus underline the continued significance of fictional spaces for (re)negotiating the present and future shapes of Holocaust remembrance.

Selection of Texts and Chapter Outline

This study analyzes a representative yet by no means exhaustive cross-section of contemporary German-language Jewish writing from a range of renowned authors who all engage with the memory and cultural afterlives of the Holocaust from a transgenerational, transnational, and/or transmedial perspective; they approach the event from in- and outside of the framework of the family and/or under the conditions of hypermediation and globalization. They thus engage less with the event, or with personal and/or intergenerational memories of the event, but rather tackle its discursivation and memorialization.

These concerns bind together a group of writers from biographically, culturally, and stylistically diverse backgrounds, although they all belong to the so-called generation after. They thus approach Holocaust memory from the perspective of the secondary or "non-witness,"[145] although the degree of their personal and cultural distance to the event varies. What furthermore brings these texts together is their publication in or after 2000, which makes them part of the growing body of Holocaust literature in the new millennium. According to Torben Fischer, Philipp Hammermeister, and Sven Kramer, this literature offers qualitatively new approaches and fields of inquiry: "Dabei hat die Literatur, so unsere These, gerade in den letzten Jahren noch einmal Zugänge eröffnet, die sich von jenen der siebziger und achtziger, aber zum Teil auch von denen der neunziger Jahre unterscheiden."[146] This study aims to investigate the nature of these new and shifting constellations in recent Jewish German-language Holocaust literature, both on an aesthetic and on a thematic level. In this context, I will pay particular attention to what I call the self-reflexive and metadiscursive or -memorial quality of the texts analyzed here, that is, the fact that they engage with the Holocaust less as a personal trauma than as a deeply ritualized, canonized, and hypermediated memory. This focus also implies that I have selected the texts in this study based on aesthetic merit. They are all characterized by heightened self-reflexivity, narrative complexity, and intertextuality, as well as the use of irony and humor. This general awareness of form is the main precondition for the critical potential that these texts unfold both in the context of contemporary hypermediated Holocaust memory and relation to established tropes surrounding the family narrative and postmemorial discourse more broadly.

While it would be an overstatement to claim that contemporary German-Jewish literature has abandoned the conventions of the family narrative, and of postmemorial discourse more broadly, this book aims to shine the spotlight on texts that engage critically with the—potentially exhausted— tropes that govern these debates and point to possible new directions. The goal is thus to take stock of innovative engagements with important issues in contemporary German-language Jewish as well as global Holocaust discourse. These include questions of hypermediation and authenticity, of post-Holocaust Jewish authorship and writing traditions, of transnational memory cultures, and of Holocaust fatigue and metadiscursivity.

Chapter 1 concentrates on the transmedial travel of Holocaust memories and the renegotiation of authenticity, testimony, and transmission in the age of re- and hypermediation. I read Benjamin Stein's novel *Die Leinwand* and its engagement with the infamous Wilkomirski affair through the framework of Bolter and Grusin's concept of "remediation." Stein's novel draws our attention to the inseparability of (Holocaust) testimony and (re)mediation, thus complicating notions of authenticity, immediacy, and witnessing in post-Holocaust discourse. I also illustrate how Stein's text develops the above-mentioned ethics of self- and metareflexivity by engaging with the remediation of Holocaust memory and its own entrapment therein. This leads to a rejection of fixed notions of (Jewish) identity, particularly those that are rooted in trauma and victimization. The (self-)reflexive potential of the novel is, however, undermined by its folklorization of post-Holocaust Jewish identity.

The topic of post-Holocaust Jewish identity links Stein's writing to Maxim Biller's novella *Im Kopf von Bruno Schulz*, which I discuss in chapter 2. I examine Biller's text as a renegotiation of transgenerational Holocaust memory and post-Holocaust Jewish (male) identity. I will highlight the importance of intertextuality and intermediality for Biller's postmemorial exploration of tradition, which pitches Eastern European (Jewish) aesthetic traditions against the German literary canon, epitomized by Thomas Mann. Applying Harold Bloom's concept of "influence"[147] to Biller's latest novella and the autobiographically inspired *Der gebrauchte Jude* (2009), I illustrate how *Im Kopf von Bruno Schulz* constructs intertextual genealogies in order to stage violent and oedipal conflicts of belonging and dissociation. In a similar vein to Stein, Biller's oeuvre is characterized by a contrast between self- and metareflexive techniques and a rather unsophisticated notion of Jewish masculinity as well as an appropriative relationship with the character and works of Bruno Schulz.

Chapter 3 remains within the Eastern European context: I analyze Vladimir Vertlib's novel *Das besondere Gedächtnis der Rosa Masur* and its engagement with the transnational travel of Holocaust memory. Engaging with the allegedly "cosmopolitan" nature of transnational memory discourse, the chapter stresses the clash between Germany's culture of guilt-ridden and redemptory Vergangenheitsbewältigung and Russia's narrative of heroism and triumph in the novel, which produces conflict rather than transcultural understanding. The chapter also shows how the particular life and memory of an individual can never find expression in the type of narrative templates that have shaped the collective national memory of the Second World War and the Holocaust. Inspired by Mikhail Bakhtin's work on polyphony and dialogism,[148] I argue that, for Vertlib, a discourse that pays tribute to the complexities of history, memory, and individual experience can only ever be instigated in the realm of literature. I thus illustrate how contemporary German-language Jewish literature allows us to scrutinize some of the broader trends in Holocaust and memory studies, while further building the case for an ethics of fictional discourse.

The final chapter brings together the transgenerational, transmedial, and transnational travels of Holocaust memory via an examination of Eva Menasse's *Quasikristalle*. I situate the novel within the context of recent debates about the family or multigenerational novel, arguing that Menasse's text works toward a multivocal and possibly postfamilial aesthetics. *Quasikristalle* furthermore represents a metadiscursive engagement with various stages of Holocaust remembrance that addresses the issue of empathy and apathy in the face of Holocaust hypermediation, while also scrutinizing the transformation of the Holocaust into a hypermobile, "floating," and ubiquitous signifier. Menasse's text is wary of the universalization of the Holocaust signifier, owing to its interference with various sociopolitical discourses in a manner that is moralizing and ethically unproductive. At the same time, it hints at the metadiscursive capabilities of the literary text as a possible antidote to representational and memorial oversaturation.

1: Rethinking Testimony: Authenticity, "Travelling Memories," and Post-Holocaust Jewish Identities in Benjamin Stein's *Die Leinwand*

Introduction: Remediating the Wilkomirski Affair

HOLOCAUST REMEMBRANCE in the new millennium oscillates between the acknowledgment of hypermediation, on the one hand, and a continuing desire for authenticity, on the other. This tension is reflected in contemporary German- and Austrian-Jewish Holocaust fiction, which has seen a rise of metafictional, metahistoriographical, and semiautobiographical genres that, by definition, focus on the interplay between (historical) reality and its representation. Benjamin Stein's 2010 novel *Die Leinwand*[1] is a case in point: the entanglement of authenticity, (re)mediation, and the appropriation of memories is at the heart of both the novel's content and its formal arrangement.[2] By offering a fictional reconsideration of the Wilkomirski affair, Stein's *Die Leinwand* is bound to touch on central questions concerning the issues of authenticity, memorial transmission, and testimony that have also shaped contemporary scholarly and artistic Holocaust discourse: How is the issue of authenticity renegotiated after the disappearance of the eyewitness generation? How do concepts of authenticity change in the age of remediation? Who does the Holocaust "belong to" after the dying out of the survivor generation? What new pathways of transmission will emerge after the survivor generation has passed away? What happens to the genres of memoir and testimony when memories become increasingly mobile and appropriable? And how do all of these developments affect contemporary notions of Jewish identity?

I will tackle these questions by concentrating on three interconnected issues in Stein's novel: remediation, memorial transmission, and post-Holocaust Jewish identity. I will start with a consideration of the relationship between Stein's novel and its most important intertext, Binjamin Wilkomirski's *Bruchstücke* (1997; translated as *Fragments: Memories of a Wartime Childhood*, 1995). Reading both works as well as their intertextual relationship through Bolter and Grusin's framework of "remediation," I will demonstrate how Wilkomirski's *Bruchstücke* was in itself already a product of complicated circuits of mediatization and remediation. This reading shifts the focus away from Wilkomirski's breach of the autobiographical pact, highlighting instead his (over)compliance with a certain set of literary conventions. My close reading of Stein's novel, which was published fifteen years after the Wilkomirski scandal, will investigate how the generational distance expressed in the text enables a radically changed perspective on the key issues of authenticity, "memorial propriety,"[3] and witnessing in Holocaust discourse.

The Realness of the Fake

In 1995 the Jüdischer Verlag, a subdivision of the renowned German Suhrkamp Verlag, published a book with the title *Bruchstücke: Aus einer Kindheit 1939–1948*, by Binjamin Wilkomirski.[4] The book was marketed and widely regarded as the autobiographical account of how Wilkomirski suffered through and survived several extermination camps as a child, before being adopted by a Swiss couple after the war. The idyllic postwar existence in Switzerland turns out to be treacherous, as Wilkomirski's life is disrupted by traumatic memories and his inability to play by the rules of a society that is largely ignorant of his past. The book finishes with a personal note in which the author explains that, because as a child his original Jewish identity had been suppressed, he was one of the many "Kinder ohne Identität" (*BS*, 142) who managed to survive the Holocaust in often miraculous ways. The note was apparently added because there were doubts concerning the book's authenticity as early as 1994.[5] Suhrkamp decided to publish the book regardless, and it became an immediate and international media success. Wilkomirski's fame as an "authentic" writer of Holocaust memoirs lasted until 1998, when the Swiss journalist Daniel Ganzfried published an article in *Die Weltwoche* uncovering Wilkomirski's real identity as Bruno Grosjean, a Swiss foster child who was taken in by a couple named Dössekker during the 1940s. As Ganzfried stated, Bruno Grosjean knew Auschwitz and Majdanek "only as a tourist."[6] Suhrkamp subsequently had to withdraw the publication. Ganzfried's article sparked heated discussions in both the media and academia, resulting in the by now widely accepted view that Wilkomirski's memoir is a fake, although Wilkomirski/Grosjean/Dössekker never admitted as much.

I want to focus here not so much on Wilkomirski's/Grosjean's/Dössekker's possible psychopathology, but rather on the reasons why so many people willingly believed in the authenticity of his memoir, as this allows us to approach the genres of testimony and the Holocaust memoir in innovative ways. Echoing Sara Jones's insights, I want to make the case of for "testimony as a performance through culture,"[7] which relies on particular authenticating devices that are embedded in specific frameworks of reception. Wilkomirski's perception as a Holocaust survivor (and *Bruchstücke*'s reception as testimony) resulted from a complex interplay between intratextual strategies and extratextual performance, which also fooled experts like Sander Gilman: "Ich habe es wirklich geglaubt, und zwar deshalb, weil dieser Text tatsächlich meiner Vorstellung eines Textes von Kindheitserinnerungen entsprach."[8] Wilkomirski's text thus achieved what I would call an "authenticity effect" by skillfully deploying some of the tropes and narrative conventions that, at the time, marked the Holocaust memoir and testimonial discourse more generally.[9] Wilkomirski's text thereby—unwittingly—revealed the increasingly "generic nature of testimony,"[10] forcing us to reconsider the authenticity imperative that defines the genre of autobiography in general and the survivor memoir in particular.[11]

A fake always points to an original whose form it tries to imitate and reproduce as accurately as possible. Fakes are possible only "in relation to a form with a clearly established genre," which carries "sufficient cultural prestige and value,"[12] so that the act of faking promises to increase symbolic capital. By the 1990s the genre of the Holocaust memoir had undergone a process of canonization that relied on certain conventions and topoi, which Wilkomirski—purposefully or not—appropriated and remediated to create a highly successful work of literature. At the same time, his audience was so acquainted with the genre's rules that Wilkomirski's text immediately triggered a specific mode of reception: the reading public received his text as an autobiographical testimony, treating the author as a survivor and witness. Susanne Düwell has pointed out that Wilkomirski's memoir belonged to a specific subcategory of the genre, which is visually oriented and aimed at creating immediacy, rather than reflecting its own constructedness:

> In Wilkomirskis Text werden die mit dem Genre der Shoah-Literatur verbundenen Rezeptionserwartungen übererfüllt: Der Text weist zahlreiche versteckte intertextuelle Bezüge zu Büchern und Filmen über die Shoah auf und bedient sich . . . gängiger Topoi der Shoah-Literatur und des Diskurses über sie. In einigen Passagen präsentiert sich der Text als literarische Umsetzung einer Konzeption des Traumas, das vergangene Erfahrung in photographisch exakten Bildern und Körpererinnerungen aufspeichert: Verwendet werden Unsagbarkeitstopi, antirhetorische Figuren und die literarische Inszenierung einer kindlichen Perspektive, die deshalb unverfälscht erscheint, weil die kulturelle Kontextualisierung von Wahrnehmung zu fehlen scheint.[13]

Düwell suggests that the emergence of this type of Holocaust memoir was reinforced by a specific notion of trauma; namely, the poststructuralist one I have outlined in the introduction.[14] Similarly, Amy Hungerford contends that "we might also note that the holocaust memoir has become a genre—with all the conventionality that term implies—because trauma theorists in the academy have been working to elaborate, explain, and theorize about the things such memories have in common."[15] And so it is that the stress on fragmentation, painful openness, and a quintessential unintelligibility, the emphasis on visual perception and flashback structures, and even the notion of literal trauma—all of which can be identified as key features in Caruth's writing—can all be found in Wilkomirski's text.

The "authenticity effect" of *Bruchstücke* thus relies on a twofold remediation: Wilkomirski's text embraced the literary conventions of the Holocaust memoir, while also emulating a specific type of traumatic memory that had been popularized by testimonial and poststructuralist trauma discourse in the early 1990s. The emergence of these conventions and tropes in turn involved their own cycles of remediation—as canonical artifacts, they were, as Aleida Assmann puts it, "destined to be repeatedly re-read, appreciated, staged, performed, and commented."[16] These acts of repetition then helped to cement their paradigmatic status and influence, which led to further recycling, and so on. The re- and hypermediated state of Holocaust discourse therefore emerges as one of the central preconditions for both the formation and the success of Wilkomirski's text. Such a perspective shifts the focus away from a moralizing or pathologizing interpretation, highlighting instead the pervasiveness and efficacy of certain discursive guidelines, even in the case of a "limit event" like the Holocaust and a supposedly "authentic" genre such as testimony.[17] I therefore agree with Barbara Staff's assessment that fakes harbor a certain reflexive potential, if they are understood as "sensible Seismographen des literarischen Marktes, die in perfekter Simulation von Authentizität den Bedürfnissen und Erwartungen des Publikums vollkommen entsprechen. Damit sind sie paradoxerweise echt und unecht zugleich; echt als Diskursphänomene ihrer Zeit; unecht als Fälschungen."[18]

Authenticity Effects in *Bruchstücke*

As argued in the introduction, the entanglement in various cycles of remediation does therefore not preclude the production of authenticity. Wilkomirski's book was praised for its raw authenticity, which was linked to its makeshift, fragmentary, or even clichéd form.[19] This paradox can be explained with reference to the aforementioned "authenticity effect." In the age of remediation, authenticity must be understood as a quintessentially performative category: "Recent engagements with authenticity highlight that it is necessarily the result of careful aesthetic construction that depends on the use of identifiable techniques with the aim of achieving certain effects for certain reasons."[20] Bolter and Grusin emphasize that, in an environment of hypermediation, the achievement of immediacy and transparency is premised on a growing number of increasingly refined and interactive media technologies. While these are necessary for upholding the illusion of immediacy and authenticity, they also threaten to destroy it. If we thus accept "the constructed and processual nature of authenticity" as something that is produced by way of specific media techniques,[21] then this suggests that the employment of these strategies can paradoxically have an authenticating force.[22]

Sara Jones describes the production of seemingly authentic testimonies by way of media technologies as "mediated immediacy."[23] A few examples from Wilkomirski's memoir will illustrate how this paradoxical idea can be put into practice: by applying a clear temporal framework, the subtitle of Wilkomirski's book—*Aus einer Kindheit 1939–1948*—already suggests that we are confronted with a historical account and not a work of fiction. In the aforementioned afterword a certain "B.W."—who can easily be identified as the author of *Bruchstücke*—tells us that what we have just read are indeed his authentic "Bruchstücke des Erinnerns" (*BS*, 143). This implies that the book's author, narrator, and protagonist are identical, which means that *Bruchstücke* is "paratextuell deutlich autobiographisch markiert."[24] This contradicts Wilkomirski's claims that the reader was free to read his text either autobiographically or as fiction.[25] The book's first couple of pages—which, unlike the rest of the text, do not have a chapter heading—appear as some kind of foreword, guiding our reception:

> Meine frühen Kindheitserinnerungen gründen in erster Linie auf den exakten Bildern meines fotografischen Gedächtnisses und den dazu bewahrten Gefühlen—auch denen des Körpers. Dann kommt die Erinnerung des Gehörs und an Gehörtes, auch an Gedachtes, und erst zuletzt die Erinnerung an Selbstgesagtes. (*BS*, 7)

Traumatic memories are presented here as exact replicas of an original event, which is stored away in a photographic archive. Wilkomirski's statement also implies a hierarchy of sensual and bodily experiences above and beyond language and reflection. He posits that the visual images are the primary and seemingly "natural" sense of memory. This version of traumatic memory interestingly concurs with the poststructuralist branch of trauma theory as put forward by Caruth, Felman, and Laub.

This idea of traumatic memory as an undistorted copy of the event is combined with a specific staging of the authorial subject: "Ich bin kein Dichter, kein Schriftsteller. Ich kann nur versuchen, mit Worten das Erlebte, das Geschehene so exakt wie möglich abzuzeichnen—so genau, wie es eben mein Kindergedächtnis aufbewahrt hat: noch ohne Kenntnis von Perspektive und Fluchtpunkt" (*BS*, 8). Wilkomirski creates here what Roland Barthes has termed the "referential illusion."[26] According to Barthes, nineteenth-century realism deployed this strategy, which originated in historiographical discourse, in order to create the impression that the reader is faced with "the advantage of the referent alone"—the thing itself and not a representation.[27] Wilkomirski too constructs language as a transparent window to the traumatic past, which fosters a sense of utmost immediacy.[28] He reinforces the "referential illusion" with statements such as "Ich bin kein Dichter, kein Schriftsteller" (*BS*, 8) and makes us believe that we encounter pure traumatic experience untouched by the hands of the authorial subject, the cultural canon, or his grown-up self. This strategy is reminiscent of Caruth's performative notion of literary language, which posits that language does not represent, but rather embodies, trauma.

The phenomenon of the "referential illusion" and the broader discourse of transparent immediacy is key to understanding why the chaotic, antilinear, vague, and at times contradictory style of Wilkomirski's book only enhanced its authenticity effect. Wilkomirski develops and performs an aesthetics and poetics of fragmentation, which is implied by the memoir's title, *Bruchstücke*:

> Meine frühesten Erinnerungen gleichen einem Trümmerfeld einzelner Bilder und Abläufe. Brocken des Erinnerns mit harten, messerscharfen Konturen, die noch heute kaum ohne Verletzung zu berühren sind. Oft chaotisch Verstreutes, chronologisch nur selten zu gliedern; Brocken, die sich immer wieder beharrlich dem Ordnungswillen des erwachsen Gewordenen widersetzen und den Gesetzen der Logik entgleiten. (*BS*, 7)

Throughout the text, the reader is confronted with an assemblage of fairly short, episodic, and often unconnected chapters, set either on the way to or in one of the extermination camps, in an orphanage in Krakow, or in postwar Switzerland. The resulting overall impression of a "Trümmerfeld" (*BS*, 7) is enhanced by the internal structure of the Switzerland-based chapters, in which the everyday life of the protagonist—and thus the narrative—is repeatedly disrupted by traumatic nightmares or flashbacks that are usually triggered by minor details such as the smell of bread or a ski lift. Although the narrative progresses more or less chronologically from the flight from Riga to the camps, to the orphanage in Krakow, and then on to life in Switzerland, the reader is under the impression that time is at a standstill, leaving the protagonist trapped in a past that simply will not pass. This atmosphere of fragmentation and disorientation is further increased by various topoi of uncertainty, expressed via, for example, the repeated phrase "ich weiß es nicht mehr" (*BS*, 15).

This interplay between fragmentation and vagueness has an authenticating effect for two reasons. First, it mimics the child's perspective, the child being unable to comprehend or logically arrange the experiences. This gives the reader the impression of having immediate access to

Wilkomirski's authentic "Kindergedächtnis," which merely recorded the events, "noch ohne Kenntnis von Perspektive und Fluchtpunkt" (*BS*, 8), that is, without a sense of interpretation or formal arrangement. Second, the structure of fragmentation and incomprehension correlates with central assumptions of poststructuralist trauma theory.[29] As outlined previously, Caruth conceptualizes trauma as a sudden or catastrophic event that shatters the subject's cognitive and psychic abilities, which is why the experience can be accessed only belatedly. Since the traumatic experience is therefore categorically split off from the subject, it is not available for representation but rather finds expression in traumatic repetition, understood as "the literal return of the past."[30]

Both traumatic dissociation and the literalness of trauma can be found in Wilkomirski's account. The dissociative nature of trauma is expressed at the level of form through fragmentation, whereas the literalness of trauma is explicitly mentioned in the text itself: "Ein Alptraum zerstörte die friedliche Ruhe des ersten Schlafes im neuen Kinderheim. Ein Alptraum, der sich in den folgenden Jahren unerbittlich wiederholte, in allen Bildern, in jeder Einzelheit, gleichsam als unaufhörlich aufeinander folgende *Kopie*, Nacht für Nacht" (*BS*, 38; italics added). Dissociation and literalness come together in the flashback structure, which defines the book's narrative style and plotline: Binjamin is frequently overpowered by his traumatic recollections, which catapult him back into a past that is edged in his mind in a pristine, unaltered fashion. The frequent use of the present tense suggests that the past events have not lost any of their immediacy; they are not remembered, which would imply an element of temporal distance and distortion, but rather recorded, so that they can be repeated in a literal fashion. Furthermore, both Wilkomirski and Caruth conceptualize traumatic memory as quintessentially visual and as categorically removed from the subject's cognitive abilities: "Die ersten Bilder tauchen auf, vereinzelt nur, als Auftakt quasi, Blitzlichtern gleich, ohne sicheren Zusammenhang, aber scharf und deutlich. Bilder nur, noch kaum begleitet von eigenem Denken" (*BS*, 8). The convergence of Wilkomirski's account and Caruth's theories indicates that Wilkomirski, consciously as well as subconsciously, drew on a number of conventions that, by the 1990s, had evolved into a veritable discourse on trauma and the testimonial form. Oddly enough, the strict adherence to these conventions made his text seem authentic, because it conformed with (and confirmed) audience expectations. Both Caruth's theory and Wilkomirski's writings are indebted to the "logic of transparent immediacy"; that is, strategic attempts to efface the medium so that we feel like we encounter the thing itself rather than its representation.[31] The main ethical problem with Wilkomirski's *Bruchstücke* is thus not so much that it invented a Holocaust autobiography—for there must be a place for fictional engagements with the event in Holocaust discourse—

but that it masked this invention as a reality and refused to acknowledge the necessary gap that always separates an event from its representation, thus creating the illusion of representation without mediation. In the following, I will demonstrate how Stein's text counters what I would call the representational naivety of *Bruchstücke* with a hyperawareness of its own mediality and an ethics of self- and metareflexivity. The novel's formal arrangement will emerge as inseparable from *Die Leinwand*'s broader ethical stance.

Representational Naivety vs The Ethics of Form

The detour via Wilkomirski's text has been necessary to understand how the negotiation of questions of authenticity, memorial transmission, and witnessing in *Die Leinwand* is fundamentally different from what is presented in *Bruchstücke*. I will illustrate how, contrary to Wilkomirski's emphasis on immediacy, *Die Leinwand* stresses re- and hypermediation and identifies these as the conditions of possibility behind what is presented as the Minsky affair in the text. I will also demonstrate how the novel probes its own implication in the cycles of re- and hypermediation by way of its form.

Stein's text is formally and thematically complex: the novel comes with two front covers, which mark the starting point for two independent storylines that converge in the middle of the book. The color red is associated with the first-person narrative of Jan Wechsler, a former writer-journalist turned publisher, whose Orthodox Jewish family life is disrupted by the arrival of a mysterious suitcase. Upon closer inspection, he finds a number of enigmatic artifacts in the suitcase, such as a book entitled *Maskeraden* by someone who is also named Jan Wechsler. In this "Enthüllungsbuch" (*DL*, W.44),[32] the other Wechsler (whom from here on I will refer to as Wechsler 2) reports on a literary scandal from the past involving a certain Minsky and his book *Aschentage*. In 1995 Minsky published an autobiographical account describing his fate as a child survivor of the Holocaust. The "memoir" was, however, eventually exposed as a "Maskerade," "ein erfundenes Rührstück, mit dem er wie ein gewöhnlicher Hochstapler Kasse machte" (*DL*, W.49) by none other than Wechsler 2, the author of *Maskeraden*. Stein's novel thus offers a fictionalization of the Wilkomirski affair, with Wechsler 2 acting as a literary double of Daniel Ganzfried, who wrote . . . *alias Wilkomirski—Die Holocaust-Travestie* (2002), and Minsky as the fictional embodiment of Wilkomirski. After having read *Maskeraden*, Wechsler suspects a case of mistaken identity; he therefore launches a criminal investigation, which gradually confirms the reader's suspicion that the recipient of the suitcase and the author of *Maskeraden* are identical. The suitcase comes from Wechsler's own past as the author of *Maskeraden*, the memory of which he has suppressed and replaced with an elaborate fiction:

Ich bin also Jan Wechsler, Schweizer Autor und Journalist mit schillernder Vergangenheit an den Rändern des politischen Spektrums. Nach meinem Enthüllungscoup bin ich aus meinem Leben geflüchtet. Die Biographie, an die ich mich heute erinnere, ist die Legende, die ich selbst aufgebaut habe. . . . Ich lebe in einem Film, den ich selbst inszeniert habe. (*DL*, W.137)

The search for his real identity takes Wechsler to Israel, where he is confronted with another specter from the past in the shape of the psychiatrist Amnon Zichroni, who was last seen alive by Wechsler before disappearing without a trace. Wechsler is locked up in an Israeli prison cell, where the memories finally return to him: he remembers that he has indeed been to Israel before, where he stayed as a guest at Zichroni's house. Their somewhat tense encounter ended with a showdown at a mikveh in Moza; the book remains inconclusive as to whether or not Wechsler had killed Zichroni.

This open ending serves as a passage into the book's other—blue—narrative strand, which is told by Amnon Zichroni. While Wechsler's narrative reconstructs the events retrospectively from the present moment (i.e., the arrival of the suitcase), jumping back and forth between the present and the (alleged) past, Zichroni's autobiographical narrative progresses chronologically from his ultra-Orthodox upbringing in Mea Shearim, his youth in his uncle's house in Switzerland, his psychiatric training and occupation in the United States, and his reluctant return to Israel. Zichroni's life is marked by the discovery of his "Erinnerungssinn" (*DL*, Z.8), which enables him to experience other people's memories by looking into their eyes or touching them with his bare hands. While he initially struggles to accept his supernatural ability, his friend Eli Rothstein encourages him to see it as a gift sent from God that should be used to help people. In the spirit of the kabbalistic concept of *tikkun olam*, that is, the idea of healing or repairing God's creation,[33] Zichroni decides to use his ability for therapeutic purposes. He eventually moves back to Switzerland after the sudden death of his uncle, and it is here that his personal and professional equilibrium disintegrates. He meets the Swiss violin maker Minsky, with whom he quickly establishes a close bond of friendship. This is why Minsky lets Zichroni in on the "secret" of his horrible life story:

Den ganzen Tag über, den ich bei ihm verbrachte, rauchte er ununterbrochen und erzählte mit vielen, langen Pausen von Auschwitz und Majdanek, vom Bild seines Vaters, der in einem kleinen Ort bei Minsk, wo er geboren sei, vor seinen und den Augen seiner Mutter von weißrussischen Milizen ermordet wurde. Er erzählte von den Baracken des Lagers, vom allgegenwärtigen Tod und den Ratten, von seiner Rettung und den Jahren im Kinderheim in Polen und schließlich in der Schweiz, in die man ihn, wie er es ausdrückte, verschleppt hatte, um ihn seiner Vergangenheit zu berauben. (*DL*, Z.172–73)

Zichroni unhesitatingly believes Minsky's claims, but "der Wunsch, Minsky und sein Leid wirklich zu verstehen" (*DL*, Z.174) provokes him nonetheless to use his "Erinnerungssinn." He sees a decontextualized scene of terror and violence, which is only afterward specified as a Holocaust memory by Minsky himself—an observation that will be of some importance. Convinced of the authenticity of Minsky's pain and suffering, Zichroni, in the spirit of *tikkun olam*, decides to support him in regaining his memories, thus acting in a similar manner to Wilkomirski's therapist, Elitsur Bernstein.[34] This process results in the book *Aschentage*, which is later exposed as a fake by Jan Wechsler. Zichroni describes Wechsler's campaign as a "Hatz" (*DL*, Z.182) that causes the complete disintegration of Minsky's life and psychic health, while also destroying Zichroni's career as a psychiatrist. Leaving his old life behind and returning to Israel, he finds work as a hypnotherapist. According to Zichroni, years after the affair, Wechsler turns up at his doorstep, determined to pretend the whole affair had not happened (the reader of the Wechsler segment knows that Wechsler in fact has no recollection of the affair). Wechsler's attitude gradually unleashes all the pent-up anger that Zichroni had harbored ever since Minsky's and his own downfall. During a showdown at the mikveh in Moza, Zichroni finally loses control and seemingly tries to drown Wechsler: "Als er wieder auftauchte und zitternd prustete, sah ich ihm direkt in die Augen und griff nach seinem Kopf. Ich hielt ihn wie einen Ball zwischen meinen Händen und drückte ihn langsam, doch so fest wie ich nur konnte, zurück ins Wasser" (*DL*, Z.193). Zichroni takes off the white gloves that normally protect him from the influx of other people's memories right before he pushes Wechsler into the water. This should give him access to Wechsler's memories, thus directing the reader (back) to the red segment of the book. The Zichroni narration thus merges into the Wechsler plotline, with the mikveh as an entry point, and vice versa, which gives the book a looplike structure.[35] The Zichroni ending appears to be more conclusive than the finale of the Wechsler narration, but this impression changes when one considers the period during which Zichroni's report was written: in the book it says, "*Sh'vat–Av 5768*" (*DL*, Z.193; italics in the original), which roughly translates as January–August 2008. The production period of Wechsler's narrative is, however, identified as "Februar–Oktober 2008" (*DL*, W.204), which means that he was still alive after Zichroni allegedly killed him. The ending of the Zichroni plotline thus inevitably leads (back) to Wechsler's narration and into the aforementioned loop.

The novel makes it clear that there is no single pathway through the thicket of its narrations and perspectives—it is entirely up to the reader where and when to start:

Zwei Hauptwege und verschlungene Nebenpfade führen durch diesen Roman. Hinter jedem Umschlag befindet sich je ein möglicher Ausgangspunkt für das Geschehen. Es ist Ihnen oder auch dem Zufall überlassen, wo Sie zu lesen beginnen. Sie können der Erzählung bis zur Mitte des Buches folgen, es dann wenden und am anderen Ausgangspunkt weiterlesen. Um einem der Nebenpfade zu folgen, wenden Sie einfach nach jedem Kapitel das Buch und lesen Sie im anderen Strang weiter, wo Sie zuvor unterbrochen haben. Sie können sich jedoch auch Ihren ganz eigenen Weg suchen. (*DL*, 5)

The reader's decision, however, is not without consequences: depending on where and how we start approaching *Die Leinwand*, the Wilkomirski/Minsky affair will present itself in two differing—maybe even dissenting—ways. The narrators use different narrative styles (chaotic and nonlinear in Wechsler's case, chrono- and teleological in Zichroni's), and interpret the Minsky affair in diverging ways. By the time readers become aware of the crux of this matter, it is actually too late: they will never be able to reverse the first decision, which was taken more or less unwittingly ("es ist Ihnen oder auch dem Zufall überlassen"), and which unavoidably colors their perception of the affair. Hence, the book's form teaches readers that there is no Archimedean point from which one can gain an objective, impartial view of (historical) reality or the truth. Just as the readership is implicated in the creation of Stein's novel—their choices determine the story that they are reading, which does not exist independently from them—so our perception of reality is always based on subjective perspectives, needs, and desires—the "truth" remains inaccessible. The novel hence issues a warning against taking the moral high ground, since the readers' interpretation of the affair is necessarily just as biased as the characters' approaches.[36]

These concerns are also reflected in the novel's title, *Die Leinwand*, as the canvas metaphor relates to the text's central topics of autobiographical remembering and writing. It also stresses the procedural and creative aspect of identity formation and remembrance, which Zichroni understands as constantly shifting and deeply transformative:

In der Analyse konnte man ihnen die Zügel wieder in die Hand geben—oder vielmehr die Palette und den Pinsel, mit dem sie auf der Leinwand ihrer Erinnerungen neue Akzente setzten. Dabei konnte man selbst ganz zur Leinwand werden, zu einer Projektionsfläche, auf der die Patienten mögliche Gegenentwürfe skizzierten und neue Möglichkeiten erprobten. . . . Dabei wanderten sie ebenso durch Tausende möglicher Welten wie beim Eintauchen in Bücher oder in Musik. (*DL*, Z.152)

Whereas the idea of the canvas points to—and, at least in Zichroni's case, celebrates—the fictional character of remembrance and identity formation, the motif of the mikveh is tied to the personal transformation and the idea of a tabula rasa. Both images therefore reflect the process of auto-biographical self-(re)construction, albeit from different angles. The Zichroni quote also points to the interrelation between the canvas and the projection screen, which implies the powers of the psyche—such as desire, fantasy, and imagination—to shape our perception of other people and of reality. This aspect of the metaphor also involves the reader, as the novel itself can be seen as a canvas for the reader's projections and desires. The reader "creates" the novel in the same way as the artist creates a painting, by adding perspective, highlights, light, and shadow. Finally, the image of the veiled or painted-over canvas, associated with Minsky, highlights the similarity between (autobiographical) memory and the notion of the pal-impsest: "Sein [Minsky's] Leben, so beschrieb er es mir gegenüber, . . . kam ihm vor wie eine Leinwand, wie ein überdimensionales verfälschtes Gemälde. Er trug die Farben ab, um die Grundierung freizulegen. . . . Er versuchte, die Konturen zu finden und zu schärfen" (DL, Z.176). The central point made in the novel, however, is that the actual "Grundierung"—the original, pristine experience—can never be excavated and might never have existed in the first place.

In the Wechsler segment, Minsky's/Wilkomirski's story is presented at a very early point in the narration as a literary scandal from the past, which has already gone through various cycles of remediation. Wechsler and the reader are thus confronted solely with mediated and mediatized second-hand depictions of the affair, since Wechsler has forgotten about his per-sonal involvement in the scandal (and the reader never finds out whether what he remembers later on is actually authentic). The first of these depic-tions is Jan Wechsler's *Maskeraden*, which is in itself a remediation of Daniel Ganzfried's book . . . *alias Wilkomirski*. Wechsler's story is thus marked by the complicated interplay between various levels of observation and (re)mediation: the original book, *Bruchstücke*, remediates the genre of the Holocaust memoir, which is then remediated in Daniel Ganzfried's text, which, in Stein's novel, becomes the model for Wechsler's *Maskeraden*. *Maskeraden* focuses on the literary success and scandal that emerged after Minsky's book *Aschentage* was published. It thus centers on the reception of the book, not the text itself (which is never explicitly quoted in Stein's novel). Furthermore, the content of *Maskeraden* is paraphrased for the reader by the narrator Jan Wechsler (the recipient of the suitcase), which adds a final layer of remediation. The remediation of Ganzfried's text via *Maskeraden* concentrates on a critique of the so-called Holocaust industry ("das Geschäft mit dem Holocaust"; DL, W.46) and the "Kult ums Erinnern" (DL, W.46), which provides the backdrop for Wechsler 2's harsh judgment of the Minsky case: he offers a brief outline of Minsky's supposed (auto)biography as it is presented in *Aschentage*, and of the suc-cess story that initially followed the book's publication. Wechsler 2 claims that he immediately knew that Minsky was jumping on the bandwagon of the so-called Shoah business, making money from a biography that was not his own:

> Für Wechsler stand fest: Minsky war kein Überlebender des Holocaust. Die Lager in Polen hatte er lediglich als Tourist gesehen, Jahrzehnte später, als erwachsener Mann. Als Kind hingegen war er nie dort gewesen, ja hatte die von Krieg und Massenmord verschonte Schweiz, wo er geboren worden war, nicht einmal verlassen. Minsky musste das Handwerk gelegt werden. Man musste ihn entlarven und gemeinsam mit ihm die gesamte Bagage, die mit dem Holocaust, mit Entschädigungsforderungen, Büchern, Filmen und sonstigem Schauerkram Geschäfte machte. (*DL*, W.49)

Wechsler's summary of *Maskeraden* ends with the downfall of Minsky and the sudden end of his literary success after exposure by Wechsler 2. Wechsler clearly does not agree with the harsh opinions expressed by Wechsler 2 ("Ich wurde das Gefühl nicht los, es mit einem Demagogen zu tun zu haben"; *DL*, W.46), which, as I will argue, holds true for the novel as a whole. By concentrating on the "Shoah business," *Die Leinwand* shifts the perspective on the Minsky/Wilkomirski scandal in three important ways: First, the Wechsler narration of *Die Leinwand* presents the Holocaust as part of an industry, or, to put it less provocatively, as firmly entrapped in a (memorial) routine or a highly discursivized framework.[37] The Holocaust is depicted as the object of literary scandals and sociopolitical debates and not as a matter of authentic memories or personal traumas. This impression is reinforced by the fact that the actual text of *Bruchstücke/Aschentage* is never quoted in the Wechsler narration; it is only the scandal, that is, the reception of the book, that is debated extensively. Additionally, Minsky/Wilkomirski himself only appears very briefly in the narration, as seen through the eyes of Wechsler.[38] Second, the rhetoric of the Holocaust industry highlights the changed status of authenticity in the "era of the post-witness":[39] the whole affair surrounding Minsky can only escalate in the way it does because the Holocaust has indeed become a commodity, a cultural and identitarian building block, which can be easily appropriated and (ab)used, as is made apparent by Wechsler 2: "Die Schilderungen der Lagergräuel wirkten auf Wechsler wie Kolportagen, Verschnitte dokumentarischer Quellen aus verschiedenen Händen, vermischt mit dem Kitsch des Grauens und legitimiert einzig durch die Tatsache, dass man einem Überlebenden nicht widersprechen durfte" (*DL*, W.48). Wechsler 2's assessment introduces a tension between the clichéd nature of the "Verschnitte" and the aura of authenticity that surrounds the survivor: it was this aura that legitimized Minsky's otherwise badly written text. Minsky's transgression concerns the appropriation of this aura and the discursive authority that comes with it. Thirdly, Wechsler's account paraphrases the Minsky affair and Wechsler 2's polemic from a moral and historical distance (intradiegetically, the affair lies in the past). Wechsler is wary of Wechsler 2's criticism, not only because it strikes him as unnecessarily harsh but also because it appears to him as polemical and outdated. *Die Leinwand* therefore reflects metadiscursively on the hypermediation of Holocaust memories in the context of the Wilkomirski/Minsky affair, while considering the criticism of this hypermediation via the rhetoric of the "Shoah business." The novel itself adopts a third position, by highlighting that hypermediation is inevitable, meaning that all we can achieve are hypersubjective and partial truths.

After having received the unsettling letter from von Dennen, Wechsler makes another discovery that calls into question his sense of identity. Reading Wechsler 2's debut novel (which is not *Maskeraden*), he realizes that Wechsler's fictions are actually rooted in his personal biography.[40] Whereas he is initially convinced that Wechsler 2 has somehow managed to steal his biography and identity, he ultimately has to admit that the opposite might also be true: "Ich selbst könnte der Dieb sein und irgendwann in den letzten zehn Jahren die Regensburgers, Hillers und Markovás [i.e., the characters from Wechsler 2's debut novel] adoptiert und ihre Familiensaga zur Geschichte *meiner* Familie gemacht haben" (*DL*, W.82; italics in the original). This insight is deeply ironic, of course, for if Wechsler's suspicions are true (which they are, as we find out), he actually committed the same crime he originally accused Minsky of: he appropriated someone else's identity to escape from an unbearable reality. The harsh judgment he passed on Wechsler 2 thus applies equally to himself: "Er hatte *mich* erzählt, ohne mich um Erlaubnis gefragt, ja überhaupt nur mit mir gesprochen zu haben. Dass er es noch weiter treiben würde, daran zweifelte ich nicht. Wer anderen die Identität stiehlt, schreckt auch vor Mord nicht zurück" (*DL*, W.81; italics in the original).

Increasingly confused, Wechsler consults another book on the matter in a search for answers: this time one written by a certain Hans Macht and entitled *Die Akte Minsky*, which is a remediation of Stefan Maechler's aforementioned study. *Die Leinwand* concentrates on those sections of Macht's/Maechler's text that give an account of Minsky's/Wilkomirski's childhood and posit that the "Urtrauma" (*DL*, W.88) of his exceptionally harsh upbringing led to "Minskys spätere[m] Rollenspiel als Holocaust-Überlebender" (*DL*, W.89)—an interpretation that does not convince Wechsler. Wechsler's summary turns to the aftermath of the affair, stressing the overall devastating turn of events for Minsky. The strong emphasis on the hard life that Minsky/Wilkomirski led before and after the affair creates a rather sympathetic outlook, although Wechsler (and Macht) is convinced that he was a fraud: "Es bestand kein Zweifel mehr darüber, wer seine leiblichen Eltern waren" (*DL*, W.90). Macht's work is depicted as the more objective and fact-based counterpart to Wechsler 2's diatribe, which makes both Wechsler and the reader more inclined to adopt Macht's view than the perspective of the "Demagoge" Wechsler 2.

Wechsler's story is an attempt to rip apart the web of multiple (re) mediations and to get to the core of what really happened between him and Minsky. He remains unsuccessful, however: his own seemingly authentic memories resurface eventually, but only in a fragmentary form. We also find out that he has gone through various identity changes, which casts doubt on the true content of his seemingly authentic memories: is he really remembering his *own* past or is he, once again, reproducing someone else's memories?

By contrast, Zichroni's perspective on the Minsky/Wilkomirski affair is entirely different. Minsky is introduced quite late in the story, on page Z.161 (out of a total of 193 pages). The Minsky the reader meets in this narration is not the epicenter of a major literary scandal but one of Zichroni's friends; he is an actual person and not a media phenomenon. It is only after establishing this personal context that the narration proceeds to Minsky's background story, which is told in fragmentary form. The reader who has read the Wechsler segment first is likely to be biased against Minsky's "memories" and Zichroni's sympathetic account in the same way that those readers who start(ed) out with the Zichroni segment are possibly biased against Wechsler. Zichroni traces how Minsky's private story and plight turns into the Minsky affair, underlining the brutality with which Wechsler and the press hunted Minsky down as part of their "Feldzug" (*DL*, Z.184). He draws an extremely negative picture of Wechsler, whose wounded pride seems to have motivated his involvement in the case. Although Zichroni is thus generally on Minsky's side, portraying him as the main casualty in a media war, he also notices the strong performance element of Minsky's behavior, which walks the line between traumatic authenticity and media spectacle:

> Wie immer las Minsky nicht selbst. Ihm hätte die Stimme versagt. Er brauchte jemanden, der für ihn aufs Podium ging, um aus dem Buch zu lesen. Meist spielte er, bevor er den Vortrag begann, ein oder zwei kurze Stücke auf der Violine. Während der Lesung selbst saß er jeweils abseits und hörte mit geschlossenen Augen zu, als ginge er noch einmal alle Orte seiner Erinnerung ab. (*DL*, Z.184)[41]

While this exaggerated behavior does not seem suspicious to Zichroni at the time—he believes in the authenticity of Minsky's trauma—it is retrospectively constructed as a hint at Minsky's disingenuousness and a possible explanation for his actions: he has a craving for attention.

The narration gains momentum when Zichroni finally uses his "Erinnerungssinn" on Minsky. As mentioned, he does this only to gain a deeper understanding of Minsky's suffering, not because he distrusts him at the time. What he sees is a historically unspecified scene of fear and menace:

> Es war das erste und einzige Mal, dass ich Minsky berührte. Als ich meine Hand auf seine Stirn legte, wurde ich von panischer Angst erfasst. Ich hockte zusammengekauert auf einem grob gezimmerten Dielenboden unter einem niedrigen Tisch. Es war dämmerig, und eine Frau stapfte brüllend durch den Raum. Ich sah von ihr nur die Beine, in großen Gummistiefeln, wie Bauern sie tragen. Sie brüllte fortwährend, dass sie mich zerreißen würde, wenn sie mich fände. Dabei schlug sie mit einem Stock oder einer Rute auf den Tisch und gegen die Wände. Die Angst, entdeckt zu werden, war so übermächtig, dass ich aufhörte zu atmen und die Hände auf meine Augen presste, weil ich hoffte zu verschwinden. (*DL*, Z.174–75)

Significantly, the context of the Holocaust is only added to this scene *afterward*, by Minsky himself: "Lederstiefel, sagte Minsky, als hätte ich ihn danach gefragt. Die Blockowa trug blank gewichste Lederstiefel, und der Stock war eine Gerte, die bei jedem Schlag wie ein Brenneisen in die Haut fuhr" (*DL*, Z.175). The vagueness of Zichroni's experience could be explained by the fact that he is confronted with Minsky's childhood memories. Without Minsky's explications, the scene that Zichroni witnesses could have taken place either in the camps or in Minsky's hiding place in Poland or in his foster home. Zichroni's act of witnessing therefore neither proves nor disproves Minsky's claim that he is a Holocaust victim. This is significant, because the "Erinnerungssinn" does not manage to provide the reader with certainty about the (in)authenticity of Minsky's memories.[42] The fact that this does not happen in *Die Leinwand* implies that there is no authority that could rightfully judge the historical accuracy of Minsky's memories. It furthermore suggests that their historical accuracy is not the main point, as the novel puts forward, as Silke Horstkotte has argued, a "funktionale[s] Wahrheitskonzept":[43] "Was . . . ist eine Wahrheit, die tötet, wert gegenüber einer Wahrheit, die jemanden leben lässt?" (*DL*, Z.179).

By contrast, the Wechsler segment presents the Holocaust as an object of literary and societal debates and not as a matter of authentic memories or personal traumas. A highly ritualized and discursivized framework of Holocaust hypermediation forms the backdrop for Wechsler's account. At the same time, it remains unclear whether Wechsler actually manages to regain his own authentic memories, and, owing to the looplike structure of the novel, the characters and the reader endlessly slip from one circuit of representations into the other. These observations suggest that in the age of remediation, Holocaust memory is depicted not so much as an issue of family traumas and intrafamilial postmemory but rather as a problem of mediatization, adoption, and appropriation. Whereas Wechsler actually has a personal connection to the Holocaust—which, however, remains unexplored[44]—neither Zichroni nor Minsky is at all genealogically tied to the event. While Minsky longs to establish this connection by fabricating a victim identity, Zichroni does not ground his Jewish identity in the experience of trauma: "In meine Familie hatte die Vernichtung keine Lücke gerissen. Meine Großeltern und Eltern kamen aus der Schweiz. Ich war . . . zuvor noch nie in Yad Vashem gewesen und hatte es immer vermieden, mir Dokumentationen über den Holocaust anzusehen" (*DL*, Z.174).

Stein's protagonists can no longer generate the same aura of authenticity as the survivor generation, since they do not have any personal experiences of the event. They furthermore—apart from Minsky—no longer aim for a Jewish identity based on trauma and victimization. By downplaying the role of historical accuracy and authenticity from the perspective of a later generation, Stein's text adopts a different, much more sympathetic outlook on the Minsky/Wilkomirski affair, as is also stressed by Horstkotte:

> Damit löst sich der Roman radikal vom Konzept des authentischen Holocaust-Zeugen wie auch vom Anspruch der historischen Forschung, Erinnerungen mithilfe von Dokumenten beweisen oder widerlegen zu können. Subjektive Erinnerung und Imagination schlagen im Roman ganz klar den Fakten- und Beweiszugang.[45]

Although Wechsler and Zichroni pursue radically different approaches to the Minsky case, they also overlap: in both cases Minsky is assigned the role of the victim who gets punished far too harshly for a crime that he—in all probability—committed unwittingly; and in both cases Wechsler features as the perpetrator who went after Minsky mainly because his own artistic ambitions remained unsatisfied. In the Wechsler narration, this harsh assessment is supported by a clever authorial move: because of his psychic dissociation, Wechsler judges his former self and publications from an outside perspective, which makes his criticism of himself appear all the more objective. *Die Leinwand* thus propagates the radical and ineluctable subjectivity of memory, along with the inescapability of hypermediation. In this way, the novel bypasses some of the larger philosophical, ethical, and political issues involved. This is why Hans-Peter Kunisch denounced Stein's novel as "viel zu unkritisch."[46] It is certainly true that Stein's novel does not consider in any detail the clash between its postmodern truisms—identities are fluid, reality is a construct—and the core assumptions governing Holocaust discourse. Furthermore, the fact that memories and identities are mobile, fluid, and open to appropriation in the age of remediation does not necessarily imply that "the issues surrounding the propriety of memory" are no longer important—in fact, the opposite is true.[47] In my view, however, the central insight produced by *Die Leinwand* is that once these memories have entered the cultural archive, there is no institution that can guarantee the rights of ownership. The novel is therefore not so much "unkritisch" (although I also find the exculpation of Minsky's character problematic) as wary of a definitive criticism and judgment. Owing to its form, *Die Leinwand* does not offer its characters or readers a point from which they could safely (in the sense of "objectively") evaluate the Minsky case.

Simultaneously, it is precisely by virtue of its form that Stein's text ultimately escapes naivety and relativism, as has also been noted by Katja Garloff:[48] as mentioned previously, the medium of literature is defined by its ability to carry out first- and second-order observations—fictional discourse offers observations and at the same time reflects on the process of observing as such; it is fundamentally self-reflexive.[49] This means that Stein's novel is able to participate in and reflect on the "cycles of remediation," alongside its own entanglements in them: it is equally self- and metareflexive. Owing to its form, *Die Leinwand* constantly points to its status as a work of fiction, which runs counter to production of authenticity effects in *Bruchstücke/Aschentage*. *Die Leinwand* thus opposes the representational naivety of Wilkomirski's account with a hyperawareness of its own fictionality and dependence on various intertexts, thereby staging and reflecting on itself as the product of various remediations. While Garloff analyzes the novel with a view to "the proliferation of paratexts . . . as an alternative to the collapse of paratextual distinctions in Wilkomirski's *Bruchstücke*,"[50] I would like to emphasize multiperspectivity, narrative uncertainty, and the evocation and remediation of various intertexts as additional pillars of *Die Leinwand*'s self-and metareflexive stance. All of these techniques ultimately require the engagement of the reader, who thereby becomes a—maybe even *the*—producer of the text. Drawing on Roland Barthes's famous distinction between "the readerly" and the "writerly" text—that is, a text that sees the reader either as a passive recipient or as an active producer—we can thus say that the particular strength of Stein's novel lies in its "writerly" mode.[51] The reader of Stein's novel is "no longer a consumer, but a producer of the text,"[52] and this also forces him/her to reflect upon his/her own implication in the dynamics presented in the text alongside the broader issue of Holocaust hypermediation. The critical potential of Stein's work is thus inseparable from its formal arrangement—the somewhat lenient outlook on Minsky's (and Wilkomirski's) character on the level of content needs to be seen in relation to the criticism delivered via the novel's form, which makes the case for an ethics and aesthetics of meta- and self-reflexivity.

The Holocaust as "Travelling Trauma": Prosthesis, Contagion, and Personification

Issues of memorial adoption and appropriation are central to the depiction of the Wilkomirski affair in *Die Leinwand*. Stein's novel stages the mobility of (Holocaust) memories in a hypermediated world as the main problem arising from the scandal: once personal memories are externalized with the help of the media, they become mobile and open to appropriation; it is therefore true that Stein's text does not so much "indict the fake Holocaust memoir" but rather "examines the mechanisms of transmission that make it possible,"[53] as observed by Garloff. Wechsler and Minsky can only construct their fake identities because they have a broad knowledge of and access to the cultural archive, in the form of literary texts, historical studies, documentary films, feature films, and numerous photographic images. These traveling memories move not only between the past and present and different individuals (i.e., interpersonally and transgenerationally) but also between national borders: Wechsler was born an Israeli Jew but adopts the identity of a GDR convert, and Minsky (as well as Wilkomirski/Grosjean/ Dössekker) originally came from Switzerland but adopts the identity of a Latvian-born Holocaust survivor. Whereas the transgenerational, transmedial, and transnational migration of mediated memories is not a new phenomenon as such, their mobility is increased and accelerated in the age of remediation: their proliferation in the mass media gives rise to what Alison Landsberg has termed "prosthetic memory."[54] This is a "portable, fluid, and non-essentialist form of memory,"[55] generated and transmitted by "an experiential site such as a movie theater or museum."[56] Through the interaction with these "experiential sites," a specific connection to the past arises: "The person does not simply apprehend a historical narrative but takes on a personal, deeply felt memory of a past event through which he or she did not live. The resulting prosthetic memory has the ability to shape that person's subjectivity and politics."[57] Landsberg's theory is situated within a wider political and ethical framework, dedicated to constructing nonessentialist "political alliances that transcend race, class and gender."[58]

In a similar vein to Caruth and Hirsch, Landsberg highlights the particularly sensuous quality of the medium—that is, cinema, in her case—and also suggests that the body, and the visceral in particular, is a realm of the authentic that can provide more direct access to the past: "Although all aesthetic experience has an affective component, the sensuous in the cinema—the experiential nature of the spectator's engagement with the image—is different from other aesthetic experiences such as reading."[59] This is why Landsberg assumes that moviegoers will automatically and inevitably identify and empathize with a media image. Like Caruth and Hirsch, she conceptualizes media as transparent carriers of affect, which function universally—she fails to culturally contextualize the production and reception of these media and "strips them of mediation," as Rick Crownshaw has rightly pointed out.[60] This emphasis on transparent affect and identification actually thwarts Landsberg's broader political agenda: while, in her view, identification is a strong enough incentive for political engagement, excessive identification can also prevent the recipients from taking any action because they are too caught up in sentiment. Landsberg's writing lacks concrete suggestions on how precisely identification "creates the conditions for ethical thinking" and instigates political action.[61]

Landsberg's approach thus grapples with some of the same issues that underlie Caruth's and Hirsch's thinking and faces similar ethical pitfalls. In spite of these reservations, the idea of "prosthetic memory" is useful for analyzing the transgenerational, transmedial, and transnational transmission of memories in *Die Leinwand*, precisely because it brings to the fore issues of hypermediation, appropriation, identification, and empathy. Landsberg ultimately abandons the distinction between reality and prosthesis altogether: "Any distinction between 'real' memories and prosthetic memories—memories that might be technologically disseminated as commodities by the mass media and worn by their consumers—might ultimately be unimportant."[62] Stein's text also suggests that fabrication and truth are categorically and inextricably intertwined in the realm of memory, which is why established notions of truth and authenticity need to be reinvestigated: "Aber es gibt diese Wahrheit nicht. Sie ist niemandes Besitz. Wir alle halten nur Bruchstücke davon in den Händen. Und weil wir nicht wissen, was wahr ist, müssen wir uns entscheiden, was für uns zählt" (*DL*, Z.61). Terri Tomsky's concerns about the ethical ramifications of "travelling trauma," its commodification, and the establishment of a "trauma economy" are not shared by either Landsberg or Stein in their respective texts.[63] The novel demonstrates that, on a personal level, "travelling traumas" might well be appropriated to gain symbolic capital (this is Wechsler 2's interpretation of the Wilkomirski affair) or to cover up a traumatic past (this is Hans Macht's interpretation and what Wechsler himself has done). *Die Leinwand* ultimately suggests, however, that this is an unavoidable consequence of hypermediation. The novel therefore establishes a middle ground between Landsberg's and Tomsky's positions by neither celebrating nor denigrating the dynamics of "travelling trauma."

Zichroni's "Erinnerungssinn"

At the same time, the novel contrasts the hypermediated mobility of "prosthetic" memories with the phenomenon of Zichroni's so-called Erinnerungssinn. As a fantasy of immediacy, Zichroni's gift seemingly enables a transmission of (traumatic) memories and histories without any mediation: "Ich konnte Zeuge längst zurückliegender Ereignisse werden. Ich konnte sie sogar *ganz authentisch* im Körper des anderen und mit all seinen Sinnen so erleben, wie sie im Gedächtnis aufbewahrt worden waren" (*DL*, Z.134; italics added). The transmission of memories via the "Erinnerungssinn" is depicted as a form of contagion that overwhelms and overburdens the subject. Whenever he touches someone else's skin, Zichroni is completely incapacitated by the violent influx of memories—

this loss of control is repeatedly described by him via an imagery of flooding, drowning, or going blind: "Wieder, wie schon die beiden Male zuvor, war ich von den Bildern überrannt worden. Ich war dem Geschehen ausgeliefert gewesen, ohne auch nur den Hauch einer Möglichkeit, den Verlauf zu kontrollieren" (*DL*, Z.98). He decides to protect himself from the contagiousness of other people's memories by wearing a pair of white gloves (*DL*, Z.124–25). Interestingly, the mechanism of transmission described here is highly reminiscent of the contagion paradigm that I have identified as a central feature of Caruth's and Hirsch's respective trauma theories. Zichroni's "Erinnerungssinn" implies a similar (over)identification with other people's experiences, memories, and traumas. He absorbs these in an act of amalgamation that is not without erotic undertones: he repeatedly speaks of the experience of becoming one with the Other. Because this is a form of transmission that functions nonverbally and literally (in the Caruthian sense), it seemingly offers immediacy. And so it is that Zichroni cannot contextualize or understand the visual impressions and intense bodily sensations that he experiences randomly, which also creates an interesting parallel with Wilkomirski's memory in *Bruchstücke*. This contagious form of transmission is able to transcend intersubjective boundaries through infectious contact.

Zichroni's gift thus appears as a literary exemplification of Caruth's theory, which raises the question whether the reader is faced with an affirmation or a criticism of the contagion paradigm. Arguably, the text gradually deconstructs this fantasy of immediacy by introducing various layers of (re)mediation. At the start of his narration, Zichroni strongly emphasizes the inherent malleability of memories:

> Erinnerung aber ist unbeständig, stets bereit, sich zu wandeln. Mit jedem Erinnern formen wir um, filtern, trennen und verbinden, fügen hinzu, sparen aus und ersetzen so im Laufe der Zeit das Ursprüngliche nach und nach durch die Erinnerung an die Erinnerung. Wer sollte da noch sagen, was einmal wirklich geschehen ist? (*DL*, Z.7–8)

Zichroni's occupation as a psychoanalyst is evident here, as this passage alludes to Freud's famous 1899 essay "Über Deckerinnerungen." Freud argues that the childhood memories that appear the most authentic have undergone multiple processes of displacement and "Umgestaltung,"[64] breaking down the boundaries between memory and fantasy while also upsetting the temporal and causal logic that links an "original" event to the memory of it. Owing to the peculiar logic of *Nachträglichkeit*, an event that happened later in time can change the perception and significance of an earlier event. Freud concludes: "Vielleicht ist es überhaupt zweifelhaft, ob wir bewußte Erinnerungen *aus* der Kindheit haben, oder nicht vielmehr bloß *an* die Kindheit. Unsere Kindheitserinnerungen zeigen uns die ersten Lebensjahre, nicht wie sie waren, sondern wie sie späteren Erweckungszeiten erschienen sind [italics in the original]."[65] Dismissing the idea that our childhood memories are based on "getreue Wiederholung des damals empfundenen Eindrucks,"[66] Freud highlights the power of retrospective construction: we see our childhood in accordance with later needs and impressions, and not how it actually was. Similarly, the Zichroni passage denies the possibility of ever reaching the original event that was at the heart of the various layers of memorial transformation and mediation. He even questions whether "das Ursprüngliche" has actually ever happened: "Wer sollte da noch sagen, was einmal wirklich geschehen ist?"[67] Contrary to his claims, Zichroni is therefore not a "Zeuge längst zurückliegender Ereignisse" (DL, Z.134): what he experiences are other people's memories of events, which in Freudian fashion are "stets bereit, sich zu wandeln."

Zichroni faces the added problem that his visions remain "vage Collage[n] aus eigenem und Fremdem" (DL, Z.99). This is why his friend Eli advises him to work on the "Verringerung des eigenen Egos" (DL, Z.99) through the practice of Bitul Azmo, a form of gradual ego depletion. His reaction to (and maybe even murder of) Wechsler, as recounted in the final pages of his narration, however, highlights the persistence of his ego, as his personal feelings of anger and resentment stop him from achieving forgiveness and reconciliation. His visions thus remain a mashup right until the end, which also calls into question the authenticity of his earlier experiences—particularly with Minsky, as we have to wonder to what extent his vision of Minsky's past was colored by his sympathy for the man. Zichroni's gift therefore fails him on two decisive occasions, as Alessandro Costazza has argued: first, he is unable to determine the truth content of Minsky's claims, and second, he is unable to establish the accuracy of Wechsler's statements.[68] Before attempting to drown Wechsler, he takes off his gloves: if we follow the fantastical logic of the novel, this means that he should be able to tell the reader which of Wechsler's memories were really his and which ones were appropriated. When writing down his version of events after the confrontation with Wechsler, however, he remains silent on the issue. Zichroni's "Erinnerungssinn" does not therefore provide him (or the reader) with access to the "truth," as it is tainted by the distortions of (other people's) memory and Zichroni's own ego. The "Erinnerungssinn" does not therefore point beyond the circuits of (re)mediation, meaning that the desire for authentic, unmediated access to the past remains unfulfilled in Stein's novel.

The Text as Embodied Experience

While Zichroni uses his "Erinnerungssinn" to connect with other people's memories, Wechsler adopts and appropriates them through the act of reading and writing. It eventually becomes clear that Wechsler has appropriated an identity that comes from his own debut novel, which is in itself based on the biography of the extratextual author, Benjamin Stein: "Die

Biographie, an die ich mich heute erinnere, ist die Legende, die ich selbst aufgebaut habe. In meinem ersten Buch habe ich sie als Geschichtenbilderbogen aufgefächert und später für mich selbst adoptiert" (*DL*, W.137).[69] Like Minsky (and Wilkomirski), Wechsler makes use of the cultural archive to construct a convincing (auto)biography.

Not everyone who reads a book or watches a film, however, identifies with the text to the extent that the lines between fact and fiction, self and other become blurred. This would be the idea underpinning Landsberg's claim that audiences, overwhelmed by the immersive experience of films, are categorically unable (or unwilling) to draw the line between reality and representation. Stein's text, however, points to a central flaw in Landsberg's argument: in *Die Leinwand*, identification is not so much the *result of* but rather the *basis for* the adoptive strategies that underpin the phenomenon and practice of "prosthetic memory." Wechsler's problems spring from his specific approach to literature, not from the immersiveness of the medium: "Es dauerte nicht lange, und ich lebte nur noch mit, in und um die Bücher" (*DL*, W.33); "Kaum eines der Bücher, die ich Buchstabe für Buchstabe *verschlang*, mir *einverleibte*, ganz und gar *aufnahm*, kaum eines dieser Bücher hat mir je gehört" (*DL*, W.37; italics added). These images of consumption highlight Wechsler's highly identificatory reading practice: literature is something that he devours in order to compensate for a life that, in the context of the oppressive GDR system, he could not live himself. This attitude paves the way for the later adoption of his own fictions, which allow him to escape from a life and self that he cannot accept. In her essay "Memorizing Memory,"[70] Amy Hungerford argues that poststructuralist trauma theory "conflate(s) reading and experience" by way of the "personification" of the text,[71] which attributes to written words the characteristics of a person. As a result of this conflation, writing is imagined as "the embodiment (rather than the representation) of the kind of experience—of 'life'—that only persons can be said to have."[72] For Hungerford, Dössekker is a case in point:

> And this is precisely what I take Bruno Dössekker also to have done. He absorbed the accounts of camp life, the stories of extreme violence, the testimonies and histories and photographs, and they finally became him, finally made him Binjamin Wilkomirski. I want to suggest that . . . in the case of Bruno Dössekker, memorizing and memory have become the same thing.[73]

Hungerford thus interprets Wilkomirski's text as symptomatic of larger developments in Holocaust discourse, which can also be found in *Die Leinwand*. Both Wechsler and Minsky obliterate the ontological difference between reality and fiction by transferring literary representations into their personal experiential repertoire. It is therefore not so much the mobility and possible appropriation of "prosthetic memory" that poses a problem but rather the identificatory and appropriative attitude toward representations of other people's experiences and traumas. The hypermediation of Holocaust memories as such does not necessarily lead to appropriation and overidentification; these are a consequence of the personification of the mediatized accounts, which deny their mediality and cast them as embodiments of experience.

In addition to the problems of authenticity and witnessing, Stein's text thus also tackles the issues of memorial transmission in a hypermediated age. In a similar vein to Bolter and Grusin, Stein's novel seems to suggest that the inescapability of remediation actually spawns fantasies of unmediated transmission of experiences and memories—be it in the form of a magical "Erinnerungssinn" or via the personification of texts. These problematic notions of the transgenerational and transmedial travel of traumatic memories are countered by the novel's own take on the theme of transmission: as argued before, *Die Leinwand* critically reflects on these fantasies of immediacy on the level of content, while contrasting them with a hyperawareness of its own fictionality and materiality and of its implication in the "cycles of remediation" on the level of form,[74] as is also emphasized by Garloff:

> Stein engages with the ethical dilemmas arising from the transfer of memories and identities in a different way, through his creative use of paratext. Through a *fictional inflation* of paratext and an emphasis on the gaps between text and paratext, Stein adds the layer of mediation that Wilkomirski's *Bruchstücke* so sorely lacks. By highlighting the defining power of paratext, Stein promotes a more responsible transmission of memories to new generations [italics in the original].[75]

It thus transpires that Holocaust hypermediation as such is not the problem in Stein's text—or at least not a problem that the novel sets out to remedy. Rather, is it our reception of these highly mobile and ubiquitous texts and images—that is, *how* we approach them—that constitutes a potential ethical stance. By fostering, through various techniques, a hyperawareness of its constructedness, form, and mediality, *Die Leinwand* develops what I have called an aesthetics and ethics of meta- and self-reflexivity that also invites readers to reflect upon their position vis-à-vis Stein's and other Holocaust texts. Echoing Gillian Rose's suggestions, literary form and its critical reflection thus emerge as possible responses to the problems of Holocaust representation in the hypermediated age.

Performing Jewishness in a Post-Holocaust World: Religion and Nation

Stein's novel questions notions of Jewish identity that are based on the (appropriated) experience of trauma and victimization. While the survivor and eyewitness generation can still draw on an aura of authenticity that comes from having lived and suffered through the wartime period, this is no longer the case for present and future generations of Jews whose personal and familial ties to the events are about to (or have already) dissolve(d). *Die Leinwand* highlights how, for these generations, the Holocaust has turned into a "travelling trauma," increasingly mobile, free-floating, and adoptable. The trauma of the past no longer defines the narrator-protagonists' sense of Jewishness—a sentiment that has also been expressed by the author Stein in an interview: "Für mein Judentum, . . . brauche ich keinen Zionismus und keinen Holocaust. Das spielt zwar eine Rolle, kommt aber von außen."[76] In contrast to both Wechsler and Zichroni, Minsky builds his (fake) Jewish identity on appropriated Holocaust trauma. An extreme example of "affiliative" postmemory and/or "prosthetic memory," his case challenges both Hirsch's and Landsberg's claim that the postmemorial position is always ethical. Both narrator-protagonists judge Minsky, albeit for different reasons: while Wechsler criticizes him for profiting from his alleged victim status, Zichroni has reservations about his lack of religion. If Jewish self-understanding thus no longer resides in the Holocaust, then this raises the question what other forms of Jewish identity the text explores in a post-Holocaust world.

Religious identity plays an important role for both of Stein's protagonists and for the text as a whole, which offers detailed depictions of Orthodox Jewish life. With both protagonists being Orthodox Jews, the text introduces the non-Jewish reader to various religious objects and customs, such as the mikveh, tzitzit binding, the learning routines at the kheder and the yeshiva, and festive and everyday religious rituals. While Jewish religious life serves as a possible anchor point for Jewish identity in a post-Holocaust world,[77] the novel's promotion of religious Jewish identity is not as unequivocal as one might think. When starting with the Zichroni narration, the reader is plunged into a rich religious world in which the main character gains considerable stability from his religious attachments. Although Zichroni is critical of his ultra-Orthodox upbringing in Mea Shearim, he never questions his uncle's modern Orthodox lifestyle, which is based on the conviction that godly wisdom and worldly knowledge need to coalesce in order to attain perfection—a philosophy that, for Nathan Bollag, is exemplified by his favorite gemstone, the demantoid, famous for its inclusion of impurities (*DL,* Z.28–29). This positive evaluation of Jewish religiousness is further strengthened when Zichroni comes across his patient Lauren, who suffers from a traumatic family history linked to her Christian fundamentalist upbringing. While Christian belief is portrayed as a disturbing mélange of unatonable sins, eternal guilt, and punishment, Zichroni stresses his "nahezu familiär anmutenden Umgang mit dem Ewigen" (*DL,* Z.137). The juxtaposition of Jewish Orthodoxy and Christian fundamentalism creates the impression that the Jewish faith is more forgiving and humane:

> Was unser Verständnis des Ewigen anging, kamen wir wie von entgegengesetzten Enden des Universums. Nicht einen einzigen Tag in meinem Leben hatte ich Gott als Scharfrichter empfunden. Er mochte mitunter grausam sein, aber wenn ich einmal das Gefühl gehabt hatte, er hätte sich von mir abgewandt, folgte auch wieder eine Erfahrung, die mich ganz davon überzeugte, von ihm angenommen und fürsorglich, wenn nicht sogar liebevoll geleitet zu werden. (*DL*, Z.135)

The text thus employs a strategy of othering Christianity to promote a positive sense of Jewish religious identity. While Zichroni never doubts his religious convictions on a personal level, however, his overall concept of the divine is called into question throughout the text. The ambiguity of the Zichroni narration blossoms more fully in the Wechsler segment. We get the impression that Wechsler's belief in the Orthodox lifestyle is less firm than Zichroni's when he concedes that his turn to Orthodoxy might just be another episode in a rather long line of life changes: "Ich habe Erfahrung darin, ein Leben für ein anderes aufzugeben" (*DL*, W.149). This suggests that his observant life is a further manifestation of his many identity crises and "Maskeraden." Wechsler's character therefore highlights the performative dimension of a religious Jewish identity, which is underlined by metaphors of dressing up and masquerading that permeate his narration. Religious identity thus appears as something that one can slip in and out of, that can be changed at will, which is further accentuated by Wechsler's name. Ironically, this aligns Wechsler with Minsky, whose Jewish identity is also created and established through a performance. Through the Wechsler narration the text thus questions the stability and authenticity of a religious Jewish identity.

Nevertheless, the protagonists' turn to Orthodox Judaism can still be read as a response to the disappearance of the eyewitness generation and the increasing hypermediation of Holocaust memory. Both protagonists are drawn to the religious domain because it offers experiences of deep connectedness, authenticity, and transcendence, which feature in both parts of the novel. In the Wechsler segment the motif of the mikveh articulates this idea of transcendence as transformation. While in Zichroni's narration the mikveh is connected to the idea of healing, repairing, and cleansing, Wechsler links it to absolute renewal and rupture: "Nichts würde mehr gelten von dem, was gewesen war. Aus dem Wasser steige man auf als ein neuer Mensch" (*DL*, W.148). The transformation in the mikveh cuts established (generational) links and thus promises to fulfill the protagonist's desire for an experience of authenticity outside the circuits of mediation.

While the Wechsler narration stresses the desire for violent self-transformation, Zichroni links transcendence to the concept of "das Unermessliche," which can only be glimpsed in the transformation of everyday reality. Art and literature play an important role in this respect:

> Doch wenn ich an Phantastisches dachte, dann an Bilder, die anstelle der Porträtierten altern [i.e., Oscar Wilde's *The Picture of Dorian Gray*] oder an verschüttetes Sonnenblumenöl [i.e., Mikhail Bulgakov's *The Master and Margarita*]—kurz: an Dichtung, an Magisches, das womöglich der menschlichen Phantasie entsprungen ist, vielleicht aber auch nicht. (*DL*, Z.63)

The Zichroni segment stages a clash between the values of a rationalized and "entzauberte" modernity and the magical powers of "das Unermessliche," which is personified in Zichroni's uncle Nathan Bollag. This conflict relates back to the issues of truth and objectivity and hence to the Minsky/Wilkomirski affair. For Bollag, the seemingly objective truths of a rationalized modernity that is marked by "Messbarkeit und Kategorisierung" (*DL*, Z.61) are nothing but "ausschnitthafte . . . Vermessungen" (*DL*, Z.60). They are far from objective, as they are bound to overlook "das Vage, in keine gängige Theorie Passende, . . . das der Messbarkeit und Kategorisierung Verschlossene" (*DL*, Z.61). This "Unermessliche" is out of the subject's reach and can only be glimpsed in rare moments of transcendence. Zichroni, too, critically comments on "die Wahrheit der Wissenschaftler" that attempted to destroy Minsky's Holocaust identity: "Was . . . ist eine Wahrheit, die tötet, wert gegenüber einer Wahrheit, die jemanden leben lässt?" (*DL*, Z. 179). A similar tension is at work in the Wechsler narration, which focuses less on the clash between the everyday and the transcendental than on the opposition between the truth of official documents and a subjective approach to historical reality. While Wechsler, in the guise of Wechsler 2, advocates "die Wahrheit der Wissenschaftler," the confusing discoveries he makes about his own identity (unknowingly) sway him toward a more subjective concept of truth as it is promoted by Zichroni.

Although both characters thus strive for transcendence to break free from the entanglements of the ego and a rationalized and hypermediated (post)modernity, they do not succeed: Wechsler remains caught up in the entrapments of his ego and does not manage to transcend his old life. His attempted transformation in the mikveh of Moza is a failure, since the past comes back to haunt him in the form of the suitcase. At the end of his narration he is confronted with an absolute emptiness: "Gleich werde ich in das eiskalte Wasser sinken, und alles wird sein, wie es einmal war. Aber ich sinke nicht. Ich falle. Das Becken, in das ich stürze, ist leer" (*DL*, W.204). Zichroni is equally unable to catch a glimpse of "das Unermessliche" or to transcend his selfish anger toward Wechsler: although he believes that there is a "tiefe Poesie im göttlichen Lenken unserer Geschicke" (*DL*, Z.145), he seems unable to decipher God's plan, as he becomes bitter and resentful toward the end of his story. Readers are also denied an experience of transcendence, as they are forced to remain within the looplike structure of the novel. While religion is thus presented as a possible anchor point for post-Holocaust Jewish identities in Stein's text, the novel seems wary of presenting it as an entirely unproblematic alternative to the identity politics of victimization. While I therefore agree with Katja Garloff's assessment that "Stein's literary project . . . seeks to broaden the range of identities, and especially religious identities, that can be expressed in German-language literature," I would question whether the novel really *affirms* "Orthodox Judaism as a way of life,"[78] as Jewish religious identity is ultimately presented as no less precarious than any of the other constructs we encounter in the book.

In the quote at the beginning of this section, Stein mentions that he needs neither Zionism nor the Holocaust to define his sense of Jewishness. While he seemingly promotes a faith-based approach in both the interview and his novel,[79] I have demonstrated that religious identity is not affirmed as unequivocally as one might think. How about the third component mentioned by Stein: namely, Zionism and the issue of Jewish national identity? The exploration of Jewishness in *Die Leinwand* takes place within various national settings, particularly those of the GDR and Israel.[80] Wechler's character provides a rather bleak assessment of Jewish identity in the GDR: "Anders zu sein als die Mehrheit, ist in jeder Diktatur ein Problem. Jüdisch zu sein, war im Kleinen Land eine Variante des ultimativen Andersseins" (*DL*, W.128). This sense of radical otherness, however, does not weld together the few who are Jewish. On the contrary, it corrodes their sense of community, as they live in fear of one another: "Die jüdische Gemeinde war vermutlich die am besten ausgekundschaftete Religionsgemeinschaft des Landes, und jeder beargwöhnte jeden, zu den Informanten zu zählen" (*DL*, W.129). While the Holocaust caused a violent breach of Jewish traditions in East *and* West Germany,[81] Jews in the GDR found it particularly hard to reestablish a solid base for their identities, as Wechsler points out:

> Ein befreundeter Autor hat mir Jahre später anvertraut, dass seine jüdische Identität auch in Westdeutschland nur zwei Anker hatte: Israel und Auschwitz. Beides fiel im Kleinen Land aus. In den KZs und Gefängnissen hatten Kommunisten gelitten. Das lernte man an den Schulen. Darüber las man in Romanen, und man sah es in Filmen. Juden waren wohl auch gestorben. Aber die Kommunisten hatten gekämpft. Im Staat der Widerstandskämpfer konnte man sich schwerlich auf Auschwitz berufen, um dreißig oder vierzig Jahre nach Kriegsende das eigene Selbstbild zu schärfen. Und Israel kam schon gar nicht in Frage. Die "Zionisten" waren imperialistische Barbaren,

die unseren proletarischen Brüdern in Palästina mit Waffengewalt alles nahmen, was ihnen rechtmäßig gehörte. (*DL*, W.130)

This polemical passage touches on Holocaust memory and Jewish identity in the GDR: the marginalization of Jewish victims of the Holocaust in favor of the antifascist, communist heroes, alongside the strong anti-imperialist, anti-Zionist stance, and the ways in which this, in some cases, gave rise to—or maybe even sustained—anti-Semitism.[82] In coexistence with and in contrast to the official memorial politics of the GDR, there also existed a private and familial memory of the Holocaust—which, however, is not accessible to Wechsler: "Meine Großeltern waren eingefleischte Kommunisten. Nach der Rückkehr aus dem Exil hatten sie bedeutende Positionen im Staatsapparat inne. Eine Synagoge haben sie nie betreten" (*DL*, W.128). The breach in tradition is thus doubled for him, since he has neither a cultural nor a personal Jewish heritage that he can relate to in his search for a post-Holocaust Jewish identity.

Israel appears to be a better homeland for both Wechsler and Zichroni. It is depicted as a place of return that both characters are strongly attracted to, either in search of inner peace (Zichroni) or of a solution to their problems (Wechsler). Neither character finds what he is looking for, however, which, in Wechsler's case, considerably complicates his relationship with Israel. He initially entertains a fantasy shared by many German Jews, who hoped to find a sense of belonging and identity in *Erez Israel*: "Dennoch glaubte ich, nur in Israel wirklich herausfinden zu können, wer ich war, wie es um mein religiöses Empfinden stand und welchen Weg ich nehmen sollte" (*DL*, W.151). These hopes are disappointed, however, as Wechsler's dream gradually turns into a nightmare:

> Es muss etwas mit diesem Land zu tun haben. Bei meiner ersten Ankunft hat es mich um meine Hoffnungen als Autor gebracht. Bei meinem zweiten Aufenthalt ist mir die Erinnerung abhandengekommen, und ich weiß nicht mehr, wer ich bin. Was mich erwartet, wenn ich zum dritten Mal in der Empfangshalle des Ben-Gurion-Airports stehe, wage ich mir nicht einmal auszumalen. (*DL*, W.159)

The reader knows that Wechsler's third visit to Israel could have ended with his death: the process of self-discovery and personal fulfillment turns out to be a story of losses. These disappointments stem, at least in part, from Wechsler's unrealistic image of Israel. His view of Israel is composed of the cliché of "bunte[s] Gedränge" (*DL*, W.182) in the Arabian bazaar as well as his experience of the West Bank as "Kriegsgebiete" (*DL*, W.192): "Als wir die Mauer passierten, die seit einigen Jahren die Westbank vom Kernland trennt, fühlte ich mich in die Zeit des Kalten Krieges zurück versetzt" (*DL*, W.194). Wechsler perceives of Israel as either the exotic, orientalized Other (the bazaar) or as an eternal war zone (the West Bank).

This perception gives rise to a tension between Wechsler as the ignorant "Jecke" and Zichroni as the slightly condescending "sabra" for whom living in a war zone is nothing out of the ordinary: "Ob es denn wirklich so sei, dass man damit rechnen müsste, als Jehudi dort [in the Arab settlements] auf offener Straße erschossen zu werden. Ja, beschied Amnon mir knapp. Die Mauer und der hohe Zaun um die Siedlung seien keine Zierde" (*DL*, W.196). This contrast is weakened and ironicized by the fact that Wechsler was actually born in Israel himself but has forgotten his original identity.

It is debatable whether the stereotypical view of Israel is attributable to the characters (or at least one of them) or a position encouraged by the text itself. *Die Leinwand* offers its readers an impression of Israel that is dominated by the (ultra-)Orthodox quarters of Mea Shearim and Geula, the Israeli policeman Ben-Or who grills Wechsler for several hours, and the zealots of Masada and the West Bank, and is thus marked by extremes rather than drawing a nuanced picture. Based on the characters' negative depiction of Israel and the GDR, one can say that *Die Leinwand* constructs Jewish identity as quintessentially diasporic, disconnected from any specific national identity. Neither the GDR nor Israel (nor indeed any of the other countries that feature in the novel) can provide the characters with a sense of belonging and integration. In Stein's novel, Jewish identity can therefore not be separated from the experience of exile: "Das hat der Ewige geschickt eingefädelt: Beim Essen und am Shabbes merkt man, dass man unter Fremden lebt, im Exil" (*DL*, W.7).

Conclusion: ". . . eine Variante des ultimativen Andersseins"; Othering, Folklore, and the Commodification of Jewishness

This diasporic conception of Jewishness fosters a sense of otherness and isolation in Stein's novel, which defines both narrative strands but is particularly palpable at the beginning of the Wechsler narration: the peace and quiet of the Shabbes is disrupted by the arrival of a deliveryman, which poses problems for the narrator-protagonist: as an observant Jew, he is not allowed to open the door, let alone accept the parcel. Wechsler's rendition of the scene evokes an atmosphere of war, conflict, and besiegement: "Will man hierzulande Shabbes halten, muss man sich eine Trutzburg bauen. Setzt man den Fuß vor die Tür, betritt man bereits ein religiöses Minenfeld, und nicht weniger gefährlich ist es, wenn jemand von außen hereintritt—indem er klingelt, am Shabbes, an unserer Tür" (*DL*, W.8). Any exchange between the (Jewish) inside and the (non-Jewish) outside is described as "gefährlich." The non-Jewish environment is portrayed as inhospitable and uncomprehending, except for laudable "Ausnahmen" (*DL*, W.7), like the neighbor José Molina, who gladly acts as the Wechsler family's "Shabbes-Goy" (*DL*, W.8). Molina is, however, a foreigner and, as we find out, gay, and thus is himself a manifestation of the Other. Whereas the Wechsler segment stages repeated clashes between the Orthodox Jewish and the non-Jewish worlds, Zichroni's narrative completely separates the two spheres. Zichroni's story unfolds within hermetically sealed, exclusively Jewish environments—such as Mea Shearim, the yeshiva, and, later on, his hermitage in Ofra—which adds a claustrophobic quality to his narrative. Whenever he is forced to briefly step out of his familiar surroundings, he is overcome by a sense of alienation, perceiving himself as an "Abgesandter aus einer anderen Welt" (*DL*, Z.107). This is especially the case when he goes to New York for the first time: "Obwohl ich nie in einem Ghetto gelebt hatte, fühlte es sich nun so an, als käme ich aus einem" (*DL*, Z.106). This assessment is not without irony, as New York harbors one of the world's largest Jewish communities. Still, Zichroni perceives the urban environment as shrill, godless, and hostile:

> Immerhin gab es Inseln, einzelne Quartiere in dieser fremdartigen Welt. . . . Aber ich fragte mich täglich unwillkürlich, wie lange der Moloch diese Inseln noch dulden würde. Ich war davon überzeugt, dass sie überhaupt nur geduldet wurden, eben weil es sich um Inseln handelte, die man ja umschiffen konnte und von denen gelegentlich auch mal eine im Meer des Mainstreams untergehen mochte. (*DL*, Z.107)

The fear of disappearance, of being swallowed up by the "Moloch" is even more pronounced in Zichroni's uncle Nathan Bollag, who warns his nephew against the "Gefahren der *yevonnischen* Sitten dort draußen" (*DL*, Z.62; italics in the original). Bollag fears the "Zerstörung des Volkes durch Assimiliation" (*DL*, Z.62), a tactic that, according to him, has been employed by goyim ever since the time of the Ancient Greeks. Against the backdrop of assimilationist discourse, the overt religiosity in *Die Leinwand* could be read as a strategy that protects the protagonists' sense of identity and community against a world that is disenchanted. The radical otherness of Orthodox Jewish life would then be a form of resistance, as it confronts the contemporary world with something that that world cannot easily absorb or consume. The density of religious rituals and customs in the text would thus be a means of protecting a heritage that is continuously under threat.

A key question arising from these observations relates to whether or not *Die Leinwand* embraces the oppositions, clichés, and stereotypes it employs. Katja Garloff has argued that Stein's use of paratext not only offers a critical comment on the Wilkomirski affair and the genre of testimony but also "challenges the notion of contemporary German-Jewish authors as ethnic authors."[83] While I strongly support Garloff's argument on testimonial discourse in *Die Leinwand*, I am less convinced by the alleged challenge to folkloristic notions of Jewishness in the text. In fact, I perceive *Die Leinwand* as characterized by a peculiar tension between a highly self- and metareflexive approach to debates around testimony and a much less sophisticated stance on Jewishness, which, in the book, is caught up in a series of binaries—between the self/the (exotic) Other, inside/outside, religious/nonreligious Jewish existence, Jews/"goyim," etc.—in a manner that suggests exclusion as a primary mechanism for constructing a sense of self. These concerns also implicate readers in a specific way, as depicting religious Jewishness as something radically alien and inaccessible forces them into a difficult outside position: they are ultimately conceptualized as the Other of the Jew, and, as a consequence, as that which turns the Jew into the Other. This is definitely the case at the start of the Wechsler narration, which forces the reader into a voyeuristic and intrusive position: "Für gewöhnlich öffnen wir am Schabbes nicht die Tür, wenn es läutet. Familie und Freunde würden nicht klingeln" (*DL*, W.7). Through the act of reading, the recipient—who is not part of the "we" that denotes the inner circle of family and friends—performs an act of transgression. The reader is staged as an intruder in Wechsler's life and story. A similar scenario is created in the Zichroni segment, which introduces the reader to the ultra-Orthodox quarters of Mea Shearim. Although Zichroni's family eventually leaves this particularly restrictive setting, the narration continues in an Orthodox milieu that, in all likelihood, is foreign to the majority of readers. Once again, the reader is in the position of either the ethnographer or his evil twin, the voyeur, who tries to catch a glimpse of a (Jewish) world that embodies otherness and is inaccessible under normal circumstances. This position is reinforced by the glossary that is situated at the end of each narration. It provides short explanations of the many religious customs and terms presented in the novel, thus trying to make (religious) Jewishness accessible. At the same time, however, "the glossary creates the impression that Judaism constitutes a realm of its own into which non-Jewish readers first have to be initiated,"[84] as Katja Garloff herself has observed. The glossary thus presents and constructs Jewishness from an external perspective, inviting the reader to adopt what I would term an ethnographic gaze.[85] According to Clifford Geertz, the ethnographic gaze starts from "a state of general bewilderment as to what the devil is going on."[86] Geertz stresses, however, that this "puzzlement" is only the first step;[87] what must follow is an "understanding [of] a people's culture [that] exposes their normalness without reducing their particularity,"[88] so that one can ultimately "converse with them."[89] Stein's novel, in my view, fails to achieve this balance between "normalness" and "particularity." Instead, it resorts to what Geertz introduces as the opposite of dialogic thick description—namely, "turning culture into folklore and collecting it."[90]

The overly detailed descriptions of Orthodox life and customs in Stein's text often verge on cliché and folklore. One example of this is the lengthy excursion into the practice of tzitzit-binding, which stretches across several pages (*DL*, Z.44–51). Although there is a point to this passage—the fact that Zichroni's father binds the tzitzit differently from the family tradition implies a moment of genealogical rupture—the extremely detailed account has a bewildering effect, to employ Geertz's terminology. This also holds true for the novel's discourse on the mikveh. Although it is a central metaphor in both stories, it is a fairly self-explanatory image, which does not require in-depth introductions into Talmudic tractates or the history and geography of various mikvot (all of which the novel provides). Arguably, these peculiarly elaborate excursions create a folkloristic and exoticizing image of Jewishness. The folklorization of Jewish identity in Stein's novel also implicates the reader, who is invited to adopt an ethnographic gaze vis-à-vis the novel's Jewish worlds. This can be interpreted as part of a broader marketing strategy that advertises the author as "die neue Stimme der jüdisch-deutschen Literatur."[91] Apart from the book's novelty value, such marketing commodifies the author's (German-) Jewishness as a major selling point, feeding on the persistent German "fascination for all things Jewish."[92]

The folklorization and commodification of the Jewish experience in Stein's novel clashes with the ethics of self- and metareflexivity in *Die Leinwand*. Whereas the book opts for a subjective and relational approach to the issues of authenticity and identity, its folkloristic tendency supports the opposing logic of reification. Folklorization also clashes with the performativity of identity because it produces essentialism. If used in an exaggerated or ironic manner, folklorization, cliché, and stereotype can have the opposite effect. In Stein's novel, however, these processes are not ironized or reflected, as they are, for example, in Vladimir Vertlib's *Das besondere Gedächtnis der Rosa Masur*. Vertlib's protagonist skillfully plays with the expectations of her audience and thereby exposes the unspoken rules and assumptions of Germany's discourse on the (Eastern European) Jew. The text furthermore metareflexively engages with the transformation of experiences of trauma and suffering into marketable goods.

Stein's novel fails to question the hyperreligious, Othered, and folklorized notion of Jewish identity, which thus reintroduces a longing for immediacy and authenticity into the otherwise hypermediated and self-reflexive scenarios of *Die Leinwand*. This raises the question of whether a recourse to (folklorized notions of) religion and/or certain cultural traditions has replaced the identity politics of victimization as a means for generating a sense of Jewish identity in the age of remediation. This suggestion will be corroborated to an extent by the next chapter, which examines Maxim Biller's novella *Im Kopf von Bruno Schulz*. Biller's text also resorts to Eastern European (Jewish) traditions, and the works of Bruno Schulz in particular, to generate authenticity in a post-Holocaust world. Stein's and Biller's works also tap into larger, transnational trends that shape, for example, the writing of American-Jewish authors like Jonathan Safran Foer and Nicole Krauss. Both of these authors use the Eastern European shtetl setting—and, interestingly enough, Bruno Schulz—to stage a seemingly authentic, yet always lost, Jewishness.[93] Additionally, Foer has recently published a reedition of the *Haggadah*, together with his Jewish writer-colleague Nathan Englander.[94] This suggest a (re)turn to(ward) religion among contemporary third-generation authors, who potentially approach and appropriate religion and/or certain cultural traditions in an attempt to generate new forms of authenticity in a hypermediated, post-Holocaust age.

2: "Im Land der Väter und Verräter": Intertextuality, Influence, and the Problem of Symbiosis in Maxim Biller's Writing

Introduction: Patriarchal Poetics

MAXIM BILLER UNDENIABLY made a comeback in 2013, when his novella *Im Kopf von Bruno Schulz* earned him the praise of influential critics such as Michael Krüger and Ijoma Mangold.[1] In the wake of his success, Biller kicked off a debate about the state of German *Gegenwartsliteratur* in early 2014,[2] and the ensuing discussions consolidated his position as a controversial literary commentator. These developments certainly influenced the decision to appoint him as Marcel Reich-Ranicki's successor for the 2015 revival of the legendary *Literarisches Quartett*. Given the long and well-documented struggle that tied Biller to Reich-Ranicki,[3] his appointment equaled an "Oedipal coup,"[4] which finally allowed the son to mount the father's throne. The takeover ended abruptly, though, when Biller announced his decision to leave the *Literarisches Quartett* in early 2017, shortly after the publication of a monumental nine hundred-page novel entitled *Biografie*, which has received mixed reviews.

Characterized by a profound concern for questions of tradition, legacy, genealogy, and post-Holocaust Jewish identity, Biller's latest work foregrounds the perspective of the writer—"*Judesein* (ist) Schriftstellersein" (*DgJ*, 70; italics in the original)—putting intertextuality at the center. His 2013 novella *Im Kopf von Bruno Schulz*[5] continues on a path that started with his earlier "Selbstporträt," *Der gebrauchte Jude*: both texts engage extensively with seminal writers and cultural figures—such as Thomas Mann, Marcel Reich-Ranicki, and Bruno Schulz—who are cast as literary (anti-)fathers. The following chapter will thus analyze how Biller's recent publications relate to these three authors via the oedipal dispositive, by investigating strategies of connection and distinction, of belonging and dissociation, which Biller employs to stage intertextual feuds with his precursors. Focusing on Biller's textual relationship with the works of Bruno Schulz, I will show that *Im Kopf von Bruno Schulz* has to be read in connection with the figures of Thomas Mann and Marcel Reich-Ranicki, who feature prominently in Biller's writing.[6] Intertextual references to these three writers connect to the central topics of Holocaust (post)memory, German-Jewish identity, and the German-Jewish (negative) symbiosis and engage with two key questions: Which traditions are still available for the (male) Jewish writer in post-Holocaust Germany? And under what conditions can he relate to them? While Stein's writing arguably breaks free from the negative symbiosis by propagating a sense of Jewishness that is no longer tied to the Holocaust, Biller's work, by contrast, continues to articulate a Jewish self-understanding that is based on the experience of victimization. As a consequence, the Jewish writer is trapped in the "Land der Väter und Verräter,"[7] without any positive role models or traditions to relate to.

Biller's recent writing emphasizes the importance of intertextuality and intermediality for negotiating contemporary post-Holocaust Jewishness. In a recent article, Kirstin Gwyer makes the case for an entire "sub-category of recent Jewish post-Holocaust fiction" in which intertextuality is used to negotiate the postmemorial position and come to terms with the legacy of the first generation.[8] Gwyer argues that the anxiety these authors experience relates to the first generation and the concern that "in the wake of the first generation's experience of atrocity, their own life story and narrative can only ever be derivative."[9] They respond to these feelings by creatively appropriating a number of fictional intertexts—among them the works of Bruno Schulz—in an attempt to combat both the "predominantly citational use of intertextuality" in much Holocaust fiction and the notion of the postmemory generation as a passive recipient of the traumas of previous generations.[10] While I will demonstrate that the anxiety of influence in Biller's writing relates to Thomas Mann and German "perpetrator poetics" more broadly rather than to the first generation, I do agree with the gist of Gwyer's brief analysis of *Im Kopf von Bruno Schulz* and her contention that intertextual relationships are a central battleground for present-day second- and third-generation authors in search of a renewed and often posttraumatic sense of Jewish identity.

When reading intertextuality in terms of anxiety and (oedipal) conflict, one cannot ignore Harold Bloom's seminal study *The Anxiety of Influence* (1973). Bloom famously construes literary history and intrapoetic relationships as a (narcissistic) struggle between the "ephebe" and his precursor (i.e., between father and son), centered on the issues of priority and originality: all poets will eventually realize that their work is influenced by other poets who came before them, and that their inability to create something truly original endangers their creativity. While mere imitators might be able to accept that they did not come first, the so-called strong poets cannot,[11] which is why they seek to fend off the influence of preceding writers by misreading them:

Poetic Influence—when it involves two strong, authentic poets—always proceeds by a misreading of the prior poet, an act of creative correction that is actually and necessarily a misinterpretation. The history of fruitful poetic influence, which is to say the main tradition of Western poetry since the Renaissance, is a history of anxiety and self-saving caricature, of distortion, of perverse, willful revisionism without which modern poetry as such could not exist [italics in the original].[12]

This "poetic misprision" has to be understood as a form of blindness or delusion that is necessary for the creative process,[13] "for poems arise out of the illusion of freedom, out of a sense of priority being possible."[14] The strong poet therefore *only thinks* that he wrote something genuinely new, when he is merely repeating what someone else has already said. Bloom, however, understands influence as fundamentally dialectic: the poet's act of repetition is at the same time a form of innovation, as the successor's misinterpretation forever changes the way we read the precursor.[15] These processes take place on an unconscious level: the struggle between the ephebe and the precursor is rarely an explicit one—in the sense of an explicit intertextuality—and the poet does not even have to know the precursor's work in order to be influenced by it. Bloom's broad understanding of intertextuality is based on the assumption that there is no pre-textual access to "reality," so that every verbal expression necessarily refers to a preceding text: "The meaning of a poem can only be another poem."[16] For creativity to emerge, this all-encompassing influence or intertextuality needs to be warded off, and Bloom dedicates most of his book to the six main ways—the "revisionary ratios"—in which this is done in literature.[17]

Praised as a "colossus" by some, while considered an "outdated oddity" by others,[18] Bloom has repeatedly sparked controversy. Apart from Bloom's endorsement of the Romantic ideal of the poetic genius in *The Anxiety of Influence*, the question of gender agitated feminist critics in particular—the "strong poet" is cast as a male poet and his connection to tradition is shaped by patriarchal models. This led Sandra M. Gilbert and Susan Gubar to formulate a different theory of authorship in their seminal book *The Madwoman in the Attic*. For them, Bloom's understanding of authorship and literary tradition was inapplicable to the experience of female authors (and critics): "Bloom's model of literary history is intensely (even exclusively) male, and necessarily patriarchal. For this reason it has seemed, and no doubt will continue to seem, offensively sexist to some feminist critics."[19] Gilbert and Gubar situate Bloom's theory within a century-old Western genealogy of "patriarchal poetics," which welds together authority, creativity, and paternity:

In patriarchal Western culture, therefore, the text's author is a father, a progenitor, a procreator, an aesthetic patriarch whose pen is an instrument of generative power like his penis. More, his pen's power, like his penis's power, is not just the ability to generate life but the power to create a posterity to which he lays claim.[20]

As a result, female authors are constantly crowded out by patriarchal metaphors and male writing practices, which cause an "anxiety of authorship," that is, "a radical fear that she cannot create, that because she can never become a 'precursor' the act of writing will isolate or destroy her."[21] Gilbert and Gubar's book focuses on the strategies of nineteenth-century female writers who attempted to revitalize and establish a distinctively female writing tradition.

In the light of this valid critique the question arises whether and to what extent the application of Bloom's framework can be useful. Bloom's theory feeds on (Romantic) lyric poetry as the primary genre of influence. This is not surprising, as lyric poetry is the genre that gives expression to the poet's individual voice. Bloom's own struggles with Freud and Friedrich Nietzsche and his exploration of Thomas Mann's anxieties of influence suggest, however, that his concept is adaptable to genres other than poetry. While Bloom's theory does not focus on the explicit, conscious struggle between a writer and his precursors as it is carried out in Biller's text, his theory helps to illuminate Biller's writing practices.[22] Bloom frames intertextuality as a question of how authors relate to literary traditions, and this is exactly what my analysis of Biller's texts will center on. His theory shows that the ideas of influence and tradition are not intrinsically positive, but that they can be a form of contagion that needs to be warded off: "Influence is *Influenza*—an astral disease. If influence were health, who could write a poem?"[23] The idea of influence as a disease that needs to be fought off provides a productive angle for scrutinizing how Biller's work negotiates the triangle Schulz-Mann-Reich-Ranicki and German and (Eastern European) Jewish relations more broadly. Finally, Bloom's paradigm helps to account for the strong patricidal elements in Biller's writing,[24] which make his postmemorial relationship with Schulz appear as a form of *Vatermord* that is (compulsively) repeated in the case of Reich-Ranicki. This double "Oedipal coup" exemplifies once more that postmemory and the postmemorial response to the work of another author is not necessarily as ethical as Hirsch presupposes. Biller's homage to Schulz, perceived as a humble elegy by most critics,[25] will emerge as the expression of anxiety and the assertion of Biller's writerly ego.[26]

Biller's work establishes a clear connection among writing, authority, and paternity, thereby endorsing what Gilbert and Gubar denounce as "patriarchal poetics." The question of literary tradition and German-Jewish relations is negotiated in terms of a father-son-conflict, so that Bloom's model can be applied "not as a recommendation for but an analysis of . . . patriarchal poetics," as suggested by Gilbert and Gubar.[27] At the same time, his position as a Jew in post-Holocaust Germany paradoxically brings Biller close to Gilbert's and Gubar's understanding of the female writer. As a Jewish author "im Land der Väter und Verräter," he is forced to write within a literary tradition that he cannot identify with. This results in the creation of alternative textual (all male) genealogies in his writing, which, however, do not question their own patriarchal bias.

Depictions of the Holocaust:
From Polemics to the Apocalyptic Mode

The Holocaust and Polemics in *Harlem Holocaust*

Biller's writing style is generally marked by polemics, exaggeration, and his inclination toward the pornographic, the obscene and the grotesque. The 1998 short story *Harlem Holocaust*[28] is a case in point, as these narrative modes are used to expose the ritualization and commodification of Holocaust discourse in postunification Germany, alongside the impossibility of a German-Jewish symbiosis. Some of the central literary modes employed by Biller—such as polemics, exaggeration, and the grotesque—can already be found in this very early short story and play an equally significant role for the more recent novella *Im Kopf von Bruno Schulz*. It is therefore necessary to analyze these modes more closely in the two texts to prepare my exploration of the grotesque portrayal of Thomas Mann and the German-Jewish symbiosis in *Im Kopf von Bruno Schulz*.

Harlem Holocaust examines the problematic triangular relationship between Efraim Rosenhain, a German son of perpetrators, his German (ex-) girlfriend, Ina Polarker, and the American Jewish linguistics professor turned writer Gerhard "Gary" Warszawski. The first-person narrator, Rosenhain, delivers a deeply unsympathetic portrayal of Warszawski, who, as a "Zerrbild deutscher Schuldprojektionen,"[29] has come to haunt Germany and destroy everything Rosenhain holds dear. Warszawski's oeuvre endlessly recycles a story of Holocaust survival, which he has stolen from his cousin Leo Schneider, while his public career and personal relationships are built on the masochistic German "Gier nach Schuld und Entsöhnung" (*HH*, 9). According to Rosenhain, this is the only reason why Warszawski is successful in Germany. He is unable to sell his gruesome account in the United States, but the German public greets him with an enthusiasm that is fueled by the "Atem historischer Anteilnahme und reumütiger Erlösungsbegeisterung" (*HH*, 41). Because of his "Auschwitz-Bonus" (*HH*, 52), Warszawski has managed to turn his mediocre writing into a literary success:

> Das war in Deutschland ganz anders, seine Stimme bekam hier schnell Gewicht, man lud ihn viel ins Fernsehen ein und machte mit ihm

lange Interviews, denn er sorgte mit seiner Exaltiertheit und seinem Durchblick für jene Sorte anspruchsvoller Unterhaltung, die wir uns anderweitig immer nur bei Zadek, Gysi, Reich-Ranicki und den anderen Kerlen holen mußten. Ich nenne es das Alfred-Kerr-Syndrom. (*HH*, 41)

The "Alfred-Kerr-Syndrom" designates a form of confrontational and polemical Jewishness, which appeals to a German audience that receives a masochistic pleasure from being scolded by the Jew. Rosenhain accuses Warszawski of willingly contributing to this German-Jewish farce by playing the role of the raging and outrageous Jew: "Ich bin euer Dybbuk! Ein aschkenasischer Zombie! Die sprechende Seife! Der schreiende, schreibende Lampenschirm!" (*HH*, 48). Warszawski's success exploits a deeply ritualized German *Vergangenheitsindustrie* that uncritically celebrates all things Jewish. Anti-Semitic discrimination has turned into a philo-Semitic espousal of Jewish Otherness, leaving the underlying patterns of exclusion intact. Biller's short story also engages polemically with the hypermediated and commodified state of Holocaust commemoration in postunified Germany, which has eroded any real sense of empathy with the victims.[30] The Holocaust is presented either as a globalized media cliché—the TV series *Holocaust* (1978), Claude Lanzmann's documentary *Shoah* (1985), and Steven Spielberg's film *Schindler's List* (1993) feature prominently in the text—or as a commodity. As Norbert Otto Eke has pointed out, Biller's narrative thus questions the transformation of the Holocaust into a "Diskursfiguration."[31] The historical events and traumatic experiences have become inseparable from their representation and deformation in the media or in cultural and political discourse. Biller's text exposes the—often implicit—norms, clichés, and regulations that structure these discourses in German society, exposing them as a "Vexierspiel mit Klischees und Projektionen."[32]

These clichés and projections also shape German-Jewish (love) relationships in the novella: Rosenhain and his (ex-)girlfriend Ina Polarker find themselves in a sadomasochistic ménage à trois with their Jewish counterpart, in which they succumb all too willingly to the lure of the Jewish monster Warszawski. While Rosenhain, who embarks on a desperate search for the long lost "Seelenverwandtschaft" (*HH*, 49) between Germans and Jews, is in equal parts attracted and repelled by Warszawski's demeanor and physique, Ina has become totally enslaved by Warszawski's irresistible air of "'Angst' und 'Reue' und 'Todeserotik'" (*HH*, 24). Warszawski wields power over the two Germans by physically and mentally abusing and demeaning them (especially Ina, who is repeatedly coerced into humiliating sex acts). He seems to draw considerable sadistic joy from the arrangement, which is why the reader cannot help but sympathize with the victimized Germans. Throughout most of the story, the reader therefore willingly embraces Rosenhain's anti-Semitic portrait of Warszawski as the sex-hungry, money-grubbing Jew. The reader's sentiment is radically called into question, however, by the story's ending: *Harlem Holocaust* finishes with a note written by a man called Hermann Warschauer, which uncovers the entire narrative as the posthumously released manuscript of a certain Friedrich (not Efraim) Rosenhain, who, he claims, was mentally ill. It remains unclear whether Friedrich imagined the entire story (along with his hyper-Jewish name) or whether Warszawski/Warschauer, in a final masterstroke, added this note to permanently discredit the (by then dead) Rosenhain. In any case, this ending makes the reader question the picture painted by the first-person narrator Rosenhain—was his portrayal of Warszawski rooted in his paranoid, anti-Semitic fantasies? And why did the reader embrace it so willingly?

Biller's literary sleight of hand thus forces readers into a critical self-examination as to why they took the parodic image of Warszawski as the "jüdische[s] Ungeheuer" at face value,[33] especially since Rosenhain is presented as an unreliable narrator from the start.[34] The disturbing relationship between Rosenhain and Warszawski (and the readers' reaction to it) can then be seen as an illustration of what Dan Diner has identified as the "negative Symbiose" between Germans and Jews after the Holocaust—an unsolvable, unintended, and mostly undesirable bond between perpetrators and victims:

Seit Auschwitz—welch traurige List—kann tatsächlich von einer "deutsch-jüdischen Symbiose" gesprochen werden—freilich einer negativen: für beide, für Deutsche wie für Juden, ist das Ergebnis der Massenvernichtung zum Ausgangspunkt ihres Selbstverständnisses geworden; eine Art gegensätzlicher Gemeinsamkeit—ob sie es wollen oder nicht. Denn Deutsche wie Juden sind durch dieses Ereignis neu aufeinander bezogen worden. Solch negative Symbiose, von den Nazis konstituiert, wird auf Generationen hinaus das Verhältnis beider zu sich selbst, vor allem aber zueinander, prägen.[35]

The story demonstrates exactly this "gegensätzliche Gemeinsamkeit," albeit in a grotesquely exaggerated manner. It shows that neither Rosenhain nor Ina can free themselves of their obsession with Warszawski and their feeling of perpetrator guilt, while Warszawski—at least according to Rosenhain's portrayal—cannot stop tormenting them (and the German public). The central characters are unable to construct an identity that does not take the Holocaust as its "Ausgangspunkt," which gridlocks them (and the Other) in the roles of either perpetrator or victim. This results in a situation where Germans and Jews are perpetually "aufeinander bezogen," without, however, being able to meaningfully relate to one another. The text demonstrates that, for Germans and Jews alike, the perception of the other is not possible beyond the level of clichés, stereotypes, and projections. The perverted and darkly grotesque depiction of German-Jewish (love) relationships in *Harlem Holocaust*—and in most of Biller's other stories—is thus the "Wiedergabe einer Situation, in der Deutsche und Juden alle Unmittelbarkeit im Umgang miteinander eingebüßt haben und nur noch in Rollen und Masken miteinander reden und so verkappt sogar miteinander ins Bett gehen."[36] From the vantage point of Biller's story, however, a *loss* of "Unmittelbarkeit" is not the central concern, as this would presuppose the existence of a harmonious symbiosis. By contrast, the text suggests that any notion of a German-Jewish "Seelenverwandtschaft"

> war, im kleinen, genauso eine Illusion und ein eskapistischer, verzweifelter Rettungsanker gewesen wie, im großen, die von so vielen propagierte deutsch-jüdische Symbiose, der historische Schulterschluß zweier Völker, der mal Genies, mal Leichen produzierte. Ja, und wir Idioten glaubten immer noch daran, an die einträchtige Kraft von George, Musil und Kisch, an die Einsichten von Freud und Schopenhauer, an die gemeinsamen Visionen von Rilke, Fritz Lang und Billy Wilder, an diese ganze romantische, germanisch-hebräische Mitteleuropa-Idee also, an die Metapher von Kultur und Kaffeehaus (*HH*, 50).

The illusory character of the German-Jewish symbiosis is also central to *Im Kopf von Bruno Schulz*: the novella explores German-Jewish relations through the sadomasochistic relationship between the Polish Jewish writer Bruno Schulz and the cultural icon Thomas Mann. In *Harlem Holocaust*, the sadomasochistic configuration is produced by Rosenhain's paranoid obsession, which, following German anti-Semitic traditions, imagines the omnipotent Jew as a threat to himself and his culture. In *Im Kopf von Bruno Schulz*, it is Bruno Schulz, the Jew, who uses sadomasochistic imagery to illustrate the dominance of German cultural and literary traditions. While the constellation is thus reversed in Biller's latest text—here it is the German who enslaves the Jew(s)—*Im Kopf von Bruno Schulz* still resorts to similar literary modes, such as polemics, exaggeration, and the grotesque alongside the sadomasochistic constellation, in a continued effort to come to terms with the negative German-Jewish symbiosis.

The Holocaust as Apocalypse in *Im Kopf von Bruno Schulz*

Before analyzing the use of sadomasochistic imagery and the figures of Bruno Schulz and Thomas Mann more closely, I want to return to the issue of Holocaust representation in Biller's writing. Whereas *Harlem Holocaust* depicts the Holocaust as a hypermediated "Diskursfiguration" to denounce the ritualization and commodification of Holocaust memory in postunification Germany, *Im Kopf von Bruno Schulz* resorts to a different historical framework: the novella is set in 1938 and focuses on a letter, written from the first-person perspective of the Polish Jewish writer and art teacher Bruno Schulz and addressed to the world-famous German author

Thomas Mann.[37] Schulz uses the letter to inform the iconic German writer that a doppelgänger of his is on the rampage in Schulz's (then) Polish hometown of Drohobycz. His detailed account of the fake Mann's grotesque and atrocious behavior is frequently interrupted by a frame narrative in which a third-person narrator provides further insights into Schulz's mind. The contents of Schulz's letter become increasingly surreal as the novella progresses; in an absurd twist the fake Mann is eventually revealed as a secret agent who was sent to investigate and eventually eliminate Drohobycz's Jewish community. This revelation also sheds light on the real motives behind Schulz's letter: in all likelihood, the fake Thomas Mann is Schulz's invention, created to attract his famous colleague's attention, in the hope that he may save the Jewish writer from the advancing German troops. Schulz's endeavors are hopeless, however, and the novella ends with an imagery that clearly anticipates the extermination policies of the Holocaust.

Set in a fictional universe where the Holocaust has not yet happened, the novella can of course not represent it as a historical reality. The Holocaust is still present throughout the novella, however, in the form of visions that plague the protagonist and some of the other characters. Schulz in particular is overwhelmed by an inexplicable sense of fear and dread, which, from the retrospective angle of the reader, appears as a premonition of what is to come:

> Er [Bruno Schulz] rechnete seit vielen Jahren damit, dass es passieren würde, aber doch nicht jetzt, sondern erst viel später—in einer unendlich fernen Zukunft, die bevölkert wäre mit seinen riesigen Wandechsen, Schlangen und Urvögeln, die ihre eigenen Schwänze aßen, mit grauuniformierten Menschenarmeen, deren lange, unordentliche Züge bis zum Horizont reichten, mit Millionen nackter Männer, Frauen und Kinder, die sich nur noch auf allen Vieren fortbewegen konnten. Und überall im Land brannten große und kleine Feuer, und wer durch den Rauch und die um sich schlagenden Flammen etwas erkennen konnte, betete, er möge nicht wie sie von einer unsichtbaren Hand auf seine Knie und Hände gezwungen und auch in diese Feuer getrieben werden. (*IKvBS*, 30–31)

In these passages Biller's text remediates biblical templates and apocalyptic literature to approach a catastrophe that has not happened yet on the level of the narrative. Apocalyptic literature often expresses future-oriented dystopian visions and prophecies through a specific imagery that involves, for example, apocalyptic beasts.[38] The prehistoric reptiles and birds in Schulz's imagination are reminiscent of these beasts, and of biblical monsters such as Leviathan and the terrifying bird Ziz.[39] The depiction of masses of naked people, the collapse of the human/animal divide, and the images of smoke and fire in this passage evoke Christian depictions of the apocalypse, such as Pieter Brueghel the Elder's *The Triumph of Death*, or

Hieronymus Bosch's nightmarish visions of hell in *The Last Judgment*. Bosch's work might indeed be the primary source of Schulz's visions, as it often features reptilelike creatures and human-animal hybrids. These visual allusions are fused with the iconography of the Holocaust (gray uniforms, fire, smoke, ashes, masses of naked people), which suggests that Schulz does anticipate the extermination of the Jews. Schulz's visions of the intradiegetic future are thus glances into the extratextual, historical past that frame the Holocaust as an apocalypse: from the perspective of the characters, they remediate apocalyptic templates that can be found in the Bible and in Early and Late Netherlandish Renaissance painting to voice fears of a nameless future, while, from the vantage point of the reader, they recycle key images in Holocaust discourse.

The representation of the Holocaust as an apocalypse has deeper implications: whereas biblical references—for example, to the destruction of the First and Second Temples—are common in Holocaust discourse,[40] the apocalyptic template is unusual and problematic: both Judaism and Christianity convey the "end of days," which imagines an apocalyptic ending of the world as part of God's creation. This event is also seen as a turning point, an end-time scenario that is also the beginning of something new, either the Second Coming or the coming of the Messiah. The apocalypse brings forth a crucial moment of revelation in which things that have been hidden become visible. While, in the Christian tradition, this is connected to the idea of the Last Judgment, in Jewish eschatology the outlook on the "world to come" is more important. The application of this template to the Holocaust may, however, be seen to imply a certain logic and teleology as the unavoidable part of a larger eschatological process. The allusion to the Last Judgment would be even more problematic because it connotes the idea of "just" punishment.

The reader is thus left wondering whether the apocalypse is a powerful metaphor through which the characters in the novella read an event that they cannot possibly fathom, or whether the text as such encodes the Holocaust as an apocalypse. In light of the novella's ending, the second interpretation seems more accurate. Apocalyptic visions anticipate a future catastrophe that will take place, regardless of human agency. The same holds true for Schulz's premonitions, which become a reality when the German troops approach Drohobycz at the end of the novella:

> Doch nach einigen Hundert Metern erblickte Bruno plötzlich einen großen, roten Feuerschein über der nächtlichen Stadt, er hörte Motorengeräusche und laute Befehle, und wenn er nach links oder rechts schaute, sah er immer wieder am Ende einer Gasse ein riesiges, schwarzes, prähistorisches Insekt vorbeirennen, dessen Füße wie Panzerketten klirrten. . . . Er war, obwohl seit fast einer Stunde unterwegs, gerade erst beim Portikus des Stadtparks angekommen, er atmete schwer, seine Knie waren wund und blutig, und die Tauben

im Himmel über Drohobycz flogen eine nach der anderen in den roten Feuerschein hinein, wo sie wie Zunder verbrannten. (*IKvBS*, 68–69)

It thus transpires that the visions that have plagued Schulz throughout the story were anticipations of his actual future (i.e., the German invasion). The ending of the novella coincides with the end of days: the apocalypse has come in the form of the German troops, and the prophetic protagonist turns into a dog: "Er schob sich den dicken Briefumschlag zwischen die Zähne, knurrte ungeduldig, löschte die Lampe und fiel auf die Knie" (*IKvBS*, 67). Schulz only expected this to happen in the hellish "unendlich fernen Zukunft" (*IKvBS*, 30) that his visions depict. When he turns into a dog at the end of the novella this future and the end of days have come. Biller's representation of the Holocaust as an apocalypse can be regarded as an extreme form of polemics. It entails, however, the highly problematic suggestion that the Holocaust is somehow part of an eschatological pathway—and even a form of "just" punishment. The character Schulz's peculiar oscillation between paranoiac and prophet will furthermore be important when investigating the novella's portrayal of the relationship between Bruno Schulz and Thomas Mann.

Face(t)s of the Father

Bruno Schulz, "Ghetto Writing," and Jewish Literary Genealogies

The life and works of Bruno Schulz are a central point of reference for Biller's novella. The text is dotted with countless allusions to Schulz's writing and graphic work, most of which concentrate on Schulz's short-story anthology *Die Zimtläden* (2014; translated as *Cinnamon Shops, and Other Stories*, 1963; also published as *The Street of Crocodiles*, 1963; originally published as *Sklepy cynamonowe*, 1934), whose main characters (the father, the mother, Adele/a) and motifs (the birds, the so-called cinnamon shops, the dog Nimrod) resurface throughout Biller's narrative, along with explicit references to the famous "Traktat über die Schneiderpuppen." Biller's intertextual engagement is seen mostly at the level of character constellations and motifs, rather than at the level of language and style, even though the text is inspired by Schulz's surreal aesthetics. The novella draws on two aspects of Schulz's writing in particular: Eastern Jewish traditions of so-called ghetto writing, on the one hand,[41] and sadomasochism in Schulz's work, on the other.[42] In its adaptation of Schulz's sadomasochistic universe, Biller's text also relies on Schulz's graphic oeuvre, specifically on a German edition of his drawings from 2000.[43] Some of Schulz's drawings are explicitly reproduced in the text, while others are implicitly remediated by way of ekphrasis.

The recourse to Bruno Schulz in Biller's novella can be read as an attempt to (re)connect with traditions of Eastern European Jewish literature. The focus on Schulz's Polish hometown of Drohobycz conjures up the lost world of Austrian Galicia (which Drohobycz used to belong to) and thus the issue of the "ghetto" and "ghetto writing." According to Anne Fuchs and Florian Krobb, the "ghetto" can be understood as "broadly . . . any location of traditional Jewish life. In our context, the ghetto is a real or imagined space where polarized conceptions of German-Jewish identities such as openness and closure, assimilation and orthodoxy, are constructed, negotiated, and evaluated."[44] Fuchs and Krobb differentiate between Yiddish ghetto stories, on the one hand, and stories by German Jewish writers, on the other. While the first, "authentic" strand of stories was based on firsthand experience, written in Yiddish, and addressed toward a Jewish audience, the stories produced by German Jewish writers targeted an assimilated readership that was out of touch with the ghetto as a lived reality. As Florian Krobb points out in relation to Leopold Kompert's ghetto stories, this second strand served a "compensatory function": as "imagined location(s)," these literary ghettos were meant to satisfy nostalgic urges by providing a sense of identity and connection, which had been lost or never existed in the first place.[45] This nostalgic ghetto fiction was "clearly an attempt to narrate this lost identity, and hence, within the logic of fiction, to overcome the sense of estrangement."[46] Schulz's and Biller's texts can be situated within the nostalgic tradition of "ghetto writing": while Schulz still experienced the ghetto as a geographical space, the traditional structures of ghetto life no longer existed when he wrote *Die Zimtläden*. Biller's writing is even farther removed from the ghetto as a lived reality, which ended, both as a geographical space and a form of community, with the German destruction campaigns in the East. Both authors therefore encounter the ghetto "primarily as a poetic space recollected through distance,"[47] although the degrees of this distance vary.

The ghetto, as a literary topos, thus connects to the issues of identity, authenticity, and nostalgia in Biller's writing. In its engagement with "ghetto writing," *Im Kopf von Bruno Schulz* draws heavily on Schulz's depictions in *Die Zimtläden*, which I will examine a little more closely here. Drohobycz and its Jewish surroundings were still a lived reality for Schulz, although Austrian Galicia had undergone significant transformations by the time he published his stories. Depictions of Jewish life and customs are not the central themes of *Die Zimtläden*, which concentrates on the topography of a nameless and dull town with only a few landmarks, such as the "Marktplatz," the "Krokodilstraße," and the eponymous "Zimtläden." The majority of the stories featured in *Die Zimtläden* focus on the first-person narrator's family life (and thus the domestic realm), portraying the tribulations and eventual breakdown of the Oedipal family and of the father in particular. The absence of central topoi of "ghetto writing" (such as the depiction of religious rituals) highlights the distance that separates Schulz's modernist account of the ghetto from more traditional examples of ghetto fiction. The nameless town is steeped in an atmosphere of phantasmagoria:

> Im Inneren der Stadt tun sich gewissermaßen Zweifachstraßen auf, Doppelgängerstraßen, Lug- und Trugstraßen. Die bezauberte und irregeführte Phantasie erzeugt illusorische, vermeintlich längst und wohl bekannte Stadtpläne, auf denen diese Straßen zwar ihren Platz und ihren Namen haben, doch die Nacht in ihrer unerschöpflichen Produktivität hat nichts Besseres zu tun, als fortwährend neue und imaginierte Konfigurationen zu liefern. (*DZ*, 87)

Passages like these highlight that Schulz's writing remediates Eastern European Jewish traditions through the lens of a Kafkaesque and modernist surrealism. Devoid of historical and geographical specificity, the town is a fantastical place, weighed down by a general sense of inertia—"jede angefangene Bewegung bleibt in der Luft hängen, alle Gesten erschöpfen sich vorzeitig und können den toten Punkt nicht überwinden" (*DZ*, 112). This atmosphere of degeneration, decay, and passivity turns the town into a backward space, which is continuously threatened by the developments of capitalist modernity and is therefore about to perish. This fear of disappearance reflects the actual dissolution of the shtetl, which was already well under way by the time Schulz wrote and published his stories in the early 1930s. The nostalgia of Schulz's writing does not so much reimagine "a place of wholeness, of Jewish solidarity and community spirit, a metaphorical refuge,"[48] but rather mourns a lost world. In a desperate attempt to go with the times, the town puts on the mask of flamboyant urbanity: "Die Krokodilstraße war eine Konzession unserer Stadt an großstädtische Modernität und Verderbtheit. Wir konnten uns sichtlich nichts anderes leisten als eine Imitation aus Papier, eine Photomontage aus Schnipseln der stockigen Zeitungen vom Vorjahr" (*DZ*, 114). Schulz's text thus conforms to a certain strand of "ghetto writing" that sees the ghetto as an underdeveloped space.[49] *Die Zimtläden*, however, lacks the enlightened impulse that usually drives this form of "ghetto writing": the stories reveal a fascination for decay and the moribund, representing the ghetto as a doomed and dying space without vigor, liveliness, and authenticity.

Die Zimtläden features only one scene that explicitly depicts traditional Jewish life:

> Anderswo hatten sich Juden in farbigen Kaftanen und mit breitkrempigen Pelzhüten auf dem Kopf um die hohen Wasserfälle der hellen Stoffe gruppiert. Dies waren die Männer des Hohen Rates, würdige und überaus salbungsvolle Herren, die ihre langen, gepflegten Bärte glattstrichen und zurückhaltende, diplomatische Gespräche führten.

Doch auch in dieser förmlichen Konversation, in den Blicken, die sie
tauschten, blitzte feixende Ironie. (*DZ*, 139–40)

Although the narrator is sympathetic toward the Jews, he depicts them
as somewhat outdated, formal, and stiff. With their colorful clothing and
unusual headdress, they come from another time and space, although they
are still in a position of authority in the town's community. It is noteworthy that Schulz's drawings from the same time feature several variations of
exactly this scene.[50] The drawings depict gatherings of Hasidic men in
traditional attire (kaftan, schtreimel, kippah, pajes), who are in conversation and display signs of physical closeness and affection. These images
invoke a sense of lively community that is absent from Schulz's writing.
With their focus on Orthodox Jewish figures, however, these drawings are
in themselves remediations of a certain ghetto or shtetl iconography rather
than representations of actual life. Arguably, they serve the purpose of
creating the illusion of community and authenticity at a time when the
underlying structures of ghetto life had ceased to exist. *Die Zimtläden* is
not part of the "authentic" tradition of "ghetto writing" but a surrealist
reimagination that redeploys existing literary traditions and iconographies
to come to terms with the end of the ghetto as a living space.

Many of Schulz's story elements resurface in Biller's text. For example,
the "chaotischen Läden hinter dem Marktplatz, die immer nur am späten
Abend für einige Stunden öffneten und manchmal auch das nicht"
(*IKvBS*, 13) and the "Marktplatz" itself refer to Schulz's written and
graphic works. The ghetto in Biller's novella is thus a space that exists
solely in the literary imagination or as a literary quote. While Schulz was
still able to draw inspiration from personal experience and actual topographies, this is obviously not the case for Biller: as a third-generation,
German Jewish author, his approach "is characterized by intellectual, historical and physical distance towards the ghetto as a lived reality."[51] He
employs an imagery that was already the result of multiple remediations in
Schulz's work, while echoing the elegiac tone of Schulz's writing by
depicting the ghetto as a precarious space that is under threat: Drohobycz
is doomed not only by the impending danger of the German invasion but
also by its own provincial backwardness. It offers little or no resistance
against the tidal waves of (fascist) modernity:

Zu lange schon leben sie [the people of Drohobycz] ohne Kontakt
zur Welt, das Provinzdasein macht sie ängstlich, verrückt und neu-
gierig. Einen Tagesausflug nach Stryj planen sie Monate vorher, und
bevor einer von ihnen in die Hauptstadt fährt, regelt er bei Notar
Reynisz seine Geschäfte. (*IKvBS*, 32)

Apart from reproducing a Schulzian atmosphere, this feeling of
impending doom in *Im Kopf von Bruno Schulz* also fuels a sense of nostal-

gia. Svetlana Boym defines nostalgia as "a longing for a home that no longer exists or has never existed. Nostalgia is a sentiment of loss and displacement, but it is also a romance with one's own fantasy."[52] In Biller's story, home is a place "that no longer exists" *and* that "has never existed": after the Holocaust, Drohobycz is a lost world that cannot be restored. At the same time, this lost world is staged as a literary intertext, remediating Schulz's writing, which assimilated ghetto reality into a surrealist tale. The ghetto in Biller's novella is thus a multiply mediated phenomenon: it is a home that indeed "has never existed" outside the realm of literature and the writerly imagination. Nostalgia in Biller's novella is thus a manifestation of "reflective nostalgia," which "is more concerned with historical and individual time, with the irrevocability of the past and human finitude. . . . The focus here is not on recovery of what is perceived to be an absolute truth but on the mediation of history and passage of time."[53] Rather than pretending that a pretraumatic fullness can be restored, "reflective nostalgia" accepts the irreversibility of loss and instead focuses on the ways in which we approach and construct the past from the perspective of the present. In the famous words of L. P. Hartley, "reflective nostalgia" accepts that "the past is a foreign country"[54] and that we cannot phantasmatically close the gap that separates us from earlier periods of history.

Distance and mediation are thus at the heart of reflective nostalgia, which accentuates the irretrievability of what is lost. While Biller's novella does not try to rebuild the destroyed world of Eastern Jewry, however, the recourse to ghetto writing still serves an authenticating purpose. Biller uses Schulz's writing to insert himself into a specifically Eastern European Jewish tradition, thereby establishing a literary genealogy. This genealogy is extended by an epigraph of the Nobel Prize-winning Galician writer Shmuel Josef Agnon, who was a prime exponent of the literary tradition of "ghetto writing": "Gelobt sei, der seltsame Wesen schafft" (*IKvBS*, 6). It is further complemented by several references to Franz Kafka's *Die Verwandlung* (1915), most notably via the novella's protagonist, who is trapped in a basement, undergoing a transformation from human to animal.[55] Paradoxically, Biller's writing hence tries to achieve an authenticating effect by relying on an author whose "ghetto writing" was steeped in intertextuality. *Im Kopf von Bruno Schulz* thus fuses an awareness of (re) mediation with an ongoing longing for authenticity in a manner that is similar to Benjamin Stein's *Die Leinwand*. While Stein's novel uses religious traditions and customs to (re)establish Jewish identities after the Holocaust, Biller's novella invokes the lost world of Eastern European Jewry to achieve this effect.

These inscriptions into Eastern European and Jewish traditions function as conscious demonstrations of belonging that are pitted against the German tradition represented by Thomas Mann. One should note in this context that in Biller's earlier text *Der gebrauchte Jude* Marcel Reich-

Ranicki was shown to reject Kafka in favor of Mann: "Und Thomas Mann sei ihm lieber als Kafka. . . . Kafka, sagte er, habe nur ein geniales Buch geschrieben, den *Prozess*, Mann dagegen sei an sich genial gewesen" (*DgJ*, 106). Biller's assertion of a Jewish literary genealogy is therefore also an act of defiance, intended to ward off the influence of German tradition. At the same time, this genealogy is steeped in a patriarchal poetics, as is illustrated by the Agnon quote, which fuses the act of writing with paternity and literary genealogy, casting the male writer as a creative, godlike force. By opening with this quote, Biller's text endorses the "paternity/creativity metaphor" that is at the heart of "patriarchal poetics."[56] This intimate connection between masculinity and creativity also informs *Die Zimtläden*, which, in the famous "Traktat über die Schneiderpuppen," stages a conflict between the male creator-genius (the "Demiurg"; *DZ*, 51) and matter, which is "formbar wie ein Weib" (*DZ*, 51). Schulz's text also, however, employs the sadomasochistic constellation to ironize the nexus between father/god/creator. While Schulz's *Zimtläden* thus unsettles the notion of "patriarchal poetics" up to a point, *Im Kopf von Bruno Schulz* fully embraces "the metaphor of literary paternity" in an attempt to create an alternative sense of Jewishness.

From Venus in Furs to Thomas Mann in Furs

Apart from Eastern European writing traditions, Biller's novella also reworks the sadomasochistic constellation in Schulz's oeuvre. While there is some continuity on the level of imagery, the two authors depict sadomasochism very differently in their respective works. In *Die Zimtläden*, the sadomasochistic figuration defines the relationship between the first-person narrator's father and the young housekeeper Adela, who rules the household (and the paterfamilias) with an iron fist and an acute awareness of her powers. Adela, who represents matter, the body, sensuality, and the lower regions of the house, uses her might to control the narrator's father, who occupies the house's upper realms, along with those of the mind. The gendered dichotomy of above/below is central to the story, as it encapsulates its main themes.[57] Above/below first and foremost describes the spatial location of the characters: Adela, although able to move freely around the house, usually works on the lower levels, sweeping and scrubbing the floors, while the father prefers to spend his time in the attic, at times sitting on top of various pieces of furniture. Birds are his favorite animals, and he spends substantial amounts of time and money on importing and hatching exotic bird eggs. These locations and attributes carry symbolic significance, of course: Adela's association with the lower regions of the house can be read both in terms of class and in terms of her alignment with the lower regions of the body, that is, those parts that are the furthest removed from the brain and the powers of reason. She is all body (or rather: matter) whereas the father is all mind.

This very dichotomy is destabilized (and maybe even reversed), however, in the sadomasochistic scenario, in which Adela alternates between playfully teasing and openly challenging the father and his patriarchal power. When the father explains the conflict between the (male) demiurge and the (female) material world in his speech on the "Schneiderpuppen," Adela repeatedly disrupts his deliberations by tantalizing him with her foot. The father reacts "wie ein Automat" (*DZ*, 56) and falls onto his knees. Ironically, this turns him into the type of mannequin that is the topic of his treatise—he is thus himself transformed from a (wannabe) active, male creator into a lifeless, passive automaton, while also being brought down from the realm of the mind (the above) onto his knees (the below).[58] Any scenes of explicit sadomasochistic punishment, however, are literally blanked out in Schulz's text:

> Adela erhob sich vom Stuhl und bat uns, die Augen zu schließen vor dem, was nun gleich geschehen würde. Sie ging auf meinen Vater zu und verlangte, die Hände in die Hüften gestemmt, was den Anschein betonter Entschlossenheit verstärkte, mit aller Deutlichkeit . . . ------
> ----------" (*DZ*, 60; ellipsis points and hyphens in the original)

Biller's text makes these allusions and omissions in Schulz's writing explicit: he transforms the multilayered sadomasochistic discourse in *Die Zimtläden* into a rather clichéd scenario of dominance, submission, and frequent physical punishment. The complex dependency and role play between the father and Adela is translated here into the openly sadomasochistic and violent relationship between the protagonist, Bruno Schulz, and Helena Jakubowicz, one of his fellow teachers. Schulz's masochistic urge is presented as a form of compulsive acting out that was caused by the frequent physical abuse he suffered from the housekeeper Adele as a child. While being locked up in a wardrobe by Helena, Schulz begins to fantasize about other forms of punishment:

> Vielleicht, fügte sie hinzu, würde sie selbst kurz mit ihm in die Kammer kommen, sie könne, wenn er es wolle, in einem der chaotischen Läden hinter dem Marktplatz, . . . einige Dinge kaufen, die sie schon lange mit ihm ausprobieren wollte. Er konnte sich denken, was sie meinte! Nein, hatte er geantwortet, lieber nicht, obwohl er sich beim Gedanken an diese Dinge—venezianische Colombina-Masken aus schwarzem Leder, mit Sägemehl ausgestopfte, penisgroße Pierrots, aus Weidenruten geflochtene und mit dünnen Stahlketten durchwirkte Osterpeitschen, silberne Nippelklemmen und japanische Schungakerzen, deren tropfendes Wachs keine Brandblasen hinterließ—sofort sehr sicher und wohl fühlte. (*IKvBS*, 13–14)

Biller's representation of Schulz's deepest desire is more reminiscent of pop-cultural depictions of sadomasochism à la *Fifty Shades of Grey*

(2011) than of Schulz or Leopold von Sacher-Masoch.[59] In their depiction of the sadomasochistic figuration, both Sacher-Masoch and Schulz rely on allusion, omission, and—as Gilles Deleuze has argued—deferral and suspension.[60] Imagination and fantasy are generally more important than execution. Moreover, the dominant/submissive relationship is used to reflect on a whole range of topics, such as the relationship between the sexes, power, performativity—or, in Schulz's case, the connection between mind and matter—and the nature of creation and creativity. Despite these similarities, Schulz's stories already transform Sacher-Masoch's model in significant ways: In *Die Zimtläden*, Sacher-Masoch's cruel mistress loses her opulent gowns and furs and reemerges as the housekeeper Adela. The sadomasochistic constellation is thus translocated from the aristocratic to the bourgeois milieu, while also being oedipalized via *Die Zimtläden*'s focus on the nuclear family. In Schulz's graphic work in particular, sado-masochism is supplemented by a foot fetish, which is not overly relevant for Sacher-Masoch's narrative. By going through yet another cycle of remediation, in Biller's writing sadomasochism turns into a cliché, reduced to a few potent images—such as the whip or the genuflection—which are invoked mainly, albeit not solely, for the purposes of provocation.

Apart from these intertextual references, sadomasochistic traditions are also present in Biller's novella on a visual level. I here want to explore in more detail the role of Schulz's drawings, particularly a German edition entitled *Bruno Schulz: Das graphische Werk*. The relationship between Schulz's drawings and Biller's novella is not a straightforward one, and the remediation of Schulz's oeuvre in the text has multiple layers: *Im Kopf von Bruno Schulz* includes six drawings by Schulz, which are inserted into the novella at regular intervals. While not intended as illustrations of any specific scenes in the text, they rather function as a general comment on the discourse of sadomasochism by adding an additional, visual layer. Five of the drawings show scenes of social or sexual domination: the female's position of power and superiority is expressed either in the form of a spatial elevation (*IKvBS*, 25) or by way of the upward movement of her head (*IKvBS*, 64). Furthermore, parts of Schulz's oeuvre are remediated in the text by way of ekphrasis: the character Bruno Schulz, for example, describes his own (and the real Bruno Schulz's) drawings, using them as an inspiration for the letter he writes and the story he invents (*IKvBS*, 34). Finally, an examination of *Bruno Schulz: Das graphische Werk* reveals that, apart from the six drawings that are *explicitly remediated* in the novella, several more of Schulz's drawings have been *implicitly remediated* in the text, which draws on Schulz's works as an inspiration for central scenes, motifs, and constellations. This, for example, concerns Bruno's transformation into a dog (118), the human cart horses used by the fake Mann (61), as well as the scenes of collective adoration and submission that return in the bathroom sequence (57–59; 113).

Schulz's graphic works were allegedly intended as illustrations of Leopold von Sacher-Masoch's *Venus im Pelz* (1870).[61] They clearly draw on the precursor's imagery by reiterating scenes of physical domination by a cold and aloof female, or by showing acts of flagellation. Biller's novella, however, downplays certain crucial aspects of Sacher-Masoch's influence on Schulz while highlighting others: *Im Kopf von Bruno Schulz* does not center on the figure of the unattainable, cruel woman and its complementary image of a man lying at the feet of his cold mistress, which are integral to literary and visual traditions of sadomasochism. Instead, Biller's textual rendition foregrounds scenes of violent punishment, especially the practice of whipping or flagellation. The topic of male adoration for a cold female thus plays a significant role on the visual level of Biller's novella—via the inserted drawings—while being downplayed on the level of narrative. Although the male/female sadomasochistic relationship is present in Biller's narrative (Schulz/Adele, Schulz/Helena), it is of secondary importance. Rather, the core sadomasochistic scenario is enacted through the relationship between Schulz and the town's Jews/Thomas Mann. While sadomasochism, in accordance with the literary tradition, is represented as an exclusively male/female scenario *on the visual level, on the level of narrative* it is coded as predominantly Jewish/German. Biller's text thus transposes the sadomasochistic complex from the realm of gender onto the domain of ethnicity and culture. This transposition only works, however, with the help of a gendered strategy that feminizes the fake Thomas Mann and aligns him, in various ways, with the cruel and dominating females who play a role in Sacher-Masoch's, Schulz's, and Biller's texts.[62] Sacher-Masoch's and Schulz's cruel mistresses are thus reinterpreted and reemerge in the guise of the character Thomas Mann—Venus in furs becomes Thomas Mann in furs.[63] This alignment becomes even clearer when considering the collection of Schulz's drawings that served as an inspiration for Biller's novella. The drawings demonstrate that one of the central scenes of degradation in *Im Kopf von Bruno Schulz*—the fake Thomas Mann uses the town's Jews as cart horses—redeploys an existing piece of art by Schulz in which a female does the exact same thing to a group of naked men.[64] It is worth noting that the drawing is entitled *Auf Kythera*; in Greek mythology Cythera is the island belonging to Aphrodite, the goddess of love and seduction. Another drawing by Schulz, which shows men crawling at the feet of a powerful woman, is entitled *Mademoiselle Circe und ihre Truppe*, evoking yet another dangerously seductive female from the realm of Greek mythology.[65] By implicitly remediating these drawings, Biller's novella aligns the fake Thomas Mann (and German culture as a whole, which he epitomizes) with traditions of the seductive femme fatale whose presence proves to be fatal for the town's Jews.

As a manifestation of "travelling memory,"[66] the sadomasochistic constellation thus moves from Sacher-Masoch's text into Schulz's written and graphic oeuvre, to then enter Biller's novella. Along the way, certain aspects of the sadomasochistic complex are highlighted while others are suppressed, and the issues attached to it change accordingly. Schulz's collection of stories sticks to the gendered constellation at the heart of Sacher-Masoch's writing but reinterprets it in terms of class and a conflict between (male) mind and (female) matter. Furthermore, Schulz's transformation of the aristocratic and cruel mistress into the housekeeper, the translocation to the realm of the bourgeois nuclear family, and the reversal of the dichotomy above/below can all be interpreted as forms of ironic debasement. Biller's text seemingly abandons the gender aspect by conceptualizing sadomasochism as an illustration of the (failed) German-Jewish symbiosis. At the same time, *Im Kopf von Bruno Schulz* incorporates certain misogynistic tendencies that are present in Schulz's oeuvre[67] by revitalizing the topos of the femme fatale.

The Seductiveness of German Culture

While Eastern European (Jewish) artistic traditions represent one important set of influences for Biller's novella, the other central reference point is Thomas Mann. Biller's engagement with Thomas Mann in *Im Kopf von Bruno Schulz* and in *Der gebrauchte Jude* demonstrates a visible anxiety of influence, which relates to Mann as a literary forefather and rival and as a symbol for German culture in its entirety. Biller's representation of the sadomasochistic German-Jewish relationship can be read as a polemical demonstration of the dangerous seductiveness of German culture. According to Biller's narrative, Thomas Mann lured Jews like Bruno Schulz and Marcel Reich-Ranicki into a submissive state, sustained by the illusion that an untainted love for German culture and a German-Jewish symbiosis are possible.

In order to better understand this argument, it is important to consider the portrayal of Mann in Biller's novella, which encompasses three facets: first, there is the Thomas Mann whom Schulz's fictional letter is addressed to. Known to Schulz only "von Fotografien und aus Zeitungen" (*IKvBS*, 7), this noble gentleman remains silent and absent throughout the text.[68] This idealized Thomas Mann is gradually overwritten by, second, the fake Thomas Mann, a "bösartiges Abbild" (*IKvBS*, 33), who roams the streets of Drohobycz and is physically and morally repulsive. Not only is he dirty, a slovenly dresser, and generally unkempt, he also abuses the town's Jews in increasingly sadistic ways and turns out to be an agent of Germany's secret police. Third, there is the actually existing author Thomas Mann, who still is an intradiegetic figure and supposed to help Schulz. It eventually becomes clear that both the ideal and its grotesque reversal spring solely from Schulz's imagination. There is no fake Thomas Mann in Drohobycz; Schulz has made him up to gain the actual Mann's attention and protection. The split Mann therefore exists exclusively in

Schulz's mind as an expression of the writer's ambivalent love-hate relationship with the idol. The sadomasochistic relationship between the fake Mann, on the one side, and Schulz and the town's Jews, on the other side, is thus uncovered as a fantasy entertained by the book's protagonist. The neat separation between the protagonist's fantasies and the author's opinions is complicated, however, when considering Biller's autobiographically inspired "Selbstporträt" *Der gebrauchte Jude*.[69] The text circles obsessively around Thomas Mann and Biller's personal love-hate relationship with the idol,[70] so that Schulz's fantasies can be said to also convey Biller's own negative sentiments toward the precursor:

> Thomas Mann ist der neue Goethe, und den Deutschen ist egal, dass fast alle seine Bücher einen dunklen Hinterausgang haben, durch den man direkt in die schmutzige Phantasiewelt der Rassentheoretiker des 19. Jahrhunderts gelangt. Die Juden bei Mann sind schnell, schmierig, gewissenlos und Demokraten. Sie haben platte Nasen und wulstige Lippen, und wenn sie wie Sieglinde und Siegmund in *Wälsungenblut* Geschwister sind, schlafen sie miteinander. (*DgJ*, 42)

Biller's novella thus uses an allegedly "real" historical event—Schulz writing a letter to Mann—to continue his own dialogue with Thomas Mann and to cope with the anxiety of influence. The novella's doppelgänger theme therefore extends to the relationship between Biller and Schulz, in the sense that Schulz represents Biller's alter ego or, more accurately, his mouthpiece.[71] This makes both Thomas Mann *and* Bruno Schulz into victims of Biller's anxiety: the last of Bloom's "revisionary ratios," termed "*Apophrades* or The Return of the Dead," involves "the triumph of having so stationed the precursor, in one's own work, that particular passages in *his* work seem to be not presages of one's own advent, but rather to be indebted to one's own achievement [italics in the original]."[72] Although Bloom refers to the level of style, which is not central to Biller's intertextual engagement, Biller's novella attempts to achieve this triumph on the level of plot. The eponymous project of getting inside the head of Bruno Schulz is an attempt to raise the dead on certain conditions: "The mighty dead return, but they return in our colors, and speaking in our voices."[73] The necromancy practiced in *Im Kopf von Bruno Schulz* is thus a form of ventriloquy: through the hand and head of Bruno Schulz, Biller expresses his own issues und anxieties as an author. This demonstrates that the postmemorial affiliation performed in Biller's novella is not an exclusively ethical one—it is both an act of homage and an act of appropriation, a continuation of tradition and a form of patricide. The nostalgic longing for the lost writing traditions of Eastern European Jewry is thus the flip side of anxiety.

While expressing the anxiety of influence, the sadomasochistic relationship between Mann and Schulz/the town's Jews also connects to the larger issue of the Jew in German culture and the (im)possibility of a German-Jewish symbiosis. Framed within the sadomasochistic constellation, Thomas Mann and German culture are imagined as feminine and highly seductive[74] but also as deceitful and dangerous. Schulz, for example, dwells on the fake Mann's "Betrügergesicht" (*IKvBS*, 39), while also taking note of his inappropriately revealing clothing, in the form of a "blutroten persischen Chalat . . ., der nur lose mit einer abgerissenen Gardinenkordel zusammengebunden war" (*IKvBS*, 49). Biller's novella here picks up on the misogynistic undercurrent in Schulz's prose, in which women are also presented as, on the one hand, mindless, passive, and hypersexual matter, while, on the other hand, being dominating and deceptive.[75]

Im Kopf von Bruno Schulz features various scenes in which the people in the town are inexplicably drawn to the fake Mann, and this is so in spite of his repugnant physical appearance and atrocious behavior:

> Die vielen wichtigen Leute aus unserer Stadt, die ihn seit seiner Ankunft wie der Bienenstaat die Königin umschwirren, ducken sich kurz, und danach tauchen sie—die Mundwinkel zum unterwürfigen Lächeln hochgezogen, die Augen vor Schrecken gerötet und glasig— wieder auf und bitten ihn, ihnen weiter seine aufregenden Geschichten zu erzählen. (*IKvBS*, 17)

The comparison of the town's community to a "Bienenstaat" puts the fake Mann in the position of the proverbial queen bee. This link is further emphasized by Schulz's choice of words when describing the fake Mann. He mentions that the phony writer has come to the town to make everyone's head spin (*IKvBS*, 32), and he admits, "Und so habe ich mich neulich auch, sehr verehrter Dr. Mann, wie jeder andere von Ihrem Doppelgänger einwickeln lassen" (*IKvBS*, 32). Verb constructions such as making someone's head spin and deceiving them form an imagery of seduction, ensnarement, and manipulation that is usually associated with the misogynistic topos of the femme fatale.[76] And even though the character of Schulz seems to take up a rather distanced, maybe even critical, stance toward this senseless admiration, he himself is not immune to the charms of Mann and finds himself trapped in his love for the German language and German culture as a whole:

> Die biegsamen Regeln der Mischna, die fast beschwingte Schwermut des Predigers, die sanfte Klarheit des Schulchan Aruch? Nein, das war nie etwas für mich. Ich sehne mich eher mit Malte Laurids Brigge und Gustav von Aschenbach nach einem Ende, das uns alle ohnehin erwartet, dessen Schönheit und Zeitpunkt wir aber selbst bestimmen sollten. (*IKvBS*, 62)

Yet, as is well known, flirting with the femme fatale usually does not end well for the male characters. This is not any different for the Jews who have fallen prey to the temptations of Thomas Mann and German culture. The fake Mann lures them into a profoundly sadomasochistic constellation of dominance and submission that eventually leads to their deaths. This is epitomized in the bathroom scene, which is at the center of the narrative arc and forms the climax of Biller's text (and Schulz's fantasy). The scene hinges on the provocative image of the doppelgänger giving the town's Jews a whipping inside a bathroom that evokes the iconography of the gas chamber:

> Sie hatten ihre Kleider an die Haken gehängt, sie saßen stumm oder übertrieben leise miteinander sprechend auf den beiden Bänken und warteten. Als der Meister mit dem Direktor und mir reinkam, erhoben sie sich fast gleichzeitig, sie verdeckten mit den Händen ihre nackten Brüste und Genitalien, und auch die letzte, allerleiseste Unterhaltung brach ab. (*IKvBS*, 34–37)

References to the gas chambers are of course anachronistic from the viewpoint of the novella, which is set in 1938. They also suggest, however, that Schulz's fantasies are *a form of premonition*, as has been observed previously in connection with the character's apocalyptic visions. The superimposition of the iconographies of sadomasochism, the Holocaust, and anti-Semitic violence in the bathroom scene indicates that the blind and masochistic Jewish love of German culture makes Jews follow Germans like lambs to the slaughter, which anticipates future historical events. The violence is sparked when the Jews start to beleaguer the fake Mann in response to his announcement that he is leaving Europe for America to escape the advent of German fascism. The physical contact made by the Jews is thus a cry for help; but their actions could also be interpreted as the culmination of their desire for symbiosis and amalgamation, which, however, provokes fear and violence in the German. What begins as a sadomasochistic orgy eventually turns into a pogrom, an act of anti-Semitic destruction. The fake Mann is positioned within a genealogy of anti-Semitic excess, which logically leads to the Holocaust as the endpoint, making him part of the perpetrator collective:

> Doch allmählich wurden die Hiebe des Deutschen schwächer, seine Stimme auch, in der silbernen Rauchwolke formten sich für einen Moment die wabernden Konturen des traurigen Kindergesichts von Leutnant Alfred Dreyfus, aus dem französischen Offizier wurde die weinende und blutende Jagienka Łomska, dann schaute ich mich selbst aus dem Rauchschleier an, und schließlich drehte sich die Wolke, sie zog sich zusammen und stieg zur Decke auf, wo sie mit einem lauten Zischen in den Düsen der Duschen verschwand—und gab so den Blick frei auf einen großen Haufen nackter Körper, die leblos um den vor Erschöpfung knienden, falschen Thomas Mann herumlagen. (*IKvBS*, 40–41)

The recourse to Holocaust imagery—and of the gas chamber in particular—is undeniable in this passage. The fake Thomas Mann, suddenly addressed solely as "de(r) Deutsche," is represented as a Nazi perpetrator, executing anti-Semitic violence, while the townspeople are integrated into a community of eternal victims, with the prophetic Schulz as their latest addition. This scene suggests that German-Jewish relations can only ever result in anti-Semitic excess because, sooner or later, all Germans will turn into perpetrators. According to this scenario, German-Jewish relations function as a one-sided dependency, based on an act of delusional submission on the side of the Jews, which inevitably entails their destruction. The introduction of Mann as "Meister" at the beginning of the scene thus carries multiple meanings: he is not only a master commanding words and slaves but also the "Meister aus Deutschland" that haunts Paul Celan's "Todesfuge" (1948) and thus an emblem of Nazi extermination policies.[77] The Schulz in Biller's story aims to exploit the difference between his grotesque invention and the actual Thomas Mann, who he hopes will save him. But the fact that Mann remains silent and Schulz's fantasies eventually become real—Drohobycz is overrun and destroyed by Nazi troops at the end of the novella—implies that the difference between the fake and the real Mann is not that big, and that Schulz himself fell prey to a delusional belief in German culture as the opposite of and antidote to Nazi barbarism. The novella hence employs Schulz's *pre-Holocaust interpretation* of German-Jewish relationships as a masochistic dependency on the side of the Jews to express a *post-Holocaust consciousness*. In contrast to Schulz's illusions, the logic of the novella is supported by the conviction that, after the attempted extermination of an entire people, Jews and Germans are "für immer geschiedene Leute" (*DgJ*, 107).

The Return of the Grotesque?

This interpretation of German-Jewish relations brings us back to the beginning of this chapter and the question of literary mode: Is the depiction of the German-Jewish symbiosis as a sadomasochistic death trap a grotesque exaggeration, or does it represent a radical post-Holocaust Jewish stance on the matter? Although *Im Kopf von Bruno Schulz* is not as openly polemical and grotesque as, for example, *Harlem Holocaust*, it still taps into the surrealist legacy of Schulz's written and graphic work, so that the reader is made to question the factual accuracy of what is described (by both Schulz and the third-person narrator). The town of Drohobycz is presented as a topsy-turvy world in which the most fantastical things are happening: "Sehen Sie, Dr. Mann, was für ein Irrenhaus dieses Drohobycz ist? Keiner hier denkt und benimmt sich, wie er sollte!" (*IKvBS*, 27). The events happening in the "Irrenhaus" of Drohobycz could be described as "carnivalesque" in Bakhtin's sense, implying a temporary suspension of the existing order, which is replaced by the peculiar logic of the "inside out" (*à l'envers*), of the "turnabout," of the continual shifting from top to bottom, from front to rear, of numerous parodies and travesties, humiliations, profanations, comic crownings and uncrownings. . . . it is to a certain extent a parody of the extracarnival life, a "world inside out" [italics in the original].[78]

The notion of the grotesque, which is intimately connected to the "carnival spirit" in Bakhtin's work,[79] would also account for the hybrid bodies (mostly Helena's border-crossing physicality, but also the repeated destabilization of the human-animal divide) and the strong emphasis on sexuality in the novella. There are, however, also aspects of Biller's text that do not reflect the "carnival spirit": a carnivalization of German-Jewish relations would also entail a reversal of the roles of victim and perpetrator, oppressor and oppressed. This is ultimately not the case in *Im Kopf von Bruno Schulz*: the sadomasochistic configuration ultimately reinforces the existing power structures instead of inverting them. Bakhtin showed that the carnivalesque suspension of hierarchies and rules is a temporarily limited phenomenon, which is followed by the reinstatement (and possible reinforcement) of the existing order. If the arrival of the German troops toward the end of the novella can be interpreted as the violent intrusion of historical reality into the surreal fantasy world of Drohobycz, then this would suggest that fascism is the "correct" order, which is reinstated after the carnival period. Finally, the carnivalesque grotesque in Biller's novella does not carry any of the positive connotations associated with the grotesque as it merely signifies the monstrous and the abject, death, demise, and decay, while lacking the crucial aspects of renewal, comic laughter, and rebirth. The grotesque in Biller's novella therefore conforms to the negative grotesque, which, following Bakhtin, is the main manifestation of the grotesque in European culture ever since Romanticism.[80] The novella's employment of the grotesque thus highlights the negative aspects of the German-Jewish relationship, without challenging the underlying power structures in a carnivalesque manner. Although Schulz uses the metaphor of the "Irrenhaus" to describe Drohobycz, the fact remains that the madness is in the end revealed as an anticipation of historical reality, turning Schulz from a paranoiac into a prophet. Far from discrediting Drohobycz, this turn of events condemns the historical reality of the German invasion, which is presented as the manifestation of Schulz's worst nightmares.

Apart from the apocalyptic template, another biblical intertext is key for our interpretation of Biller's novella: namely, the rather obscure story of King Abimelech and the town of Sichem. It is brought up more than halfway through the book, when Schulz starts wondering whether he might be taking things a little too far: "Ich meine, dass sich jemand als er ausgibt, könnte zwar sein, aber dass er so brutal und überheblich ist, gerade zu denen, die ihn achten und rühmen, klingt ziemlich unwahrscheinlich, oder?" (*IKvBS*, 47). (His) Fear, who is personified throughout the text, replies as follows: "Kennst du die Geschichte der Bewohner von Sichem, . . . weißt du, wie es ihnen erging, nachdem sie Abimelech zum Herrscher der Philister gewählt hatten?" (*IKvBS*, 47). Section 9 of the book of Judges centers on Abimelech, a judge who desires to become the new ruler over the town of Sichem and secretly plots to kill his seventy brothers, who would have been a competition for the throne. This is backed by the people of Sichem, who have become ensnared by Abimelech and his lust for power. He succeeds in murdering all of his brothers except for one, Jotam. Jotam retreats to the mountain of Garizim, where he curses the people of Sichem for their act of betrayal and asks God to deliver a just punishment:

> 16 Habt ihr nun recht und redlich getan, dass ihr Abimelech zum König gemacht habt? Und habt ihr wohlgetan an Jerubbaal und an seinem Hause, und habt ihr ihm getan, wie er's um euch verdient hat?
> . . .
> 19 Habt ihr nun heute recht und redlich gehandelt an Jerubbaal und an seinem Hause, so seid fröhlich über Abimelech und er sei fröhlich über euch.
> 20 Wenn nicht, so gehe Feuer aus von Abimelech und verzehre die Männer von Sichem und die Bewohner des Millo, und gehe auch Feuer aus von den Männern von Sichem und von den Bewohnern des Millo und verzehre Abimelech.[81]

Abimelech rules in peace for a time, but after three years God sends an evil spirit to divide Abimelech and the people of Sichem, who subsequently try to overthrow him. Abimelech hires an army of mercenaries to destroy Sichem as a punishment for this insurgency. He is successful but cannot escape divine judgment indefinitely: during the siege of Tebez, a woman throws a millstone on his head, and he has to beg his armor bearer to kill him so as to avoid the disgrace of having been slain by a woman. The end of Sichem and the death of Abimelech are presented as the result of a divine intervention:

> 56 So vergalt Gott dem Abimelech das Böse, das er seinem Vater angetan hatte, als er seine siebzig Brüder tötete.
> 57 Desgleichen alle bösen Taten der Männer von Sichem vergalt ihnen Gott auf ihren Kopf, und es kam über sie der Fluch Jotams, des Sohnes Jerubbaals.[82]

Given its position in the text, the reader is encouraged to establish a direct connection between Abimelech/Thomas Mann and Sichem/Drohobycz. The story is introduced as a warning against one-sided loyalties and false allegiances. The people of Sichem decide to support Abimelech because his uncles convince them that he is one of them, their brother (Richter 9:3). Similarly, Jews like Bruno Schulz succumb to Mann

(and German culture in general) because they think a German-Jewish symbiosis is possible, that Germans and Jews can (or even have) achieve(d)
"ewige Brüderlichkeit" (*DgJ*, 117). Schulz believes that the idealized
Mann is not capable of the atrocities committed by the fake Thomas
Mann. The story of Abimelech demonstrates that the difference between
the two is not that great: a king/an idol can turn into a slaughterer and
vice versa. As such, the story of Abimelech is not meant to denigrate the
fake Mann but to highlight the dangers of misjudging the original.

The story is taken up again on the last pages of the novella, when
Schulz tries to make sense of what is happening to him and his town:

> Was ist das?, dachte er.
> Keine Antwort.
> Was ist das?!
> Das ist die Armee von Abimelech, sagte schließlich die Angst, sie ist
> gekommen, um all die zu vernichten, die ihn zuerst zum König
> machten und sich später daran erinnerten, dass er siebzig ihrer Brüder
> ermordet hatte. (*IKvBS*, 68)

By the end of the novella, the fire unleashed upon Sichem by Jotam's
curse has reached Drohobycz; its destruction therefore appears as a just
punishment for an act of betrayal. Altering the biblical narrative, Fear tells
Schulz that Sichem/Drohobycz is being punished for the betrayal of its
seventy brothers in the service of a foreign king. The biblical original,
however, states that it is not Sichem's but Abimelech's seventy brothers
who are murdered. This fairly minor change in fact has big consequences:
the misreading of the biblical original suggests that Drohobycz's Jews have
betrayed their brothers (i.e., their Jewishness) in their blind devotion to a
foreign king (i.e., Thomas Mann) and are now paying the price. The implications of this are extremely problematic, if not downright inacceptable,
since the Holocaust is made to appear as a just punishment for the blind
belief in the possibility of a German-Jewish symbiosis.

"Er war, wie ich werden würde": Marcel Reich-Ranicki

Biller's fixation on Thomas Mann is matched by his obsession with Marcel
Reich-Ranicki, and both are brought together in the space of his autobiographically inspired *Der gebrauchte Jude*. The text stages repeated, violent
attacks against Thomas Mann in an attempt to ward off the influence of
the German *Übervater*, while seeking to gain the attention of his Jewish
"literarischer Ersatzvater" (*DgJ*, 80) Reich-Ranicki. What is at stake in this
love-hate triangle among Biller, Mann, and Reich-Ranicki is a specific
understanding of German-Jewish relations and the status of the Jew in
German (postwar) culture, which provides the nexus between Biller's
2009 text and his later novella *Im Kopf von Bruno Schulz*. Tensions arise
from a generational difference between the wild pop-journalist Biller and

the established bourgeois critic Reich-Ranicki, but they go beyond a cliched clash between the young rebel and the establishment. What truly separates Biller from Reich-Ranicki is their different understanding of Jewish identity in present-day Germany and the relationship between Jews and German culture. The key issues that Biller addresses in his fictionalized encounters with Reich-Ranicki thus converge with the central themes in *Im Kopf von Bruno Schulz*: What does it mean to be Jewish in the land and culture of the perpetrators? What traditions can the Jewish writer still relate to after the Holocaust? What is the role of literature and writing in negotiating these issues? In the search for answers, Reich-Ranicki acts as a role model for Biller—after all, he was one of the most visible Jewish public intellectuals in postwar German culture. Biller stages their relationship as an antagonistic struggle over Thomas Mann and introduces a constellation that is similar to *Im Kopf von Bruno Schulz*, in which a Jew falls prey to the seductiveness of Thomas Mann and German culture more generally. Biller's verdict on Reich-Ranicki is even harsher, however, since, unlike the turn-of-the-century Galician writer Schulz, Reich-Ranicki has experienced the Holocaust firsthand and, in the eyes of Biller, should know about the futility of the German-Jewish symbiosis. Thomas Mann is a particularly unacceptable role model for Biller, who accuses the German writer of having been an incorrigible anti-Semite: "Thomas Mann hasste die Juden!" (*DgJ*, 42). Mann's bigotry extends to his German audience, which chooses to ignore the blatant anti-Semitism of his oeuvre to protect their cultural heritage. In Biller's eyes, Reich-Ranicki goes even further, by identifying with Mann and his oeuvre rather than with the Jew Franz Kafka:

> "Er schrieb *Tonio Kröger*! Hier war der Konflikt, den ich seit meiner Kindheit kannte. Konnte ich Künstler sein? Hatte ich den Mut, das Talent, die Geduld?" Und Gregor Samsa waren Sie nicht? [asks Biller.] "Damit hab ich nichts zu tun, das ist jüdische Schizophrenie. Jüdischer Selbsthass!" (*DgJ*, 106)

Reich-Ranicki's sentiments are, of course, reminiscent of Bruno Schulz's previously mentioned admiration for Malte Laurids Brigge and Gustav von Aschenbach—that is, Rilke and Mann—in *Im Kopf von Bruno Schulz*. This parallel further strengthens my claim that Biller's texts fictionalize Bruno Schulz's and Marcel Reich-Ranicki's relationships with Thomas Mann to deal with similar issues. Biller's scathing critique is aimed at both the German-Jewish literary critic and the more or less forgotten Polish Jewish writer, since, in his eyes, they both fell in love with the wrong person and culture:

> Nicht Kafka, sondern Thomas Mann. Nicht der Jude, der das schönste Deutsch des zwanzigsten Jahrhunderts schrieb, weil er den tadelnden Blicken der Nichtjuden standhalten wollte—sondern der

Deutsche, der sich bis zu seinem Tod in der jüdischen Moderne so wohlfühlte wie ein niedersächsischer Pastor auf dem Geburtstagsfest des Zaddiks von Przemysl. (*DgJ*, 107)

Biller calls the belief that German culture can be isolated from the atrocities of German fascism the "Reich-Ranicki-Syndrom" (*DgJ*, 117). Part of this syndrome is the unshakable investment in the possibility of a German-Jewish symbiosis: "Seit zwei Jahrhunderten glaubten die Deutsch sprechenden Juden Mitteleuropas, deutsche Worte und deutsche Melodien seien eine einzige große Hymne auf die ewige Brüderlichkeit" (*DgJ*, 117). Jews like Reich-Ranicki cannot let go of this belief and their love of German culture, even in the face of the Holocaust:

> Wie gern wäre er [Reich-Ranicki] Deutscher gewesen . . . aber das ging wirklich nicht mehr. Und wenn doch? Also subtrahierte er sich seine Lebenswahrheit zurecht, wie so viele Davongekommene: Deutschland minus Hitler, Goebbels und Auschwitz gleich Heine, Rilke und Thomas Mann. (*DgJ*, 82–83)

Biller claims that this delusional desire for a German-Jewish symbiosis, which ignores the Holocaust, is a phenomenon associated mainly with the "Deutsch sprechenden Juden Mitteleuropas." This suggests that Biller's conflict with Reich-Ranicki is also marked by an East/West divide (although they share their Eastern European origins), which forms around the question of assimilation. And so it is that Biller transforms the generationally coded rivalry between Reich-Ranicki and himself into the opposition between an assimilationist and radically antiassimilationist notion of Jewish identity. The combination Thomas Mann/Reich-Ranicki stands for a bourgeois, Central European, and assimilated form of Jewishness, from which Biller sets himself apart. In *Der gebrauchte Jude* he mobilized an American Jewish genealogy of writers (Saul Bellow, Bernard Malamud, Philip Roth) to achieve this separation effect; a few years later, he rediscovered Eastern European Jewish traditions to reach the same goal. Biller is, however, faced with the conundrum that he also occupies a prominent position in mainstream German culture, as his nomination for the *Literarisches Quartett* exemplifies. His attacks on Reich-Ranicki are thus fueled by his own fear of assimilation: "Er war, wie ich werden würde, ob ich es wollte oder nicht" (*DgJ*, 81). In this context, Thomas Mann is an overdetermined signifier, evoking oedipal rivalry, anxieties of influence, and the lures of German culture, alongside the fear of assimilation and annihilation. Biller's critical engagement with Mann in *Im Kopf von Bruno Schulz* therefore also addresses Reich-Ranicki, warning him that the unconditional love of German culture and the abandonment of Jewish tradition can only lead to one of two things—assimilation or extermination.

Conclusion: From Patriarchal
Poetics to "Perpetrator Poetics"

Harold Bloom's theory of influence is driven by the question of how authors relate to literary heritages. While Bloom demonstrates that the inscription into tradition usually involves severe conflict, aggression, and murderous impulses, he still supposes that all male writers eventually join the patriarchal family that is the canon of Western literature. Bloom focuses on the question of *how* authors adopt and transform their precursors, and not on the problem *if* they (are able to) do so in the first place. Gilbert and Gubar's criticism of Bloom posits that such an understanding of literary tradition reinforces patriarchal dominance; they also challenge the feasibility of Bloom's model for all those who are not part of that canon. The "anxiety" of the woman writer results from her inability to relate to masculinist traditions, as they do not provide any potential for a positive identification. The woman writer's literary orphan status fuels a fear of being creative/a creator that obstructs her artistic potential. Curiously enough, Maxim Biller is faced with a similar problem as a German Jewish writer in post-Holocaust Germany: certain traditions are not available to him, either because they have been violently destroyed or because they are part of a culture from which the Holocaust emerged. This leads to a recurring engagement with literary paternity and the integration into tradition in Biller's latest writing, which does not tackle the logic of "patriarchal poetics" but rather tackles what I would call "perpetrator poetics."

This term points to the central predicament Biller faces as a Jewish writer in Germany: he cannot positively identify with the influence of German "perpetrator" culture—epitomized by the writer-father Thomas Mann—while at the same time being cut off, historically and geographically, from vital Jewish writing traditions. While Biller cannot relate to German culture and writing traditions, however, he is still a part of them. Bloom's approach ultimately posits that writing is never free of influence, that it is always "infected" with the ideas of the precursors, who, in Biller's case, belong to the perpetrator collective. This causes a profound sense of "dis-ease" in Biller's writing,[83] fueled by the inability to escape the contagious influence of German culture and "perpetrator poetics." This "dis-ease" is the essence of Biller's hateful relationship with Mann, who, as a prewar author, is employed to express Biller's post-Holocaust consciousness, marked by the unavoidability of German cultural influence and the "negative Symbiose."

Gilbert and Gubar show that female writers perceive the infectiousness of a male-dominated tradition as "profoundly debilitating" and respond with images of sickness, deformity, and confinement.[84] Biller's texts, however, choose a more belligerent path: fending off the anxiety caused by the influence of "perpetrator poetics," Biller's writing constructs "positive" and "negative" intertextual genealogies. A positive intertextual relationship is established with the works of Bruno Schulz, which inscribes Biller into a specifically Eastern European Jewish tradition. This heritage encompasses "ghetto writing" and sadomasochistic discourse (Sacher-Masoch, Agnon, Schulz), alongside a Kafkaesque surrealism, all of which intersect in Schulz's oeuvre. Biller's novella furthermore uses a fictionalized Schulz to act out the anxieties of creative obstruction and infection that are associated with Thomas Mann in Biller's work. The text's relationship with Schulz's oeuvre can thus be described as a form of appropriative postmemory, which diverges from the ethical trajectory suggested by Hirsch. *Im Kopf von Bruno Schulz* demonstrates that the postmemorial generation's relationship with the past and certain cultural traditions comprises ambivalent feelings, encompassing both love and hate, commemoration and erasure, adoration and patricide. The relationship with Thomas Mann is less ambivalent and is marked by hatred. Since Biller's texts do not engage with Thomas Mann's oeuvre as such, the German writer fulfills a synecdochical function, representing German cultural tradition as a whole. There is an obvious patricidal element to this relationship, since Biller's texts try to expose and degrade the idol in order to break free from its spell. In *Im Kopf von Bruno Schulz*, this is achieved by imagining alternative yet masculine genealogies, while also associating Mann with the female, which is constructed as a site of abjection. By contrast, the relationship with Reich-Ranicki is defined by identification—Biller sees himself in Reich-Ranicki and claims that the opposite is also true. Nonetheless, Biller's writing discredits Reich-Ranicki by merging him with the character Bruno Schulz, accusing both of a blind infatuation with German culture. The danger of this infatuation is highlighted in the sadomasochistic submission of the Jews by Thomas Mann, which can only end in assimilation or annihilation.

My analysis has thus concentrated on Biller's use of explicit intertextual references to deal with the (un)relatability and (un)availability of certain traditions after the Holocaust. In Biller's latest work, intertextuality becomes the battleground on which conflicts of belonging and dissociation are staged and acted out, as his texts employ intertextual allusions to connect to some traditions, while aggressively warding off the influence of others, as has also been noted by Gwyer: "Intertextuality and intermediality are working together here in the dual aim of allowing Biller to take his place in Jewish world literature and position himself against the narrowly German literary canon."[85] Intertextuality thus emerges as a central literary technique for (re)negotiating contemporary, post-Holocaust Jewish identities. In their recent volume on contemporary German-Jewish literature, Katja Garloff and Agnes Mueller have suggested that many younger contemporary authors—such as Alina Bronsky, Mirna Funk, Olga Grjasnowa, and Katja Petrowskaja—actually move beyond a preoccupation with the Holocaust and conceptions of a negative German-Jewish symbiosis.[86] While Biller's fixation on the "negative symbiosis" thus seems potentially outdated, it is worth stressing here that his preoccupation with certain intertextual and intermedial relationships is highly current, as is also highlighted by Gwyer.[87] Biller thus appears as an ambiguous figure, who in some ways represents a slightly older generation of German-Jewish writers whose concerns are maybe not entirely shared by the younger cohort. At the same time, his attempts to (re)connect with a seemingly more authentic, untainted version of Jewishness, represented by the lost world of Eastern European Jewishness, reflect a highly current moment. He is also ambiguous in the sense that, in a similar vein to Stein, his writing combines highly self- and metareflexive elements with a less sophisticated stance on certain issues. Whereas his engagement with intertextuality and certain writing traditions, such as "ghetto writing," is ironically distanced and self-reflexive, his overall approach to Schulz's work relies on an appropriative and instrumentalizing "act of dispossession."[88] As I have illustrated in relation to Stein's work, the mix of vanishing eyewitness accounts and hyper-mediated cultural memories makes certain notions of Jewishness increasingly unavailable for present and future generations. While Stein's writing attempts to compensate for this loss of authenticity by turning to religion and folklorized notions of Jewishness, Biller—and other present-day second- and third-generation authors—appear to be grappling with similar issues but have instead decided to revisit, re-create, and (re)claim the literary and artistic legacies of Jewish Eastern Europe. As Biller's writing shows, they often walk the line between (self-)reflexive appreciation and acts of appropriation.

3: Contrapuntal Memory, Dialogism, and Irony: Challenges to Transnationalism in Vladimir Vertlib's *Das besondere Gedächtnis der Rosa Masur*

Introduction: Scrutinizing the "Transnational Turn"

TRANSNATIONAL AND/OR TRANSCULTURAL perspectives on the Holocaust are undoubtedly *en vogue*, as is demonstrated by the many recent conference calls, publications, and research clusters on the theme. This boom is indicative of a larger transnational or transcultural turn,[1] which, over the last ten years, has reached disciplines as diverse as sociology, history, modern languages, and, most importantly, memory studies.[2] Transcultural/-national memory can be understood as an intervention into the field of memory studies, which promotes the fundamental interrelatedness of cultural and mnemonic phenomena. It focuses on literal and metaphorical instances of border crossing, intermingling, travel, and translation, drawing attention to "the palimpsestic overlays, the hybrid assemblages, the non-linear interactions, and the fuzzy edges of group belonging."[3] The idea of transnational memory ties in with a broader dynamization of memory studies, which entails a shift in focus away from (cultural) memory as a "product" to the procedural character of memory formation, transportation, and translation.[4]

The increasing globalization of almost all spheres of social life, coupled with a new sense of "connectivity" brought about by digital technologies,[5] has called into question many of the core assumptions guiding memory studies. This particularly pertains to what Astrid Erll and others have identified as the "methodological nationalism/culturalism" of memory studies,[6] that is, the implicit understanding of cultures as separate and clearly delineated "spheres" or "containers," and the "assumption of an isomorphy between territory, social formation, mentalities, and memories."[7] In response to this, cultures and memories have been increasingly conceptualized as dynamic, porous, and constituted through exchange—they are not discrete and uniform but entangled and hybrid. In terms of research, this has brought forward a focus on phenomena that emerge at the intersection of nations and cultures or cut across them. This concentration on national,

cultural, and mnemonic interlinkages also challenges traditional under-
standings of the nation or culture. Lucy Bond and Jessica Rapson therefore
regard transcultural memory

> as describing two disparate dynamics in contemporary commemora-
> tive practice: firstly, the travelling memory *within* and *between*
> national, ethnic and religious collectives; secondly, forums of remem-
> brance that aim *beyond* the idea of political, ethnic, linguistic or reli-
> gious borders as containers for our understanding of the past [italics
> in the original].[8]

Transcultural memory brings into view the cross-fertilization of various national and/or cultural memories while also promoting the transformation and eventual transcendence of the nation-state. This shows that
the transcultural or transnational is frequently "deployed not only as a
descriptive tool but also as a prescriptive term that carries normative implications."[9] Underpinning a lot of research in the field—especially in the
realm of cultural studies—is the utopian idea(l) of a borderless world,
premised on peaceful transcultural/-national exchange, a cosmopolitan
ethos, and "transcultural empathy."[10] More-recent research in the field
has adopted a critical stance toward these celebratory agendas, and scholars like Michael Rothberg have arrived at a more nuanced understanding
of the ethics involved in acts of cross-cultural, multidirectional
remembering.[11]

The shift toward a transnational and transcultural memory paradigm
not only denotes a certain *subject matter* but also a specific *research perspective*, which unsettles established assumptions about what (cultural) memory is and does. Astrid Erll takes these two dimensions of transnational or
transcultural memory as a starting point for initiating a more fundamental
paradigm shift in memory studies, which she captures in the notion of
"travelling memory":

> The term "travelling memory" is a metaphorical shorthand, an abbre-
> viation for the fact that in the production of cultural memory, people,
> media, mnemonic forms, contents, and practices are in constant,
> unceasing motion. . . . I claim that *all* cultural memory *must* "travel,"
> be kept in motion, in order to "stay alive," to have an impact both on
> individual minds and social formations. Such travel consists only
> partly in movement across and beyond territorial and social bounda-
> ries. On a more fundamental level, it is the ongoing exchange of
> information between individuals and the motion between minds and
> media which first of all generates . . . collective memory. "Travel" is
> therefore an expression of the principal logic of memory: its genesis
> and existence through movement [italics in the original].[12]

Transculturality, fluidity, and entanglement are thus the basic modes of
memory formation—cultural memory is never stable and monolithic; it

depends on travel and exchange in order to constitute itself and survive.[13]

While the transnational and transcultural memory paradigm has thus been widely embraced in the arts, humanities, and social sciences, there is a general confusion as to what the differences between these two terms are and how they relate to a host of buzzwords that have evolved alongside them, such as the inter-, multi-, and cross-cultural; the postnational; the global; and the cosmopolitan. The difference between the transnational and the transcultural is not simply one between national-geographic and sociocultural dynamics and phenomena. Advocates of transculturality and/ or transnationalism have rightly pointed out that culture and the nation have often been imagined as congruent, making the task of neatly separating them difficult. Astrid Erll therefore suggests an understanding of transcultural memory as an umbrella term, encompassing—among other things—transnational memory as a subcategory.[14] Dagmar Brunow further broadens the term by proclaiming that transculturality should transgress "at best not only the notion of the nation-state, but also class or subcultural belonging,"[15] to include markers such as gender, sexual orientation, subcultural identification, and regional and local attachments. Erll's and Brunow's approaches are representative for the transcultural paradigm insofar as they draw on cultural and postcolonial studies with their strong focus on border-crossing, nonessentializing forms of mixing and hybridity. The transnational paradigm, by contrast, emerged in the social and political sciences and captures globalization, the impact of digital technologies, the movement of capital, goods, and people, etc. Instead of simply constituting a subcategory of a broader turn toward the transcultural, the transnational captures a research perspective that, according to critics such as Steven Vertovec, Chiara de Cesari, and Ann Rigney, is different from and preferable to the transcultural.[16] They argue that the idea of transcultural memory puts too strong an emphasis on the "study of mobility and flows."[17] In contrast, the notion of transnational memory also considers the issue of borders, and hence the blockages and hindrances of flows and mobility:[18]

> In this way, "transnationalism" proves better suited than more homogenizing cognates to highlight the frictions at play at the interfaces between different social formations and cultural imaginaries, and the varieties of currents and cross-currents at work in the exchange and appropriations of travelling narratives and mnemonic forms in a world that is not seamless.[19]

While the transcultural paradigm overemphasizes mobility, flux, and flows, however, the transnational is perhaps too Eurocentric. The very notion of the nation, which spurs the scholarly desire to transcend, transform, and translate, is modeled on the Western European nation-state as it evolved in the late eighteenth and nineteenth centuries. It is therefore not applicable to constellations involving a different genesis of the nation-state and nationality, in which the desire and need to transcend the nation can manifest itself in another manner (or, owing to prolonged struggles to achieve the status of nation-state, not at all). Eastern Europe, which is at the center of this chapter, is particularly interesting in a transnational setting, as we are generally faced with a different evolution and understanding of the nation. The Eastern European states that play a role in Vertlib's novel (such as Russia, Belarus, Ukraine, and Estonia) have changed affiliations, shapes, and political systems many times over the last centuries and decades and are relatively new in their contemporary form as autonomous nation-states. At the same time, and probably as a result of this, they share histories of fervent and at times violent nationalism. We will thus have to investigate if and how the "Eastern European turn" relates to the broader transnational turn.[20]

In my analysis of Vertlib's text I will work with concepts of transnational memory and transnationalization rather than with the framework of the transcultural for two reasons: while the travels and writings of the author, text, and characters in question span different countries—such as Germany, Belarus, the Ukraine, and Russia—they arguably still take place within a broader European memorial and cultural space. The postcolonial underpinnings of the transcultural paradigm, with its stress on counter-memory, hegemony, and hybridity, are therefore not viable in the case of Vertlib's text.[21] Furthermore, the term *transnational* seems to offer greater critical potential, as it enables a dialectic approach that probes the extent to which national, cultural, and memorial borders are criticized and/or affirmed, transcended and/or perpetuated in the entanglements of German and Eastern European memories and topographies of the Holocaust and anti-Semitic violence. I will therefore draw on Chiara de Cesari and Ann Rigney's understanding of transnationalism as a self-reflexive notion that, while paying attention to phenomena of border-crossing flows and entanglements, does not neglect the realities of boundaries and blockages. My analysis therefore "recognizes the significance of national frameworks alongside the potential of cultural production both to reinforce and to transcend them."[22]

Another problem concerns the inherently paradoxical status of transnational or transcultural memory. As mentioned before, the prefix "trans-" not only points to a movement *across* different nations or cultures but also encompasses the need to go *beyond* them. At the same time, the composites *transnational-* or *transcultural* still carry the nation or the notion of culture in their name; they are based on the very notions they are trying to abolish. While Wolfgang Welsch has reflected on the contradictoriness at the very heart of the concept of the transcultural,[23] Dagmar Brunow has accentuated that, despite their efforts to transcend the idea of a monolithic container culture, theories of the transcultural tend to work with essential-izing and ethnicizing concepts.[24] The issue of terminology points to broader conceptual frictions that have to do with conceptions of universal-ity and specificity, the global and the local. As Lucy Bond and Jessica Rapson remark, research in the field is faced with the tension between an "increasing awareness of global issues" and "the necessity of maintaining contextual specificity."[25] De Cesari and Rigney claim that although we are faced with global and multidirectional flows of people, consumer goods, ideas, memories, and data, these are produced, received, and actualized in very specific, localized contexts—the various scales of the global and the local, the transnational and the nationally bounded, the distant and the intimate thus need to be regarded as interrelated,[26] turning transnational-ism into a quintessentially multiscalar phenomenon.[27]

Arguably, the medium of fiction might be particularly suited to express such contradictory, intermingled, and multiscalar perspectives. The novel in particular is quintessentially dialogic; it is therefore able to accommo-date conflicting viewpoints, while also analyzing them from a metaperspec-tive.[28] Vertlib's *Das besondere Gedächtnis der Rosa Masur* is permeated by multiple tensions and conflicts between the East and the West, national(istic) and transnational memory discourses, the particular and the universal, male and female acts of remembrance, and oral and written history. This raises the question of how the text deals with these frictions and whether or not it arrives at the dialectical position advocated by de Cesari and Rigney. The issues raised here involve a string of additional questions about the relationship between "travelling memory" or "travelling trauma" and historical context that need to be addressed: Can all memo-ries be easily and seamlessly transplanted into any context? What happens to the sociocultural specificity of locally produced memory (i.e., its per-sonal, historical, material, local dimension) when it travels? Can it be com-pletely stripped of this and turn into a transparent, entirely appropriable signifier, emblem, or template? If so, do we conceive of this as an ethical challenge or do we simply accept it as the way in which memory works? What is it that constitutes the seemingly universal appeal of some memo-ries (such as the Holocaust)? Instead of concentrating on the seamless exchange and flow of memories, we need to ask what are the obstacles that hinder a memory's translation? What are the unexpected side effects, unforeseeable constellations that come with memory's travels?

The last set of questions particularly benefits from the analysis of Eastern European memory narratives: whereas, from a Western perspec-tive, the Holocaust has indeed turned into a free-floating, easily appropri-able signifier, the Eastern European context is quite different. In Vertlib's novel issues such as silence, denial, (forced) forgetting, repression, and memorial competition play a far greater role than the boundless mobility and universal applicability of the Holocaust emblem. *Das besondere*

Gedächtnis der Rosa Masur stages the clash between a culture of German Holocaust remembrance and Vergangenheitsbewältigung and an Eastern European setting in which Jewish suffering has been systematically blocked out for the most part. These different approaches to memories of the Second World War and the Holocaust spring from diverging narratives about who was the primary victim of Nazi policies and warfare. Although Vertlib's text thus situates the Holocaust within a transnational narrative framework, it shows how nationalist agendas challenge the idea of a universal, cosmopolitan (Holocaust) memory.

As Astrid Erll has remarked, "Holocaust memory, with its wide reach and its significance for a discussion of the ethics of memory, has proved the most important case of transcultural memory studies so far."[29] And indeed, ever since Daniel Levy and Natan Sznaider's 2001 publication *Erinnerung im globalen Zeitalter*, there has been a growing interest in trans- or cross-cultural and -national perspectives on the Holocaust. Their groundbreaking work on the Holocaust as a global "Erinnerungsemblem"[30] has been considerably extended and advanced in recent years, mainly by Stef Craps, Michael Rothberg, and Max Silverman.[31] These authors are interested in how Holocaust discourse provides a cross-cultural framework for exploring the interrelatedness between diverse histories of violence and victimization. Their research is driven by the quest for an ethically and socially productive form of transnational or transcultural remembrance, ideally resulting in the emergence of a cosmopolitan ethics (Levy and Sznaider), "differentiated solidarity" (Rothberg), or "transcultural empathy" (Rothberg, Craps). Apart from merely describing the travels of Holocaust memory and trauma, these scholars are thus invested in exploring (and maybe even fostering) the conditions under which these movements can be noncompetitive and enabling. Marked by a postcolonial perspective, the works by Craps, Rothberg, and Silverman focus predominantly on the role of Holocaust memory in the context of colonialism and decolonization, mainly in non-Western countries.

My exploration of Vertlib's writing will build on this work, while at the same time querying its strong ethical impetus. Distancing himself from his own celebratory affirmations of multidirectional memory, Michael Rothberg notes in his more recent work that multidirectionality is a description of the fundamental character of all memory, rather than an ethical program:

> If, as I argue, public memory is *structurally multidirectional*—that is, always marked by transcultural borrowing, exchange, and adaptation—that does not mean that the politics of multidirectional memory comes with any guarantees. Indeed, given the ubiquity of Nazi and Holocaust references and analogies in contemporary public spheres on a global scale, it is clear that the articulation of almost any political position may come in multidirectional form [italics in the original].[32]

Rather than assuming that the transnational travel of memories auto-matically produces cosmopolitanism and mutual understanding, we there-fore have to carefully investigate *what effects* the comparative approach toward the memory of the Holocaust and the history of anti-Semitic pogroms in Belarus, Russia, and/or the siege of Leningrad engender in Vertlib's text. Does this approach foster competition or, by contrast, the illumination of the historical specificities of these events? What happens, for example, when Vertlib's text constructs its protagonist both as a Jewish victim of the Holocaust *and* a Russian woman desperately trying to survive the siege of Leningrad? The broader question at stake here relates to how the Eastern European approach to transnationalism challenges or affirms the notion of the Holocaust as a cosmopolitan memory emblem and a universal moral touchstone. Levy, Sznaider, and Rothberg not only con-struct the Holocaust as the traumatic memory par excellence; they also implicitly champion the Western European way of collectively dealing with this memory—that is, the ideas of working through and learning a lesson from the past—as the principal route toward coming to terms with legacies of violence and atrocity.[33] As Uilleam Blacker, Alexander Etkind, and Julie Fedor have remarked, however, this model does not necessarily work for the post-Soviet condition:

> These tortured, warped memory developments have been quite dif-ferent from the public and consistent narrative of the Western mem-ory boom, which centers on German contrition for the Holocaust and the Second World War. In this sense, East European countries are closer to West European countries such as France and Spain, Israel, or to many postcolonial countries whose processes of memory and mourning have also been suppressed and convoluted.[34]

It therefore seems important to scrutinize the depictions and dis-courses of trauma in Vertlib's text in order to establish whether or not it conforms to the dominant Western European model of working through and Vergangenheitsbewältigung.

While thus focusing on the transnational travels of the Holocaust sig-nifier, this chapter aims to add an additional facet to the mobility of trauma in contemporary literature and theory by highlighting its interaction with specific spaces and places and the political entanglements this produces. I will furthermore demonstrate how the medium of literature allows us to scrutinize some of the assumptions and claims underpinning contempo-rary notions of cosmopolitan and transnational Holocaust memory by pointing to the persistence of national(istic) memory frames and obstacles to "transcultural empathy." At the same time, I will explore whether, in contrast to official political discourse, the medium of fiction enables us to overthrow binary and exclusionary patterns of thinking by way of its metareflexive and dialogic potential.

Contrapuntal Memory in *Das besondere Gedächtnis der Rosa Masur*

Vladimir Vertlib's oeuvre is part of a larger "Eastern European turn" that is currently remapping the space of German literature in general[35] and German-language Jewish literature in particular. Jewish writers from Russia and the so-called GUS-Staaten (the CIS states in the Anglo-American context) include Alina Bronsky, Lena Gorelik, Olga Grjasnowa, Wladimir Kaminer, Kat Kaufmann, Katja Petrowskaja, Julya Rabinowich, Sasha Marianna Salzmann, and Vladimir Vertlib. They represent a new type of Jewish literature, which, owing to the migratory and/or cross-cultural movements of its authors and protagonists, is inherently transnational and considerably broadens the spectrum of Jewish identities in present-day Germany and Austria. Some of these authors also offer a new stance on the Holocaust, either by downplaying its role in the formation of Jewish identity or by placing it within the legacy of anti-Semitic violence and fervent nationalism in Eastern Europe.[36]

Vladimir Vertlib can be regarded as an early exponent of these shifts, which are taken up in his 2001 novel *Das besondere Gedächtnis der Rosa Masur*. The text centers on the recollections of Rosa Abramowa Masur, a Jewish woman born in a shtetl in Belarus, who, together with her son Kostik and his wife, makes her way to Germany at the age of ninety-two as a so-called Jewish *Kontingentflüchtling* from the former Soviet Union. The family's disillusionment with their fictional new hometown of Gigricht leads to a growing sense of isolation and boredom. Rosa is therefore eager to partake in a book project commissioned by the municipality on the occasion of its 750th jubilee. Under the politically correct title *Fremde Heimat: Heimat in der Fremde*, the town intends to celebrate its diversity by assembling various life stories from its migrant community, and Rosa is supposed to act as a representative of the town's Russian Jews. This frame narrative provides the backdrop for Rosa's autobiographical, first-person narrative, which spans almost four hundred pages and several decades of Eastern European history, ranging from the czarist regime to the Russian Revolution, the German invasion during the Second World War, and the era of Stalinism. Her story unfolds as part of an interviewing process and amid tensions between what the German audience expects from Rosa as a representative of a certain community and the idiosyncrasies of her actual life and memory that are reflected in the novel's title.

Rosa's transnational and particular memory can thus be characterized as a contrapuntal memory. In classical music, the counterpoint is part of a compositional technique that is quintessentially polyphonic. As such, the counterpoint provides the so-called *Gegenstimme* to a dominant melody, to which it connects while at the same time retaining a degree of autonomy. The musical imagery employed here also alludes to Mikhail Bakhtin, who will be an important reference point for my analysis of Vertlib's text. Bakhtin famously developed a theory of the polyphonic novel in *Problems of Dostoevsky's Poetics*. The notion of polyphony—with its stress on dialogic interdependence—and the concept of the counterpoint allow us to capture the construction and contestation of memories as they are presented in the novel: Vertlib's text consists of a multiplicity of coexisting stories, perspectives, discourses, narrators, and voices. The counterpoint forms an integral part of this larger construction, which is defined by the *concertatio*, that is, the tension and competition between various voices. In a similar vein, Rosa's memory is inextricably interlaced with the developments of European history in the twentieth century, while, by virtue of its particularity, often providing a "Gegenstimme" to its dominant narratives. Rosa's memory therefore interacts with the various settings in which it is (re) produced, which establishes its dynamic and dialogic quality—it is influenced by its surroundings while simultaneously (re)shaping them, a process described by Bakhtin as "interillumination."[37] This is especially the case in relation to Rosa's German environment, German Holocaust memory, and perceptions of Jewish identity, which will be at the center of my analysis.

Rosa's memory is defined by the fundamental interplay between subversion and affirmation, discord and harmony, particularity and universality, with often uncontrollable and unpredictable results. The counterpoint and polyphony are therefore well suited to capture the various manifestations of memory in *Das besondere Gedächtnis der Rosa Masur*, not least because they make a productive contribution to the previously mentioned debates about transnationalism: instead of trying to eclipse all sense of contestation and difference by endorsing a universalist, borderless, and cosmopolitan utopia, Vertlib's novel highlights the tensions between boundless mobility and insurmountable borders, fluidity, and stagnation, the universal and the particular as fundamental to the way in which these (and all) memories work. This echoes Bakhtin's core conviction that language, human beings, and the social world are constantly "filled with struggle," never stable, and always in dialogue.[38]

A Modern-Day Scheherazade?
Rosa's Role as the Unreliable Narrator

Das besondere Gedächtnis der Rosa Masur comprises twenty-one chapters, most of which are narrated by Rosa as a gifted first-person storyteller who recounts her life from her childhood in a shtetl in Belarus to roughly the end of the Stalinist era in Russia, mostly in chronological fashion. Rosa's style is witty, anecdotal, and digressive and presents the reader with a series of flashes, curious incidents, and vignettes rather than a coherent life story. Her inconsistent narrative is further broken up by frequent shifts in tense, combining past and present tense. While Rosa's use of the present tense usually points to dangerous situations and painful memories, signaling heightened emotional involvement and immersion, this is not always the case. The embedded first-person narrative of Rosa's life is framed by four chapters, told by a highly ironic third-person narrator who alternates between internal and external focalization. These chapters provide background information on why Rosa came to Germany, what motivated her to take part in the book project and what happens to her after the project ends prematurely. In the course of the novel, Rosa's first-person narrative is repeatedly broken up by additional third-person chapters or paragraphs, which provide the reader with a critical glimpse into her and other Russian Jewish immigrants' everyday lives in Germany. Chapter 16 comprises a letter from Rosa addressed to her dead friend Mascha.

The intimacy and emotional transparency found in the letter to Mascha contrasts with the high degree of mediation and manipulation that characterize Rosa's other recollections. As mentioned before, Rosa remembers and narrates her life as part of an interview process; it is conducted by Dimitrij Silberman, a young man commissioned by the municipality to translate her Russian narrative into German. Dimitrij is by no means a neutral vessel, however, as Rosa points out:

> Damit möchte ich nicht behaupten, seine Rolle sei eine rein passive. Er übersetzt alles, was ich ihm erzähle, in ein gepflegtes Deutsch. Er hat Wiederholungen gestrichen, zeitliche und inhaltliche Sprünge bereinigt und einzelne Episoden in Kapitel zusammengefasst. Ich habe diese deutsche Version gelesen. Der junge Mann hat sich bei der Übersetzung einige Freiheiten erlaubt. (*DbG*, 312–13)

It never becomes entirely clear which version of Rosa's story we read as part of the novel: is it the recordings or transcripts of Rosa's narration or the edited translation by Dimitrij? Dimitrij's interventions are not the only instances of manipulation, however: in the third-person frame narrative we find out that Rosa is primarily interested in the book project because it will bring an overall reward of 5,000 DM, which will enable her to pay for her son's coveted trip to Aix-en-Provence. As Kostik grows increasingly depressed in his new German environment, Rosa is under pressure to raise the money for a journey that she hopes will make her son happy.

When Rosa arrives at the building where the interview takes place, she realizes that achieving her goals will be harder than she initially thought. The competition is tough, as several Russian-Jewish immigrants are waiting to undergo an absurd casting process. The project leader, Dr. Karolin Wepse, makes impossible demands on the applicants: "Sie müssen sowohl durch sogenannte typische Merkmale ihrer Gruppe als auch durch etwas Individuelles und über das gewöhnliche Maß Hinausgehendes beeindrucken" (*DbG*, 36). In Rosa's case the stakes are even higher because, as a Jewish survivor, her biography needs to showcase a heightened degree of universality: "Gerade in den jüdischen Biographien [sollen] die Tragik, die Umbrüche und Hoffnungen des zwanzigsten Jahrhunderts erkennbar werden. . . . Die Höhen und Tiefen der Zeit exemplifiziert am Beispiel einer persönlichen Erfahrung, wo sich in der Einzigartigkeit das Allgemeingültige widerspiegelt" (*DbG*, 37). This "Einzigartigkeit" should, however, not shatter people's preconceived ideas of the Holocaust and Eastern European Jewry. The participants' stories must therefore conform to the notion of critical openness and prescribed diversity that typifies German memory debates in the book, while not seriously threatening the overall intention to produce a "nettes Büchlein" (*DbG*, 36).

While others react to this catalog of requirements with sheer exasperation, Rosa immediately understands that she must sell her story well if she wants to be successful. She therefore spices her Eastern European Jewish narrative with a mix of folklore, shtetl romance, and suffering, while also playing into some of the stereotypes that Western Europeans harbor about Russia and the Eastern bloc. Added to this mix is an extraordinary "Trumpf" (*DbG*, 39) in the form of an alleged personal encounter with Joseph Stalin. Unsurprisingly, this works: Rosa not only gets the job; she also positively enthralls her audience: "Frau Wepse ist so begeistert von ihrer Geschichte und auch der Doktor Sambs, unser Chef, vor allem aber der Kulturstadtrat und erst der Bürgermeister—der ist richtig drauf abgefahren!" (*DbG*, 313). Among her Russian friends Rosa is unashamedly open about her intentions and her calculating attitude: "Jeder Tag bringt 50 Mark und das nütze ich natürlich aus. Je mehr ich erzähle, umso besser" (*DbG*, 108). Rosa's digressive and anecdotal narrative style is therefore not only an expression of personal preferences but part of a larger scheme to extract as much money as possible from the project. She thus assumes the role of a Russian-Jewish Scheherazade who tells intricate and captivating stories, not to save her life but to be able to afford "eine hauchdünne Scheibe von dem, was man gemeinhin als Glück bezeichnet" (*DbG*, 40). To this end, she does not shy away from bending the facts in a manner that benefits her story.

And yet, Rosa's approach toward her story and the interview process becomes more complex as the novel progresses. Her hard-nosed attitude eventually crumbles as the recollection of painful events begins to take its toll, leaving her increasingly unable to ward off the ghosts from the past. Rosa begins to suffer from nightmares and a growing sense of temporal disorientation, while also becoming more and more dependent on a weekly routine that she in equal parts anticipates and dreads: "Mit jedem Mal fürchtete sie sich mehr und konnte noch weniger darauf verzichten" (*DbG*, 402). When the 750th jubilee turns out to be based on a forged charter and all the festivities and projects are called off, Rosa is left with a sense of despair that cannot be explained by the financial repercussions alone (she can keep what she has earned on a day-to-day basis but will not get the reward of 5,000 DM).

The entire setup of Rosa's scheme satirically and metareflexively dissects the German environment in which the Other is stereotyped and in which Jewish stories of suffering have become a commodity. The casting process situates her story within a larger "trauma economy,"[39] forcing her to compete against the other migrants and their hardship and suffering. She successfully highlights her unique selling points, presenting herself and her story in terms of a tradeable good. Her calculating attitude is thus the flip side of a German approach that also commodifies stories of hardship and suffering and distributes recognition and compassion accordingly. The novel demonstrates how this climate hinders the development of empathy, which requires a willingness to listen and dialogic openness, which are not possible within the framework of the book project. Vertlib's text criticizes a broader German discourse in which the Other is perceived primarily as a victim or a folkloristic attachment to a politically prescribed "Fremdenliebe" (*DbG*, 416), which masks an ongoing culture of xenophobia. As Brigid Haines has argued, already the title of the project, *Fremde Heimat. Heimat in der Fremde*, presumes a binary division between the Self and the Other and thus leaves the politics of exclusion untouched,[40] despite the institutionalized displays of xenophilia. Rosa's cool examination of the rules of this game and her decision to play along exposes these underlying scripts in a highly ironic and effective fashion.

Owing to the context in which her story is set, Rosa emerges as a fundamentally unreliable narrator on several levels.[41] Her narrative is predominantly based on her personal recollections; it is well known that autobiographical memories are inherently malleable, prone to factual errors and geared toward and influenced by the contexts in which they are produced.[42] Additionally, in the broader framework of her story Rosa acts as a modern-day Scheherazade intent on telling *and* selling her story. As a result, we can at no point in her narrative determine with any degree of certainty whether she is telling the truth or whether she is relaying what the audience wants to hear. Rosa's narrative constantly walks the thin line between affirming and subverting stereotypes, between pandering to and deliberately disappointing her audience's expectations.[43] These observations also raise the issue of authenticity and, in relation to this, questions about trauma. Although Rosa, for the most part, delivers a carefully crafted narrative, tailored to the needs of her audience, this cannot hide the fact that her life is marked by various traumatic experiences: she witnessed a string of pogroms during the Russian Civil War, lost both her parents in the Holocaust, and survived the blockade of Leningrad, only to witness the deaths of her best friend and her husband. Vertlib's text suggests, however, that Rosa has no space in which to articulate her personal pain. I would therefore contest Sebastian Wogenstein's assessment that Rosa masters her trauma through the process of narrativization.[44] Such a therapeutic success would require an environment of empathetic listening and the possibility of some form of closure, neither of which are available to Rosa. Whereas the initiators of the book project are enthusiastically absorbing her stories of hardship and suffering, they leave her entirely alone with the side effects produced by her descent into a painful past:

> Aber daß der ganze Aufwand umsonst gewesen war! Die vielen Stunden am Institut und die Alpträume in den Nächten danach. Die Selbstüberwindung. Die Erschöpfung. . . . Sobald sie zu erzählen begann, verstärkten sich ihre Zweifel, kamen alte Selbstvorwürfe wieder hoch und der dumpfe Schmerz über versäumte Gelegenheiten. Ängste, die sie mehrmals durchlitten hatte, in der Realität des Augenblicks und danach immer wieder, unzählige Male in Erinnerungen und Träumen, packten sie, hoben Zeit und Raum auf. . . . Schon vor dem Eingang zum Institut hämmerte das Herz jedes Mal wild, etwas klopfte bedrohlich in den Schläfen. (*DbG*, 402)

The unexpected cancellation of the book project long before Rosa has reached the end of her story deprives her of the possibility of narrative closure, which would certainly be an essential component of her alleged "Selbst-Therapie durch das Erzählen."[45] While she cannot fully articulate her trauma in the official, institutionalized context of the book project, the more personal space of the family is also blocked. Being symbiotically close to her son, Rosa is estranged from her daughter and her grandson; and so it is that the interview setting becomes a—flawed—surrogate for the lack of familial tradition and intergenerational transmission. Rosa's relationship with her first-born son, Kostik, is marked by his dependency on her and Rosa's inability to let go. His aggressive antisocial behavior as a child and his life-long battle with physical illness can be read as symptoms of inter-generational traumatization. When Rosa, who is struggling with her young son's behavior, consults the so-called witch, the latter explains in nonclinical words that Kostik has internalized his mother's repressed traumatic experiences: instead of taking these experiences to heart—that is, emotionally confronting them—his ancestors let them sink into their legs. Kostik has inherited their heavy legs, which contain their unaddressed issues: "Er ist zwar noch ein kleines Kind, aber er trägt schon deren [his ancestors'] Bilder in sich" (*DbG*, 200). *Das besondere Gedächtnis der Rosa Masur* stresses the lack of genuine acts of empathetic listening in Rosa's life: while still living in Russia, she was confronted with the politically motivated suppression of Jewish suffering under Soviet rule that also shaped her intrafamilial communication. Toward the end of her life, she comes across the very different German memorial culture, which, while centered on Jewish suffering, is unable to approach her personal trauma outside of the ritualized framework of Vergangenheitsbewältigung, or as anything other than a marketable good in a broader "trauma economy."[46]

A Different Optic: Challenging Collective Scripts and Templates

Arguably, the novel's central themes of Holocaust remembrance and Jewish identity bring out the full force of Rosa's contrapuntal memory, which serves to decentralize and destabilize core assumptions connected to these two issues in both the German and the (post-)Soviet context. Rosa's recollections weave the Holocaust into a transnational network, in which various instances of anti-Semitic violence interconnect with major events of twentieth-century Russian and Eastern European history. This contributes to a decentering of the genocide of Europe's Jews as the pivotal experience of Jewish suffering in the twentieth century.[47] It furthermore exposes the ritualized and exculpatory dynamics that underlie Germany's efforts to come to terms with the past, alongside the blind spots of (post-)Soviet memory discourses.

Rosa's birth coincides with a major pogrom, and this constellation foreshadows her life story, which is shaped by recurring experiences of anti-Judaism and anti-Semitism: "Der Anfang? Die erste Erinnerung? Der Schrei eines Kleinkindes. Das Kleinkind bin ich. Das Klirren der Fensterscheiben in der Synagoge am anderen Ende der Stadt" (*DbG*, 41). The pogrom emerges as a key topos and event in her life story. Rosa is subjected to various forms of prejudice and persecution, ranging from everyday racism, verbal and physical abuse, and targeted discrimination to policies of ethnic cleansing and genocide. The Holocaust appears as the climax of a long and ongoing narrative, in which certain patterns of exclusion, persecution, and violence seem to endlessly repeat themselves. Rosa's narrative perspective thus queries the status of the Holocaust as *the* traumatic core of twentieth-century Jewish existence. Her perspective reflects the fact that she only experienced the Holocaust from a geographical distance—being trapped inside the siege of Leningrad, she is not present when the German troops murder her parents and wipe out her birthplace. While Rosa is therefore not a firsthand witness to the atrocities of the Holocaust, she is directly and physically affected by the pogroms during the Russian Revolution and the Russian Civil War. These experiences constitute her indelible life trauma, which is suppressed by herself and her husband, Naum, and finds expression in physical symptoms, nightmares, and behavioral patterns that are transmitted transgenerationally: "Jahrzehntelang habe ich mich bemüht, die Bilder jener Zeit aus meinem Gedächtnis zu bannen. In meinen Träumen suchen sie mich heute noch heim" (*DbG*, 85).

Rosa's experiences of suffering are not exclusively tied to her Jewishness, however. The construction of her life narrative is centered on the German invasion of Russia and the siege of Leningrad, which make up a significant part of her story. This is noteworthy, since Rosa does not suffer as a Jew but as a Russian in these sections of her narrative. Nonetheless, her Jewishness still plays into her experience of the war, as it makes her more vulnerable—for the Germans, she is not only an enemy but also a possible target of extermination policies. Rosa's hatred of the Germans, however, expressed in her refusal to speak German, even though she had studied the language before the war and worked as a translator, is motivated by the cruel and inhumane behavior of the German troops toward the Russian—not the Jewish—population:

> Ich denke an die Deutschen, die wenige Kilometer entfernt in ihren Unterkünften sitzen und warten, bis es *uns* nicht mehr gibt. Sicherlich essen sie Sauerkraut und Würste, trinken Bier und lachen über die russischen Untermenschen, die lieber in ihrer alten Hauptstadt krepieren, anstatt sich zu ergeben. Ich gebe mir das Versprechen, keinen deutschen Satz mehr zu übersetzen. Kein deutsches Wort soll jemals wieder über meine Lippen kommen. (*DbG*, 272; italics added)

Rosa's use of the personal pronoun "uns" demonstrates her strong identification with the plight of the Russians—she sees herself not as a Jewish Holocaust survivor but as a Russian survivor of the siege of Leningrad: "Man sprach von mehr als sechshunderttausend Verhungerten und von über neunhunderttausend Gefallenen. Gefallenen an der Leningrader Front. *Für uns, die Überlebenden,* war jeder Morgen, an dem wir aufwachten, ein Sieg" (*DbG*, 283; italics added). Her memories of the German invasion and the siege of Leningrad unsettle the idea that Rosa's suffering is necessarily and exclusively tied to Jewishness,[48] further decentering the Holocaust as the most incisive experience of Rosa's Jewish life. This gains further importance in the context of Germany's culture of Vergangenheitsbewältigung, in which Rosa is repeatedly assigned the role of Jewish victim. Casting herself as a survivor of the siege allows her to destabilize the nexus between Jewishness and suffering, while also integrating her experience into a more heroic narrative: she reads her survival as a "Sieg"—she is a victor, not a victim.

While the connection to Leningrad bolsters a heroic self-image, it also allows Rosa to distance herself from the provincial, backward, and blatantly Jewish shtetl identity that she grew up with: "Ach, wie haßte ich diese Provinzjüdlein mit ihrer behäbigen Selbstgefälligkeit und dieser Städlpanik, so als wäre die Zeit der Verfolgung nicht allemal vorbei" (*DbG*, 123). Rosa despises the shtetl Jews, who have not yet understood that a new era has dawned. For her, Leningrad embodies the utopia of a cosmopolitan socialism, which knows no Jews but only good Soviet citizens and promises to break the shackles of provenance, prejudice, and persecution. These hopes are crushed as the narrative progresses, but Rosa's positive identification with Leningrad (not the Soviet Union!) remains unchanged. This underscores the importance of local attachment in Rosa's otherwise trans-national story, demonstrating the need for what de Cesari and Rigney have called "multi-scalarity" in the context of transnationalism.[49] They promote an approach that assumes the "mutual construction of the local, national and global" instead of seeing them as separate entities.[50] Such a perspective is useful for Rosa's narrative, which is defined by clashes between various memorial cultures and national outlooks, alongside strong localized tension between the periphery—as a space of tradition, backwardness, and inescapable persecution—and the center as a space of cosmopolitanism, Jewish emancipation, and an urban bourgeois culture that promises to level out all differences.

Finally, Rosa's focus on Leningrad introduces her German listeners—and the reader—to a contrapuntal perspective on the Second World War. Brigid Haines points out that Rosa's "different optic . . . illuminates one of German historiography's blind spots: the genocidal Leningrad siege."[51] While the image of the "blind spot" is probably exaggerated in the case of Leningrad,[52] it is true that Rosa's interpretation of the war experience deviates from the German script. The Russian perspective is exemplified in Rosa's summary of a speech delivered by Stalin on July, 3 1941, shortly after the end of the Molotov-Ribbentrop Pact:

> "Wir müssen alle unsere Kräfte mobilisieren, um den bösartigen und hinterlistigen Feind aus unserem Land zu verjagen, wir müssen in zertreten wie eine Schlange, ihn vernichten wie unsere Vorfahren im Mittelalter die Armeen des Deutschritterordens vernichtet hatten, die Nowgorod bedrohten! So wie wir Napoleon 1812 verjagt haben. Seid standhaft, Brüder und Schwestern!" So oder so ähnlich sprach der Diktator. (*DbG*, 235)

Stalin's speech draws on a deep-seated "narrative template" in Russian collective memory that the sociologist James V. Wertsch calls the "Expulsion of Foreign Enemies":[53] throughout history, Russia has been repeatedly and unlawfully attacked by various outsiders (including the *Deutschritterorden*, Napoleon, and now the Germans) and brought to the brink of utter destruction. In the end, however, Russia always heroically prevailed, rising from the ashes as an even greater nation. We can clearly detect elements of this template in Stalin's speech and in Rosa's description of the siege, which also delivers a tale of heroic defiance and survival. As Aleida Assmann has pointed out, this template has led to a specific perspective on the Second World War in the Soviet context, which is diametrically opposed to the German way of dealing with the past:

> We can distinguish today between two memory policies, a traditional and a new one. The traditional one is based on pride and the fortification of a positive and heroic self-image. The new one is more complex, as it includes also the responsibility for historical crimes, thereby

acknowledging the victims of former state terror. In Germany the globally recovered memory of the unprecedented crime of the Holocaust has led to the historical novelty of adopting a "negative memory" premised on guilt and responsibility.[54]

Although the Russian template has probably changed with the collapse of the Iron Curtain, Rosa's narrative confronts her (intra- and extradiegetic) German audience with the problematic tale of "pride and the fortification of a positive and heroic self-image." By bringing Rosa's Russian perspective together with the German approach, the novel stages a struggle between these two templates, which brings into focus their very existence. As the decentering counterpoint to the German discourse of guilt, responsibility, and atonement, Rosa's Russian angle foregrounds the siege of Leningrad and tales of heroic survival. Her narrative demonstrates that the perception and memory of historical events is often (if not always) mediated by powerful templates that do not necessarily function on a conscious level.[55] Rosa's particular and contrapuntal memory therefore exposes the (unconscious) scripts that underlie personal and collective acts of remembrance, both in the Russian and in the German case.

While challenging the German, guilt-focused script, Vertlib's novel is equally wary of the heroic Soviet narrative: whereas Germany's memory of the Second World War is dominated by an awareness of Jewish victimization and German perpetration, the official postwar stance in the Soviet Union was for a long time premised on the suppression of Jewish suffering.[56] Rosa experiences this firsthand after the end of the war when she visits her hometown of Witschi, whose Jewish community has been completely wiped out (except for one survivor). She decides to commission a commemorative plaque for the Jewish victims, among them her parents, and comes up with the following text: "*An dieser Stelle wurden im August 1941 alle Juden von Witschi von den faschistischen Unmenschen ermordet. Sie wurden Opfer des deutschen Hasses und Rassenwahns*" (*DbG*, 294; italics in the original). This dedication is, however, unacceptable to the new director of the Witschi sovkhoz, who instead wants to commemorate "*die in den Jahren der deutschen Besatzung 1941–1944 in Witschi von den Faschisten ermordeten 1483 Sowjetbürger*" (*DbG*, 298; italics in the original). When Rosa insists on the particularity of the Nazi genocide of the Jews, the official reacts with anger and anti-Semitic prejudice, which creates a parallel between German and Soviet traditions of anti-Semitism: "Warum wollt ihr Juden immer etwas Besonderes sein? Selbst im Leid wollt ihr besser sein als wir!" (*DbG*, 305). This episode highlights the specific dynamics of the Soviet and, more broadly speaking, Eastern European postwar discourse, which was dominated by heroism and competitive victimhood. The general refusal to remember the genocide of the Jews also stemmed from the population's complicity in some of the Nazis' genocidal atrocities. The sole

Witschi survivor, Isaak Beigel, repeatedly points this out to Rosa, but she seems unwilling to acknowledge the full extent of this collaboration and refuses to listen to him. Yet she is ultimately unable to avoid the personal confrontation with this legacy of complicity, prejudice, and suppression, which effectively hinders any public or private acknowledgment of her losses. Unable to properly mourn the death of her parents, she is forced into melancholic isolation: "Ich war allein . . ., weil ich das Denkmal nun immer in meinem Inneren tragen musste, bis an mein Lebensende" (*DbG*, 306).

These observations highlight the fact that there are different forms of decentering at work in Vertlib's text: on the one hand, Holocaust memory is being recalibrated via Rosa's narrative, which serves a critical purpose in the context of German Holocaust remembrance; on the other hand, the marginalization of the Holocaust is part of a larger politics of relativization and suppression in the Soviet context, coupled with a fervent nationalism and continued anti-Semitism. These lines of continuity become apparent in Stalin's ethnic-cleansing campaigns, which, for Rosa, conjure up painful memories and comparisons: "Die judenfeindlichen Karikaturen in der *Prawda* unterschieden sich nur wenig von jenen in Naziblättern, der Antisemitismus auf den Straßen wurde kaum mehr geahndet" (*DbG*, 353). The Stalinist purges shake Rosa's belief in a socialist utopia and open her eyes to the realities of totalitarianism. These various levels of comparison and recalibration need to be disentangled carefully by comparing the German and the Soviet positions toward Jewish Holocaust victims in the novel: whereas Rosa's status as a Jewish victim of the Holocaust is not acknowledged in her Soviet environment, her new German surroundings cast Jews as the primary victims of National Socialism, to the extent that no other identity position is available to Rosa as a Jew: "Frau Masur, wie ist es eigentlich für einen russischen Juden, wenn er gerade nach Deutschland übersiedelt, ich meine, nach allem, was Deutsche den Juden angetan haben?" (*DbG*, 25). Whereas the Soviet discourse seeks to erase all traces of Jewish victimhood, German culture zooms in on Rosa's Jewish suffering. Rosa is thus forced into a position as the victim par excellence, although the experience of victimization is not defining for her.

Against this backdrop, Rosa's unsettling Eastern European perspective has to be understood as an intervention into the dynamics of "a well-intentioned but unreflective German culture of Holocaust remembrance"[57] in the book, centered on Jewish suffering, German guilt, and a longing for redemption. Many of the elements in Rosa's story clash with the cornerstones of this culture—the Holocaust is not the single most awful event in Rosa's Jewish life, Germans are not the only perpetrators, and victimization does not always automatically connect to Jewishness—and it is only through these deviations from the official script that the latter's underlying mechanisms become clear. Vertlib's novel conceptualizes

Rosa's transnational memory as a contrapuntal memory, in the sense that its messy entanglements and complications collide with the templates of a deeply ritualized, ossified German memorial culture. We can therefore distinguish between what I, inspired by Bakhtin, would call monologic marginalization in the (post-)Soviet case—certain forms of suffering are blocked out in a competitive manner, shutting down the conversation—and the dialogic decentering that results from Rosa's narrative. By irritating our conventional perspective and shifting the emphasis, Rosa's narrative creates a space for communication and challenge, which calls into question the viability of all master narratives, be they German or Russian.

The novel further questions the German memorial template by depicting its descent into empty rhetoric. A ritualized display of sympathy with the Jew as the victim has replaced any actual empathy toward the Jew as the Other, as the story of Rosa's friend Chawa highlights: Chawa also wants to come to Germany as a Kontingentflüchtling, but she first needs to prove her Jewishness to a member of the German consulate back in Moscow, in order to be able to legally settle down. When confronted with her experiences in the ghetto of Minsk, the official reacts with what Chawa mockingly portrays as an automated and formulaic response:

"Als er vom Ghetto und vom Schicksal meiner Familie hörte, senkte der Beamte die Augen. Er, als Deutscher, trage, wie übrigens alle Deutschen, eine große Schuld für das, was den Juden in deutschem Namen angetan worden sei, hat er gesagt. Seine Eltern seien allerdings Nazigegner gewesen (hätte mich schon gewundert, wenn das nicht gekommen wäre), und er sei froh darüber, diese Zeit nicht persönlich miterlebt zu haben." (*DbG*, 225)

Chawa's ironic comment reveals the mechanisms underpinning the ritualized German discourse on Vergangenheitsbewältigung—a formulaic admission of collective guilt, coupled with a repudiation of any personal responsibility. The official's tone and behavior change when he finds out that, owing to the destruction of the Holocaust, Chawa has lost all documents or relatives that could prove her Jewishness: "Da war er nicht mehr ganz so höflich wie zuvor, und der Tonfall seiner Stimme gab mir wieder einen Stich" (*DbG*, 225). The consulate employee stubbornly insists on the necessity of documentary proof and seems unaware both of the bitter irony at play—for the same documents that Chawa now desperately needs could have once caused her death—and of the (re)traumatizing potential of the whole episode. It appears as if the rehearsed acknowledgment of German collective guilt has freed the official from the obligation to actually listen to and empathetically engage with the living Jewish Other. Chawa eventually manages to obtain the necessary documents in a rather unconventional fashion, but she pays a high price for this:

"Ja. Nur die Stimmen, die mich verfolgen, habe ich nicht bedacht, die Alpträume und die Angst. Ständig glaube ich mich von Aufsehern, SS-Leuten oder Soldaten umgeben. . . . Am schlimmsten ist es, wenn ich auf Uniformierte treffe, ob Polizisten oder Briefträger, ist egal. Sogleich bekomme ich Schweißausbrüche, beginne zu zittern, kann kaum atmen und würde am liebsten so schnell wie möglich davonlaufen, wenn ich die Kraft dazu hätte." (*DbG*, 230–31)

Apart from blocking any real sense of empathy, the guilt-focused German memorial script also fails to address the acts of typecasting, discrimination, and racism that are still part of Germany's everyday reality in the book. The prescribed, politically correct "Fremdenliebe" of a society that thinks it has learned its lessons from the past masks a problematic ambiguity toward the Other. The celebration of a double-faced "Multikulti" ideology, epitomized by the book project, cannot distract from the fact that the non-German Other can only be approached in a stereotypical manner. When the book project has to be canceled, the town of Gigricht still goes ahead with an award ceremony. Although presented as guests of honor, the participants of the book project are still perceived as a manifestation of the Other by their German environment and thus grouped into three categories: the first is that of *the victim*, which is how the Cameroonian and the two Jewish guests are introduced: "Wir begrüßen ganz herzlich Herrn Bubajamba. Nach schweren Mißhandlungen und zweijähriger Isolationshaft in seinem Heimatland Kamerun hat Herr Bubajamba in Deutschland Asyl und in Gigricht ein neues zu Hause gefunden" (*DbG*, 411–12); and "Herr Adler, 1919 in Gigricht geboren und jüdischer Abstammung, hat den Holocaust in mehreren Konzentrationslagern überlebt" (*DbG*, 412). The second category is that of *the exotic other*, whose allure is emulated by the band that accompanies the event—its members are dressed up in an absurd mix of folkloristic costumes, while performing "ein jiddisches Lied, das viel jiddischer klang als alle jiddischen Lieder, die Rosa in ihrem Leben gehört hatte" (*DbG*, 410). The third category is that of the *socially abject Other*, exemplified by Rosa's encounter with a well-off German woman who mistakes her for a toilet attendant, despite Rosa's painstaking efforts to dress nicely. This typology is tied to a hierarchy: Rosa, who represents both the victim and the exotic Other, is rewarded for the way in which she performs her Jewish Otherness. By contrast, less desirable forms of Otherness are rejected by society: during the interview period, Rosa witnesses how two German policemen arrest and abuse a man from Ethiopia, who has entered the country as an illegal migrant. The man, whose name is Tesfaye Ezana, is the double of Rosa and all the other "desirable" immigrants whose testimonials the town is chasing after. As such, the character Tesfaye Ezana calls attention to the ambivalences of Germany's *Willkommenskultur*, whose approach to the Other remains degrading and discriminatory despite the country's eager efforts to learn from the past.

In a unique mix of ironic mockery and social criticism *Das besondere Gedächtnis der Rosa Masur* scrutinizes a German culture in which the Other can ultimately not be embraced in a fashion that would break down binaries. This suggests that a border-crossing and hospitable transnationalism, as it is imagined (and wished for) in some of the current academic discussions, is not part of Vertlib's novel, at least on the level of character interaction. The cross-cultural encounters in the narrative do not automatically produce understanding and solidarity but instead bring out clashes, tensions, and the disingenuousness of a politically prescribed "Fremdenliebe."

"Ich bin nicht typisch": Female Jewish Identity between Stereotype and "Unfinalizability"

Rosa's Eastern European optic also recalibrates notions of Jewish identity, as many of the attributes commonly associated with being Jewish do not apply to her. This has to do with her Russian-Jewish background and with the essentializing logic behind the very concept of identity more generally. Rosa's narrative is marked by a conflict between what is expected of her as a Jew(ess)—either by a discriminatory (post-)Soviet system or by German society—and her personal biography.[58] What is at stake here is the complex relationship between *the universal*, that is, Rosa's role as the representative of a specific group, and *the particular*, understood as the singularity of a life story that does not conform to predefined categories. Oscillating between compliance, playfulness, and subversion, Rosa's narrative foregrounds the performative quality of her Jewish identity. Her narrative therefore achieves a de-essentializing effect by underlining that identities are nonstable and the result of continual negotiations between expectations from the outside and personal experiences and memories. *Das besondere Gedächtnis der Rosa Masur* promotes an intersectional approach,[59] emphasizing that identities consist of various interactive components whose relation to one another is not fixed—depending on her surroundings, Rosa might stress or repress the ethnic, the national, the local, the class, or the gender aspects of her identity. Her identity emerges as something that can never be fully contained by preexisting categories; it is "unfinalizable" in Bakhtin's sense:

> An individual cannot be completely incarnated into the flesh of existing sociohistorical categories. There is no mere form that would be able to incarnate once and forever all of his human possibilities and needs, no form in which he could exhaust himself down to the last word . . ., no form that he could fill to the very brim, and yet at the same time not splash over the brim. There always remains an unrealized surplus of humanness.[60]

Neither the status as a Holocaust victim nor the notion of the eternal Jewish suffering fully encapsulate Rosa's sense of identity. Yet, like many Jews from Russia and the former Soviet states, Rosa is also not a religious Jew. The novel repeatedly highlights that the Kontingentflüchtling community in Gigricht consists mainly of atheists:

> In der Synagoge von Gigricht treffen sich Menschen, die sechzig Jahre alt sind und noch nie in ihrem Leben ein Gebet gesprochen haben. Es treffen sich dort Menschen, die schon vor Jahren Gott verflucht haben, die sich offen als Atheisten bezeichnen. . . . Der junge Rabbiner aus Israel hat seine Bekehrungsversuche schon vor langer Zeit aufgegeben. Gestört vom Geflüster der "Russen" fühlen sich nur die wenigen alteingesessenen deutschen Juden. Sie sind die einzigen, die die Texte in den Gebetbüchern tatsächlich kennen. (*DbG*, 221)

Vertlib's text ironically pits the new Russian migrants against the "alteingesessenen deutschen Juden," who actually define themselves in religious terms. These tensions within the Jewish community evoke a much older divide between *West-* and *Ostjudentum*, which is at the same time inverted, as the so-called Ostjuden used to be more observant than the assimilated Western Jews.[61] The continued existence of these divides emphasizes the fact that Germany's Jews are by no means a homogeneous group. These nuances are not recognized, however, by the Gentile environment, which assumes all Jews to be religious: what keeps Rosa going during the boring and awkward award ceremony mentioned earlier is the prospect of the tasty ham sandwiches that are part of the subsequent buffet. Rosa is clearly not following the Orthodox dietary laws, although that is what her conscientious German hostess Sabine Lapka expects: "Frau Masur! Wir haben koschere Speisen. Extra für Sie und die anderen jüdischen Herrschaften" (*DbG*, 414). When Rosa instead asks for traditional German and Austrian foods such as ham, schnitzel, potato salad, and beer, this deviation from the expected norm is met with disappointment: "'Oh! Ich verstehe', murmelte Lapka enttäuscht" (*DbG*, 414).

Similar presumptions affect the Eastern European aspects of Rosa's Jewish identity. Vertlib's novel demonstrates that the German "fascination for things Jewish" has turned into a "fascination for things Eastern European Jewish."[62] The Eastern European context adds exoticism to this discourse, coupled with the sentimental touch of a world that has been irretrievably lost. As mentioned, Rosa affirms many of these clichés, delivering a narrative full of shtetl romanticism, Jewish wit, and melancholy impressions of a lost world. When reading her stories about the shtetls of Witschi, Gomel, and Gobyl, we get the impression that Rosa has added a good deal of folkloristic exaggeration. These distortions are completely lost, however, on her German listeners, who perceive Rosa's stories to be particularly enthralling and authentic, precisely because they overfulfill their expectations:

> Ich nehme ja an diesem Projekt mit dem Jubiläumsbuch teil, wie Sie wissen, und je mehr ich ihnen vom alten Städtl, von Luftmenschen, verrückten Lehrern, Rabbinern und Pogromen erzähle, desto zufriedener ist Frau Wepse, die Leiterin des Projekts. Neulich wollte sie von mir wissen, ob ich chassidische Märchen kenne. Sie hätte gern so ein Märchen in ihrem Buch. (*DbG*, 222)

Rosa thus cleverly remediates various set pieces from the tradition of "ghetto writing" that have been disseminated and popularized in mainstream culture via Broadway productions and films such as *Fiddler on the Roof* (1971) and *Yentl* (1983). She plays into her listeners' romanticized and uninformed ideas about Eastern European Jewry, which she ironically mocks when describing Karoline Wepse's fascination with "chassidische Märchen": Hasidism is a branch of Jewish Orthodoxy and thus a religious phenomenon, which, while having strong folkloristic undertones particularly in the nineteenth and early twentieth centuries, is different from the German tradition of fairy tales, as Rosa points out: "Ich kenne viele Märchen von meinem Vater. . . . Mit Chassidismus hat das allerdings nichts zu tun" (*DbG*, 222). At the same time, this romanticization of Hasidism and the Eastern Jew has historical roots: traces of this can already be found in certain traditions of "ghetto writing" in the nineteenth century, which saw a revival of Hasidism as part of a folkloristic imagery.[63] The episode emphasizes that this process has resulted in the complete conflation of Hasidism and folklore in contemporary culture. This conflation was fueled by the disappearance of the ghetto environment as a lived reality, on the one hand, and the mass-mediated popularization of a romanticized and nostalgic Eastern European Jewishness, on the other. Throughout the novel this simplified view of shtetl life is contrasted with Rosa's perspective on her upbringing, which exposes the shtetl as a site of violence in ethnic, cultural, and in social terms. The shtetl Jew represents everything Rosa wants to shake off—victimization, traditionalism, gendered suppression, and the periphery; in short, the opposite of the assimilated, bourgeois Jewish identity she is striving for. This tension between the shtetl periphery and the urban center seems much more defining for Rosa's identity than a legacy of Eastern European traditions that were already on the decline when she was a child.

Rosa's actions and her narrative dislodge many of the expectations of what a Jew is supposed to be like. Since neither ethnicity nor victimization, religion, tradition, or national belonging define Rosa's life, this leaves us with the question of what Rosa's Jewish identity is actually based on. As demonstrated, Rosa's sense of identity is defined by the complex interaction between various markers of Jewishness and other unrelated aspects of her life, which include gender, sexuality, class, and national backgrounds as well as local attachments. The ways in which Rosa expresses or suppresses her Jewishness are bound up with other factors, such as her identification with Leningrad as a city or the role she assumes in her German environment. There are crucial aspects of her identity that are not directly connected to her Jewishness, such as her strong self-identification as a mother, her sense of femininity, and her self-understanding as a survivor of the Leningrad siege. Rosa's identity is thus not fixed but a fluid, situational, and relational phenomenon, which requires a strong performative element. It never fits the "existing clothes," as Bakhtin puts it, because there is always an element that complicates, supersedes, or contradicts the expectations. By alternately affirming and subverting the assumptions she is faced with, Rosa approaches the issue of identity in a ludic manner, and this playfulness has a de-essentializing effect.

The novel as a whole features various scenes that further highlight the changeability and fictionality of identities: after the end of the Russian Revolution, Rosa takes a job in a local communal office; she is responsible for the implementation of a new decree that orders every Soviet citizen to possess an identity card. One of the women requesting such a card introduces herself with a markedly Jewish name—"Rabinowitsch, Rivka Mowschewna" (*DbG*, 113)—but Rosa knows that she is a Ukrainian Gentile named Jewdokija Karaschtschuk. When Rosa calls her bluff and asks her why she decided to adopt a Jewish identity, the Ukrainian women claims that this charade is necessary "in einem Land, wo die Krummnasigen regieren" (*DbG*, 115). Her anti-Semitic argument alludes to the fact that after the Russian Revolution, some Jews rose to power in the context of a larger flourishing of Jewish culture under the Bolsheviks. Rosa meets the woman again decades later, when the tide has turned and anti-Semitic discrimination has regained currency. The woman's son, Jascha, has grown up to be a proud Jew, eager to migrate to Israel, who reprimands his mother for the supposed denial of her Jewishness: "Du musst endlich lernen, dazu zu stehen, was du bist. Zu lange hat man auf unserem Volk herumgetrampelt" (*DbG*, 117). While the episode reveals the interchangeability of identities and the unreliability of official documents (a recurring theme in the novel), it also demonstrates quite powerfully that identities are based on fictions. In Jascha's case, these fictions have the ability to alter the physical world. In a witty reversal of the Marxist credo that the social and material conditions determine consciousness, Jascha not only acts hyper-Jewish but also looks the part, as Rosa remarks: "In der Tat erinnerte Jaschas Nase an den Hauptkamm des Kaukasus. Seine Lippen sind rot wie die Fahnen bei den Aufmärschen am 1. Mai. Das schon etwas lichte Haar ist kraus und schwarz" (*DbG*, 117). The irony here results from the fact that the staunch anti-Semite Jewdokija Karaschtschuk, who appropriated a Jewish identity for purely strategic reasons, has ended up with a son who could not look and act more Jewish if he tried. We are thus left with the darkly comical suggestion that the anti-Semite produces the perfect Jew. The episode furthermore attacks the essentializing and naturalizing logic at work in racist thinking, which is reduced to absurdity by Jascha's example: his story suggests that our looks and identity are not determined by our genes but by cultural influences, coincidence, and our interpretations of these.

Vertlib's text articulates repeated clashes between the complex, fluid, and fictional character of identities—their "unfinalizability"—and a reductive thinking intent on pinning Rosa (and others) down to (certain aspects of) her (and their) Jewishness, which are cast as "natural."[64] While these clashes often serve a comical purpose, they nonetheless convey a serious message: the essentializing patterns employed by individuals and institutions can result in exoticization, discriminatory stereotypes, and clichés, which, in the worst case, give way to racist violence and persecution. The identity games played by Rosa thus have ethical implications, as they seek to dismantle naturalizing notions of identity. This ethical impetus distinguishes Vertlib's text from Stein's novel: even through both writers emphasize the fluidity of identities, *Die Leinwand* does this as part of a broader postmodern agenda. In contrast, *Das besondere Gedächtnis der Rosa Masur* urges us to embrace the nontypical, singular, and unfinalizable as the basis of an ethical response toward the Other.

Conclusion: The Ethics of Fictional Discourse

While this chapter has thus far concentrated on the depiction of transnational memory phenomena in Vertlib's *Das besondere Gedächtnis der Rosa Masur*, it seems important to not see literature as merely an exemplification or reflection of broader cultural, social, and political discourses but as an active agent shaping the very issue of transnationalism. Instead of asking how literature can be read through the lens of the transnational, the question then is: What can fiction contribute to the transnational turn and transnational memory debates? In recent scholarship, the possible intersections between transnationalism, literary discourse, and aesthetics have not received a lot of attention. This is surprising, considering that key theorists of this turn—such as Stef Craps, Michael Rothberg, and Max Silverman—are themselves literary scholars. Their work, however, is generally centered on the various manifestations of transnational, transcultural, and/or multidirectional memory constellations in/via certain texts/cultural artifacts, alongside their political and ethical implications. Nonetheless, both Rothberg and Silverman make tentative attempts to outline a possible multidirectional (Rothberg) or palimpsestic (Silverman) aesthetic: in a recent article on W. G. Sebald and the contemporary South African artist William Kentridge, Rothberg compares their respective artistic strategies.

In the case of Sebald, he highlights "intertextuality and a metonymical narrative technique,"[65] coupled with "association."[66] Kentridge's work—consisting of drawings and animated films—is marked by a "dynamic aesthetic of juxtaposition and layered meaning,"[67] relying on techniques such as superimposition and montage. Rothberg does not reflect adequately upon the specific media these artists work with—a literary text is quintessentially different from a drawing or an animated film—and the techniques he identifies, such as intertextuality, montage, and superimposition, are not necessarily and exclusively indicative of a multidirectional aesthetics. In contrast to Rothberg, Silverman reflects a little more extensively on the specific function of literary discourse:

> I will argue that artistic works may be more suited than historical or sociological method to making visible the complex interaction of times and sites at play in memory, as a fundamental feature of imaginative (poetic) works is to overlay meaning in intertextual space and blur the frontiers between the conscious and the unconscious, the present and the past, and the personal and the collective.[68]

Silverman also identifies intertextuality and layering as quintessential techniques related to palimpsestic memory, but he comes across the same problem as Rothberg. For Silverman, a palimpsestic aesthetics coalesces with the aesthetics of literature as such, which is by definition an intertextual medium.[69] Silverman's quote furthermore promotes an understanding of literature and art as mere illustrations of certain conceptions of memory. This overlooks the specificities and inner logic of literary and artistic discourse. Artworks are never simple and unmediated reflections of individual or collective memory processes but *representations* of such phenomena, shaped by certain conventions and a specific form.

In response to Rothberg and Silverman, I suggest replacing the search for a markedly transnational, multidirectional, or palimpsestic aesthetics with an exploration of the *specific function* literary discourse can assume in relation to the recent debates on transnational memory: what can fiction do that public and scholarly discourse cannot achieve? And how and to what extent can literary discourse help to broaden or question the existing notions of transnational memory and transnationalism? Vertlib's *Das besondere Gedächtnis der Rosa Masur* offers an excellent starting point for tackling these questions, since it is in many respects a metanovel: it not only reflects on the workings of autobiographical and collective memory but also functions as a "poetologischer Text über die Rolle von Literatur in der Gesellschaft."[70] Vertlib's text focuses in particular on the relationship between literary discourse and other, nonfictional discourses, suggesting that fiction provides certain dialogic, critical, and ethical possibilities that supersede those of other forms of speaking and writing.

These possibilities are opened up by the polyphony and dialogism that pervade Vertlib's novel. *Das besondere Gedächtnis der Rosa Masur* consists of a remarkable range of different discursive modes and genres, while also accommodating a host of oftentimes conflicting personal and political agendas. Tensions exist, for example, between the discourses of official historiography and factuality (the book project), on the one hand, and autobiography, storytelling, and fictionality (Rosa's story), on the other hand. This basic conflict is complicated by opposing national and cultural outlooks (Russian vs. German, East vs. West, narratives of heroism vs. narratives of repentance), subject positions (victims vs. perpetrators, victims vs. heroes/survivors, insiders vs. outsiders, Jews vs. Gentiles, men vs. women, older vs. younger generations) and the clash between different modes of remembering (private vs. public, individual vs. collective). In addition, the novel's texture is made up of different languages (German, Russian, Ukrainian, Polish, Yiddish), different temporal and geographical layers (past vs. present, East vs. West, periphery vs. center) and frequent changes in narrative style (first- person vs. third-person narrator, inserted genres such as the letter to Mascha). What makes *Das besondere Gedächtnis der Rosa Masur* stand out is the fact that these various discourses, modes, perspectives, and voices can coexist and interact in the space of the novel.[71] Vertlib's text provides space for these tensions, conflicts, and contradictions, which necessarily arise from polyphonic mixing, without resolving them in a hierarchical manner. According to Mikhail Bakhtin, the unique potential of the polyphonic novel, as it was created by Fyodor Dostoevsky, lies in its ability to accommodate a range of worldviews without having to take sides. He describes Dostoevsky's compositional technique as "the unification of highly heterogeneous and incompatible material—with the plurality of consciousness-centers not reduced to a single ideological common denominator."[72] It is debatable whether Vertlib's text is characterized by the same degree of polyphony and dialogism as Dostoevsky's work. Our sympathies are clearly steered toward Rosa as a character, and we are invited to adopt a critical stance toward certain aspects of German culture and German Vergangenheitsbewältigung. One can therefore not speak of the "*equal rights* [italics in the original]" that Bakhtin envisaged for all the voices found in a polyphonic novel.[73] Nonetheless, these biases in Vertlib's novel do not result in crushing verdicts but in humorous, ironic observations, which are open to interpretation. Owing to its fictional and polyphonic nature, the text does not have to resolve the tensions and conflicts that exist in the narrative, as it is not bound to come up with definitive truth statements. In contrast to other forms of so-called monologic discourse (such as political, academic, religious expression, etc.),[74] the novel provides space for ambiguities and dialogic openness. We never find out for sure whether or not Rosa lied about her meeting with Stalin, and we are unable to neatly separate the parts of her story that are based on facts from those that are invented to meet her audience's expectations. While the organizers of the book project require documentary proof of the meeting between Rosa and Stalin, we as readers do not, because as a discursive mode the novel is not governed by the rules of facticity but by those of fiction. In a carnivalesque reversal, *Das besondere Gedächtnis der Rosa Masur* questions this prerogative of documented, factual proof: the end of the novel reveals that the medieval charter that the town's jubilee and self-image is based on is forged. This is only one of the many instances in the novel that openly challenge the reliability of official documents, establishing ambiguity and openness as the norm and not the exception. This echoes Bakhtin's core conviction that monologic, centralized discourse does not represent the actuality of the social world and its language but is something that needs to be artificially produced: "Alongside the centripetal forces, the centrifugal forces of language carry on their uninterrupted work; alongside verbal-ideological centralization and unification, the uninterrupted processes of decentralization and disunification go forward."[75]

The polyphonic novel instigates a dialogue between its various voices, which leads to what Bakhtin calls "interillumination": instead of canceling each other out and fighting for supremacy, two (or more) contesting concepts, perspectives, or voices can *interact dialogically* and produce a better understanding of all the components involved.[76] And so it is that the Russian and the German perspectives on the histories of totalitarianism in the twentieth century interilluminate each other in Rosa's narrative and in the space of the novel. The intersection of German and Russian history in Rosa's narrative does not engender relativization or competitive victimhood but "dialogical interaction with other histories of victimization," as also noted by Jessica Ortner.[77] These interilluminations draw the reader's attention to the neglected aspects of German-Russian history (such as the siege of Leningrad) and to the complex and transnational history and legacy of anti-Semitism and the Holocaust. They expose the shortcomings of the German narrative of guilt and redemption, while also criticizing the Soviet heroic template, which resulted in the repression of certain histories of suffering. Rosa's story therefore enables what official historiographical and political discourses often fail to achieve: the creation of an "integrated European memory" that brings together the German and the Russian legacies of war and totalitarianism without relativizing or trivializing them.[78] The point of open-ended, ambiguous novelistic discourse, however, is precisely that it does not aim to integrate or resolve (both of which imply a higher unity) but to foster eternal dialogue, predicated on "*coexistence* and *interaction* [italics in the original],"[79] as Bakhtin puts it.

Das besondere Gedächtnis der Rosa Masur thus stages the failure of various master narratives in the face of a quintessential multilayeredness of individual and collective experience. Monologic in nature, these grand narratives rely on the exclusion and hierarchization of certain aspects of personal and collective history. This problem is clearly reflected in the novel, which repeatedly contrasts the book project and Rosa's personal narrative. The initiators of the book project apply an exclusionary logic ("Fremde" vs. "Heimat," Germans vs. their Others, "good" vs. "bad" immigrants) to produce the narratives they want to hear (for example, the Jew as the eternal victim) and the outcomes they expect (the stabilization of a certain self-image, i.e., Germany as a multicultural society). They radically shut out anything that does not fit these (pre)conceptions, as is demonstrated by the initial interviewing/casting process. Rosa at first obeys the rules of this monologic discourse, before increasingly giving it a dialogical twist. She strays from the prescribed path by introducing her own emphases, by defying expectations, and by increasingly blurring the boundary between fact and fiction. Rosa's story therefore no longer promotes the self-understanding of the project initiators but emerges as a novel in the Bakhtinian sense. The fact that the book project as such eventually gets canceled while Rosa's narrative persists as part of *Das besondere Gedächtnis der Rosa Masur* suggests that novelistic discourse eventually supersedes any form of monologism.[80]

Based on these observations, I would argue that literary discourse is able and uniquely suited to express a dialectic and "multi-scalar" understanding of transnationalism as promoted by Chiara de Cesari and Ann Rigney. In Vertlib's case, however, the notion of a dialectics needs to be replaced with the idea of dialogism, which is not aimed at resolution (as is the case for traditional notions of dialectical *Aufhebung*) but allows for the continued coexistence of diverse and diverging perspectives.[81] In *Das besondere Gedächtnis der Rosa Masur*, transnational narratives and national or even nationalistic discourses intersect with border-crossing, universal, or very local concerns in a multiscalar fashion. Rosa's transnational, contrapuntal, and novelistic perspective allows for a coexistence of these various angles, while calling into question the idea(l) that the transnational movement of people and memories automatically produces cosmopolitanism and mutual understanding. This can only happen when transnational memory is understood and practiced as dialogic memory. Vertlib's text suggests, however, that the dialogic approach is limited to the realm of fiction and, in all likelihood, not translatable into other discourses.

In Bakhtin's view, the novel is not dialogic but also quintessentially metadiscursive and self-reflexive. As the omnivore among literary genres, it constantly ingests other modes of expression:

> The novel permits the incorporation of various genres, both artistic (inserted short stories, lyrical songs, poems, dramatic scenes, etc.) and extra-artistic (everyday, rhetorical, scholarly, religious genres and others). In principle, any genre could be included in the construction of the novel, and in fact it is difficult to find any genres that have not at some point been incorporated into a novel by someone.[82]

This dynamic of incorporation is so fundamental to the novel as a genre that it almost appears as if it has no approach of its own—its core principle consists in not having a principle, so to speak, as it constantly recycles other forms, genres, discourses. Bakhtin stresses, however, that the novel accomplishes much more than simply regurgitating what is already there. As a variation of the genre of parody, novelistic repetition actually serves a critical purpose: "The novel parodies other genres (precisely in their role as genres); *it exposes the conventionality of their forms and their language* [italics added]."[83] For Bakhtin, parody is always connected to (carnivalesque) laughter and comedy, but it is also a tool for metageneric or -discursive reflection: novelistic repetition and parody lay bare the underlying scripts, rules, and conventions that determine other genres and discourses. The novel draws attention to their cultural evolution, thereby denaturalizing and demystifying them. It is this potential that allows litera-ture to initiate a metadiscourse, enabling a (critical) reflection of the dynamics that underlie broader cultural (and its own) debates. In the case of Vertlib's *Das besondere Gedächtnis der Rosa Masur* this is true on various levels: the text engages critically with historiographical discourse (the book project) and with the broader discourse of institutionalized Holocaust remembrance in Germany, while also problematizing Soviet narratives of heroism and the genre of autobiography—Rosa's story at least partly *mim-ics* or *stages* processes of autobiographical remembrance. The insertion of these discourses into the novel and their dialogic intersection make us aware of the rules and scripts underpinning them. The exposure of these templates serves a critical purpose: Vertlib's novel shows that the rigid conventions and political agendas underpinning historiographical dis-course, as exemplified by the book project, or national(ist) memory cul-tures leave no space for the particularities that make up Rosa's (or any person's) individual life. Her personal pain and suffering cannot be articu-lated within the book project, as this discourse relies on universalizing or sensationalizing categories (the Jew as the paradigmatic and eternal vic-tim). In a similar vein, Vertlib's text casts doubts on the institutionalized culture of Holocaust remembrance in Germany, which allows for ritualized displays of sympathy but no real empathy for the Jewish and other migrant Others—this culture is different from the Soviet context, however, in which Jewish suffering is systematically blanked out. At the same time, *Das besondere Gedächtnis der Rosa Masur* questions the extreme valorization of eyewitnesses and their seemingly unmediated, emotionalized approach to the past by highlighting that Rosa's report is far from authentic.

Parody is connected to another central feature of Vertlib's novel and of novelistic style more generally: namely, the ironic narrative mode. Irony is a crucial device employed on various levels of Vertlib's text: in the framing narrative, the third-person narrator reports Rosa's experiences in post-Soviet Russia and in Germany in a highly ironic manner. Rosa herself repeatedly uses irony and sarcasm to respond to what she perceives as ignorance and/or impertinence: when a German friend of her grandson's wants to know whether it is true that many of the so-called Kontingentflüchtlinge are not actually Jewish, she replies sarcastically, "Ich habe die anderen Lagerinsassen nicht nach ihrer Abstammung gefragt. . . . Ich bin keine Expertin für Rassenkunde" (*DbG*, 26). Finally, the novel resorts to situational irony, mostly to highlight the absurdities of history or of certain ideologies. I already introduced the story involving Jewdokija Karaschtschuk and her son Jascha, and the account of Benedikt Hirsch creates a similar darkly comic effect—he is a Polish Jew who survived the Nazi genocide because he was deported to eastern Siberia by the Russians, so that one form of totalitarianism saved him from another (*DbG*, 210–11).

Bakhtin claims that (carnivalesque) laughter "expose[s] the disparity between his [i.e., man's] surface and his center, between his potential and his reality."[84] Irony achieves a similar effect—it stresses the gap between our expectation and reality. Ironic humor stages a clash between different perspectives, highlighting the discrepancies between what we expect the world to be like and what it is actually like, bringing out the gulf that separates people's perception of themselves from the ways in which others perceive them. By focusing our attention on these disparities, irony makes us aware of the existence of these underlying expectations, perceptions, etc. One can therefore say that Vertlib's novel ironically exposes the gap between Germany's self-image as a multicultural, open, and tolerant society and a reality based on the stereotyping and exoticization of migrant groups. By pointing out this gap, *Das besondere Gedächtnis der Rosa Masur* draws our attention to an underlying script in which a prescribed xenophilia and a failed multiculturalism spring from a desire to somehow atone for the crimes of the past. By trying to do better, the Germans in the book, ironically, make it worse. Further to this, Vertlib's novel comments ironically on the institutionalization and transnationalization of Holocaust memory as such. The hypermediation and globalization of Holocaust memory creates the fertile soil for Rosa's story and guarantees that there is an interest in what she has to say. This corresponds to the rise of the survivor and/or eyewitness as a contemporary icon and the establishment of a "trauma economy" in Terri Tomsky's sense,[85] that is, the commodification of and constant competition between stories of pain and suffering on a global scale. The broader cultural climate surrounding the book project furthermore casts the past as something that can and needs to be managed, not so much in a psychological but more in a political and economic sense. It is precisely this combination of mass-mediatization, iconization, instrumentalization, and commodification that ensures that Rosa can tell and sell her story but that no one will really listen. This creates a contrast between the ever-growing presence of the Holocaust and the survivor as global icons and the invisibility of any real pain and suffering.

The ironic criticism promoted via *Das besondere Gedächtnis der Rosa Masur* differs from other forms of engagement, as it does not seek to instruct or indoctrinate.[86] It is a fundamentally open—or, as Bakhtin would say, "dialogic"—form of criticism, since it merely highlights the discrepancies between expectation and reality and lets the recipients draw their own conclusions. Vertlib's novel at no point openly polemicizes against Germany's forced multiculturalism; this is a conclusion the reader has to draw. By illustrating that things are not what they seem, irony has a destabilizing, de-essentializing effect, which radically sets it apart from any form of monologic and naturalizing discourse. Finally, the crucial point of irony is that these disparities and tensions can be *laughed off* instead of leading to conflict, division, and aggression. Rosa's experiences in Germany for the most part make us laugh and maybe shake our heads; they do not make us hate Germany or the Germans.

Apart from dialogically interlinking a multiplicity of perspectives, the novel can expose various discursive templates and criticize them in an ironic fashion. Literature thus seems to be able to instigate a dialogic or "ironic" transnationalism that not only accommodates conflicting perspectives but is also quintessentially self-reflexive and self-critical. "Ironic" transnationalism enables us to keep in mind the historical, political, and material circumstances and realities that underpin academic and political debates (such as borders, blockages, misunderstandings), which the utopian discourse on transnationalism seems to forget. Ironic transnationalism is related to what Stuart Taberner describes as "'kynical' cosmopolitanism," which also uses "ironic distance."[87] While Taberner stresses the ethical possibilities of his concept, however, I would like to emphasize the critical and metadiscursive potential of my term. What unites both notions is their close affiliation with the logic of literary and novelistic discourse.

While I understand "ironic" transnationalism as a critical-analytical rather than an ethical term, there is a specific ethics of literary discourse and storytelling at work in Vertlib's novel. This is also what sets it apart from Stein's writing: although both authors use a metadiscursive approach to make similar points about the fluidity of identities and the subjectivity of truth, their trajectories differ. While Stein's text is concerned with the epistemological issues that arise from the hypermediation of Holocaust memory and reality more generally, Vertlib's novel favors the specificities of Rosa's memory and literary discourse for ethical reasons. In his lecture "Spiegel im fremden Wort," Vertlib reflects on the relationship between the particular and the universal as it unfolds in the realm of fiction:

> Soweit die Fiktion als Ergänzung zu Selbsterlebtem eine symbolische und allgemein gültige Dimension besitzt, kann sie, wie ich glaube, zu guter Literatur werden. Wenn ich beim Schreiben das Gefühl habe, dass das Erlebte oder das Erinnerte sowie das Erinnerte, das man

nachträglich als Erlebtes wahrnimmt, etwas widerspiegelt, das über die eigene Person hinausgeht, in dem sich also auch andere Menschen spiegeln können, dann kann daraus etwas Wertvolles entstehen.[88]

Vertlib suggests that "good" literature brings out the "allgemein gültige Dimension" of personal experiences, thus linking the particular to the universal. For Vertlib, it is *only* the medium of fiction that can achieve this effect, and this is what distinguishes it from other modes of expression. His point is exemplified in *Das besondere Gedächtnis der Rosa Masur*: although the book project tries to wed the particular with the universal, it is simply not the right medium to create this union. This is so because it approaches the particular in universalizing categories (i.e., clichés and stereotypes), while simultaneously subordinating the universal, cosmopolitan appeal of Rosa's story to the particularity of its own agenda (the consolidation of a certain self-image and image of the past). The instrumentalizing approach inherent in the book project leads to a systematic erasure of the particularities, incongruences, and ambiguities that make up Rosa's (or any individual's) life story. Bakhtin claims that "the consciousnesses of other people cannot be perceived, analyzed, defined as objects or things—one can only *relate to them dialogically*. To think about them means to *talk with them* [italics in the original]."[89] This dialogic relationship cannot be achieved by the book project, but it is attainable as part of the novel *Das besondere Gedächtnis der Rosa Masur*: while the former tends to objectify, instrumentalize, and commodify Rosa's memories, the latter urges readers to engage dialogically, to empathize and to confront and question their own assumptions, blind spots, and preconceptions. The remarkable and "unfinalizable" memory of Rosa Masur can therefore only realize its full potential as a *literary* memory, which is presented as the more viable ethical option. Hence, it is only logical that the book project fails while Rosa's story persists as part of the novel *Das besondere Gedächtnis der Rosa Masur*.

Vertlib also stresses the importance of the reader as an agent of universalization. The reader connects to the experiences presented in the text, turning them into a "Spiegel—auch einem Zerrspiegel—der eignen Gefühle, Erfahrungen, Ängste und Sehnsüchte. . . . Nur wenn das gelingt, vermag der Text wirklich zu berühren. Er kann dem Leser einen neuen Blickwinkel eröffnen oder aber helfen, Abgründe auszuloten."[90] I therefore conclude with a consideration of the role of the reader for Vertlib's novel by returning to my earlier claim about the lack of empathetic listening space in the work: Rosa cannot meaningfully articulate her trauma, either as part of the book project, in the context of the German and Russian narratives about the past, or in the space of her own family. The readers act as witnesses to Rosa's trauma, however, as they get a multifaceted insight into Rosa's personality and her suffering that none of the above-mentioned discourses provide. We get to read the first-person story she tells for the book project, but we also know the passages told by the third-person narrator, which provide background information that is missing during the interviewing process. We thus learn about Rosa's true motivation for participating in the project, but we also witness the changes in her behavior from ironic mockery to retraumatization. She begins to suffer from nightmares, flashbacks, and anxiety attacks, while the interviewing process turns from an exclusively economic enterprise into a therapeutic endeavor. Finally, it is only the reader who gets to see the letter she writes to her dead friend Mascha. This letter is the only unmediated access route to Rosa's consciousness in the novel, to the extent that it is written in private and not filtered through the third-person narrator.[91] Its position in the text is therefore significant: the letter follows Rosa's visit to her completely annihilated hometown shortly after the end of the war. Here she is for the first time confronted with the murder of her parents during the Holocaust and the brutality of the Soviet politics of prescribed amnesia. Rosa loses the battle over the memorial and leaves Witschi with a double loss: her parents have disappeared, and she has no space—literally and figuratively—to mourn or commemorate them. This descent into an extremely painful past is potentially retraumatizing for Rosa, but she holds back during the interview process. She only admits to her sleeping problems, irritability, and growing sense of temporal and geographical disorientation (*DbG*, 307; 316–18) in the intimate (imaginary) conversation with Mascha. The reader is similar to Mascha in acting as an entity that listens to and witnesses those parts of Rosa's story that are ambiguous and painful. The act of reading creates an intimate setting, as does the epistolary conversation, which is the precondition for the expression of personal pain and empathetic listening. My initial claim that there is *no space* for Rosa's personal story of suffering is therefore not entirely true—there is a space, but it is located not on the intradiegetic level of character interaction—neither the initiators of the book project, nor the (post-)Soviet or German state or Rosa's family will listen—but on the level of reception.

The role of the reader extends even further, as a number of critics have pointed out.[92] As mentioned, the book project eventually gets canceled, and Rosa's story never reaches its initial target audience. In its preliminary form, however, her narration is salvaged as part of the novel *Das besondere Gedächtnis der Rosa Masur*. Novelistic discourse thus saves Rosa's story from disappearing into the archive (or worse: the waste bin), but this recovery would be incomplete without a reader who actualizes and transmits it.[93] With the institutional and familial systems of transmission failing, it is therefore down to the reader to witness, remember, and pass on Rosa's story. Annette Teufel and Walter Schmitz are therefore only partly right when they stress the importance of the narrator in this process.[94] As demonstrated above, the third-person narrator only registers parts of Rosa's story—the other passages consist of her first-person narrative and the letter to Mascha. The preservation and transmission of Rosa's story *as a whole* therefore falls to the reader who has to join together its various pieces. The active and creative role of the reader corroborates Bakhtin's observation that there are no bystanders in polyphonic novelistic discourse: "Everything in the novel is structured to make dialogic opposition inescapable. Not a single element of the work is structured from the point of view of a non-participating 'third person.'"[95] Vertlib's *Das besondere Gedächtnis der Rosa Masur* follows through with its dialogism by making the reader an integral part of the memorial processes it describes and analyzes: considering the novel's ironic distance toward (and skepticism of) nationalistic mythologies and the discourses of institutionalized historiography and Vergangenheitsbewältigung, the reader is responsible for an alternative route of transmission. The particular memory of Rosa Masur is therefore not only a quintessentially literary but also a participatory memory that can only be fully acknowledged and realized in the act of reading.

Vertlib's ironic transnationalism thus evokes an ethical agenda of its own. This agenda, however, does not entail the automatic leveling out of all differences and erasure of the realities of conflicts and borders. By parodying dominant memory discourses, Vertlib's text seeks to create a space in which the particularity of a person's life, experiences, and memory can be articulated and acknowledged. In the context of an increasing hypermediation, globalization, and commodification of memories (especially of traumatic ones), literature, in Vertlib's view, appears as a space in which the complexities of history as well as personal and collective memory can be expressed, recognized, and (re)negotiated. This suggests a highly empathic understanding of literature and a powerful belief in the capabilities of this specific discourse. Novelistic discourse has its own limitations, however: from Vertlib's perspective, it is questionable whether the specific potentials and strategies of fiction—such as polyphony, dialogism, interillumination, ironization, participation—are translatable into other realms of life and society where they are sorely needed.

4: From the Family to the Metamemorial Novel: Eva Menasse's Fiction

Introduction: Beyond the Family Novel?

FAMILY AND MULTIGENERATIONAL NARRATIVES, which experienced a boom in the early 2000s, still dominate much recent Holocaust literature and scholarship. Countless novels have been published in recent years that explore family memories of the Nazi past through the lens of the children and, more often, grandchildren of victims and perpetrators alike. Instead of a straightforward renarration of family history and memory, these texts offer investigations into memorial and genealogical gaps and the fictions they produce, putting issues of mediation and imagination, and hence the process of remembering and writing itself, at the center. This self-reflexive potential of some (although not all) family novels, emphasized by many scholars in the field,[1] often manifests itself in complex negotiations of the relationship between fact and fiction and the rules of the autobiographical genre. Many narratives focus on the overlaps and clashes between the private realm of family memory and the public field of institutionalized historiography, supplementing established discourses on the past with alternative accounts. Numerous studies have been dedicated to the topic of the family or multigenerational novel,[2] which appears inexhaustible: "Mit dem Familienroman ist es eben noch lange nicht vorbei."[3]

This optimistic assessment is questioned in a recent study by Kirstin Frieden that probes contemporary *Neuverhandlungen des Holocaust*. Frieden rightly criticizes the increasingly clichéd nature of many family narratives, which corresponds with a stagnation in current literary scholarship on the Nazi past and the Holocaust. This assessment substantiates Frieden's central claim that we are currently facing major shifts in Holocaust memory that are not (yet) sufficiently reflected in contemporary research. Like many other commentators, she refers to the disappearance of the survivor generation and the transition from personal and familial experiences and memories of the Holocaust to a completely mediatized and institutionalized cultural memory of the events. This is not a new insight as such; Frieden stresses, however, that the search for links to the past is complicated by larger societal transformations. The "junge

Generation,"[4] those born between 1965 and 1980, have grown up in an environment in which Holocaust memory has become entrenched in cli-chéd or ritualized frameworks. The lack of personal experience is thus met by an excess of images and representational conventions that provoke a "Gefühl der Übersättigung."[5] Frieden analyzes a range of media, including literature, performance art, and new media, in her search for contemporary responses to these shifts, although the processes she is trying to grasp are, for the most part, still ongoing and in flux.

Apart from a need for new theoretical and conceptual frameworks, these shifts provoke a reshuffling "[der] Karten der Holocaust-Repräsentation und ihrer Akzeptanz."[6] Frieden's exploration thus concentrates on new aesthetic approaches in Holocaust-related art that reflect on and extend existing representational conventions and boundaries. In the case of literature, she questions the future viability of the generational paradigm by asking: "Was kommt nach dem Familienroman?"[7] Frieden's question implies that, as a result of the demographic and social changes currently under way, the family novel might indeed have exhausted itself. As a blanket statement this is, of course, problematic, not least because we are witnessing an ongoing production of family narratives in the realm of Holocaust literature also among younger authors such as Alina Bronsky, Mirna Funk, Olga Grjasnowa, and Sasha Marianna Salzmann. Many of the recent family and multigenerational novels, however, do indeed appear formulaic and/or scrutinize the viability of "family frames,"[8] as is, for example, the case in Katja Petrowskaja's *Vielleicht Esther* or,[9] more recently, Salzmann's debut novel *Ausser Sich*.

These developments thus raise the question of whether the genre still offers the same potential for critical engagement with the Nazi period as it used to,[10] while also encouraging us to investigate new gen-res and forms that might offer forward-looking (re)negotiations of Germany's past in relation to a changing present. This is the focus of my exploration of Eva Menasse's 2013 novel, *Quasikristalle*. Menasse's text is divided into thirteen seemingly unrelated chapters consisting of the observations, thoughts, and feelings of specific characters. It gradually becomes clear that these various impressions all relate to the text's central character, Xane Molin. Xane is an Austrian-born Jewish intellectual, who, in her late twenties, abandons her home country to go to Berlin, where she launches and then ruins a successful advertising company, then marries and starts a family, before returning to Vienna in old age. Each of the chapters adopts the perspective of specific characters who relate to Xane during specific phases of her life and in different roles. The impressions we get zoom in and out of Xane's life: while some characters are very close to her (her immediate family and best friends), others are mere acquaintances. The book's seventh (and central) chapter is told by Xane herself. We thus follow Xane's biography through the eyes of various people, but this multiperspectival narration does not produce a fully rounded picture of her. We are left with various biographical pieces and impressions that fit together loosely and not exactly smoothly.

Menasse's attempt to translate the structure of the quasicrystal, a scientific phenomenon discovered in the 1980s, into literature paves the way for an examination of biographical writing, of the nature of truth and female identity. I want to argue, however, that it also probes the aesthetics and poetics of a new, possibly postfamilial Holocaust literature and memory. In her latest work Menasse replaces the aesthetics of the family novel, epitomized in her previous novel, *Vienna* (2003; translated, 2007), with what I call a metadiscursive or metamemorial approach: the text depicts Holocaust memory in a number of forms and historical stages (covering the past, present, *and* future), which all coexist in the space of the novel. The more or less unifying framework of the family is thus shattered and substituted by a multifaceted depiction of Holocaust memory that combines familial and nonfamilial, individual and collective, psychological and cultural approaches to the memory of the event. The biological family does not cease to exist as a carrier of memory, but it is no longer the dominant platform for the articulation and transmission of Holocaust memories. I have already argued in the introduction that metadiscursivity is a central feature of Holocaust fiction in the new millennium; this assessment is echoed by Kirstin Frieden:

> Weil weder die aufklärerische Rekonstruktion der Vergangenheit noch die biographischen oder tradierten Erinnerungen zum zentralen Thema . . . werden, arrangieren sich neue Metadiskurse über die Reflexionen der kanonisierten Erinnerungskultur. Dies führt auf der Erzählebene zu immer neuen Konstrukten aus Vielstimmigkeit, Pluralität, sprachlichem Changieren zwischen Alten und Neuem, "Diskursgewirr" oder Diskurs-Demontage.[11]

We have already seen that multiperspectivity and metadiscursivity play a central role in Stein's, Biller's, and Vertlib's writing. This suggests that what I, at the beginning of this study, introduced as the metamemorial mode of narration is indeed a key response to the loss of personal access to the past, as well as a response to the increased globalization and discursivation of Holocaust memory. In the following, I will examine how Menasse's work uses metamemorial reflexion to complicate both the genre of the family novel and the ubiquity of the Holocaust as a global memory emblem.

Familial, Affiliative, or Postfamilial?
From *Vienna* to *Quasikristalle*

Breaking the Family Frame: *Vienna*

Vienna can be regarded as a paradigmatic example of the family or multi-generational novel and its postmemorial dynamics.[12] Menasse's text tells the story of a Vienna-based Jewish-Catholic family that encompasses four generations and grapples with the trauma of the Holocaust and the conundrums of pre- and post-Holocaust Jewish identity. *Vienna* uses the framework of the family to explore and recalibrate the larger history and memory of the Second World War in Austria, characterized by repression, denial, and a belated critical confrontation with the past.[13] The novel places a strong focus on practices of communicative memory; hence the dominance of oral genres such as anecdotes, legends, and jokes. The epicenter of the novel and the family's memory is the family table, around which the relatives regularly assemble to exchange and repeat the family's founding myths, "die alten Familiengeschichten" (*V*, 371). Whereas the reader is at first enthralled by the richness of these family stories and the witty, lighthearted tone struck by the narrator, a more critical perspective emerges as the novel progresses: what appears to be a celebration of family memory turns out to be a chronicle of its shortcomings and its gradual but inevitable disintegration.[14]

In fact, family memories and mythologies are questioned right at the beginning of *Vienna*: we find out that the narrator, who turns out to be one of the family's (grand)daughters, has only limited knowledge of the most crucial events in her family's history. Her narrative centers on the father and grandfather, whose formative experiences date back to a time long before her birth. What is presented as a chronicle of the family's history turns out to be a mix of public and private documents (such as photographs, family heirlooms, historical knowledge, etc.), "imaginative investment and creation,"[15] unverified deductions, and, most importantly, the "Heimeligkeit des familiären Sagengutes" (*V*, 372). It soon transpires that the family anecdotes are at least as historically unreliable as the narrator's postmemorial fantasies: every important story exists in several versions that continue to circulate in the family. The stories that prevail are not necessarily the most truthful ones but the ones that are the most entertaining—"bei dieser Familie, wo das Faktische oft so ungewiß war, wo alles nur gut und ganz wurde, wenn man es zu einer Geschichte mit einer Pointe machen konnte" (*V*, 389)—or encapsulate the general family ideology of "das Steuer herumreißen, against all odds, das war das geheime Thema all dieser Klassiker unserer Familienanekdoten" (*V*, 107). *Vienna* thus portrays family memory as a highly unreliable, malleable, and contested entity shaped by personal agendas, desires, projections, and defense mechanisms rather than historical reality. By openly admitting to this co-fabulation, the narrator repeatedly undermines her own authority.

The grandchild narrator's struggle with the issues of belatedness and historical distance is exacerbated by the fact that the family stories also serve a paradoxical psychological purpose—they are both a carrier *and* a cover-up of traumatic knowledge: the narrator's grandfather lost his mother in Theresienstadt and was himself taken into forced labor, her father and uncle were sent off to England on a *Kindertransport*, and their sister, aunt Katzi, tragically died from tuberculosis soon after she had managed to escape to Canada. As is often the case in survivor families, these traumas are not directly communicated, although the silences are nuanced: whereas the grandfather imposes a prohibitive silence about his own or Katzi's fate during the war years, the narrator's father cultivates the art of forgetfulness: "Doch das meiste vergaß er für viele Jahrzehnte, manches auch für immer, denn mein Vater pflegte die weniger geglückten Dinge im Leben blitzschnell zu vergessen, oder er machte daraus einen geistreichen Witz" (*V*, 23). By contrast, the narrator's uncle communicates his war trauma in a displaced fashion, as Daphne Seemann has argued: she reads the uncle's somewhat inexplicable affection for his caretaker, Mimi, as an expression of survivor guilt.[16] The family stories are thus intended to transmit the family's story of defiance and survival without tearing the delicate web of silences, taboos, and defenses meant to cover up the core traumatic experiences. The family's anecdotal and witty style represents a defense mechanism, since both the medium of the joke and narrative irony act as forms of doublespeak, designed to simultaneously communicate and conceal stories of pain and suffering.

The relative stability and cohesive power of this volatile mix of myths, jokes, and traumatic silences is remarkable: for most of the novel, the significance of the anecdotes as a means of providing reassurance and familial cohesion is not called into question. This is so not least because the family's "Sagengut" is incessantly repeated, rehearsed, and reenacted throughout the text. Phrases such as "wie es später immer wieder erzählt wurde" (*V*, 11), "in einer typischen Formulierung hieß es in meiner Familie immer" (*V*, 31), or "die hundertmal geübte Familienvorstellung" (*V*, 34) foreground family memory as a highly ritualized business that depends on the recurring appropriation, circulation, and consolidation of a few canonized events in the act of "manisches Mythologisieren": "Wenn das begann, wenn die alten Familiengeschichten zum tausendsten Mal heraufbeschworen, durchgekaut und neu interpretiert wurden, flüchteten sich die angeheirateten Frauen theatralisch eine Weile lang in die Küche" (*V*, 371–72). These ritualized retellings and reembodiments accentuate the hybrid character of the family in *Vienna*, which is presented both as a biological and a cultural unit. Hence, it is impossible to determine whether the family mythology is the product and reflection of a preexisting family identity, or whether the family unit is only created in the act of storytelling. This highlights the quintessentially performative dimension of the family in Menasse's novel, which is held together by a genealogical and a narrative chain.[17] Such performative enactment of familial identity also questions the alleged authenticity and immediacy of family memories and their access to the past: Menasse's novel not only shows that family memory is made up of various layers of mediation and fantasy; it also stresses that the family is something that needs to be actively constructed and reinforced through performance—it does not exist outside of a narrative framework. Such a perspective reduces the power of biological bonds to an extent, as it demonstrates that blood relations alone are not enough to construct a family. The family members in *Vienna* are kept together not so much by biological relationships but by virtue of the narrative and social ties that family mythology and rituals have created. When these begin to crumble, they cannot simply be replaced by the thickness of blood, and the family falls apart.

The two elements—genealogy and performance—are of equal importance for the preservation and continuity of the family (memory), and both come under attack as the narrative progresses. The narrator's brother and sister are the first ones to develop a critical stance toward the latter's "Familienwahn" (*V*, 370). The narrator's brother questions the family myths mainly in an attempt to emancipate himself from his father: "Mein Bruder, der sich, seit er studierte, den Traditionen und Ritualen der Familie, besonders aber ihren Glaubens-, das heißt ihren Anekdotengrundsätzen heftig widersetzte" (*V*, 32). By choosing to become a historian, he opts for the rigorous separation of fact and fiction, which is repeatedly undone in the acts of familial remembrance. When he exposes the questionable past of a major Austrian sports icon, Felix Popelnik, he causes a major public scandal. This course of action is completely at odds with the family policy of glossing over the personal and collective consequences of the war.[18] The brother's active contestation of family memory is complemented by the ostentatious indifference of the narrator's sister, who usually takes greater interest in her beauty regime than in the family stories. She also repeatedly breaches the unwritten family rules, either deliberately or by accident, by inquiring about the taboos and blind spots in the family's memory. Nonetheless, both of them are still active participants in the circulation of family stories, and as such they are carriers of memory.

These cracks in the family memory develop into a full-blown rupture in the final chapter, suggestively entitled "Ende" (*V*, 369). The chapter centers on a nasty fight within the family, which flares up around the issue of Jewish identity: the narrator and her siblings have a Jewish father, who was himself the son of a Jewish father. According to the rules of the halakah, they are therefore not Jewish, although both their father and grandfather were categorized and persecuted as Jews by the Nazis. Because their uncle's first marriage was to a Jewish woman, their cousins are fully Jewish in the eyes of Jewish religious law. These tensions surrounding the question of "proper" Jewishness run through the entire narrative, but they only explode when the cohesive power attached to the family narrative has finally crumbled. The narrator links this collapse to the disappearance of the eyewitness and survivor generation. The authenticity of their embodied experiences and suffering gave this generation an authority that was greater than all the conflicts, contradictions, and multiple versions of the past that made up the family memory:

> Solange mein Vater, meine Mutter, mein Onkel, die Tante Ka und die kleine Engländerin lebten, die die Widersprüche und Ungereimtheiten unserer Familie verkörperten, als Beweis für alles, was möglich ist, so lange konnten wir Kinder die besten Freunde sein und Mitglieder einer Familie. Doch als diese Generation tot war, kämpften wir traurigen Diadochen um eine Deutungshoheit, die vor uns keiner gebracht hatte. (*V*, 392–93)

The authority of the eyewitness generation is not based on the factual accuracy of their memories—the text repeatedly emphasizes that distortion, repression, and displacement shape these. Rather, it is an affective authority that stems from their personal, firsthand experience and survival, which has been inscribed into their bodies and minds. The narrator concedes that the eyewitnesses and survivors *embody* the past with all its contradictions, whereas the following generations can only ever *represent and reinterpret* it. By virtue of this embodiment, the eyewitness generation also testifies to the possibilities of survival ("als Beweis für alles, was möglich ist"). This provides them with a "Deutungshohheit" that goes beyond historical and factual accuracy: without this type of authority, the family legend turns into an empty accumulation of rituals, anecdotes, and orphaned memories that later generations can no longer connect to, not least because they have lost their therapeutic function.[19] This problem is even greater for the fourth generation, as the narrator's niece observes: "Unsere Familiengeschichte bestehe doch nur aus geschönten Anekdoten einerseits und umso auffälligeren Lücken andererseits. 'Das bildet doch keinen Zusammenhalt', sagte sie . . ., 'das ist doch nur blödes Gerede'" (*V*, 391). The disappearance of firsthand experiences of the war thus gives rise to a generational conflict centered on the issue of post-Holocaust Jewish identity. The fourth generation, represented by the niece, is no longer willing to take part in the family project of glossing over and covering up painful memories (she rejects the "geschönten Anekdoten"), because she is not personally affected by the family trauma. This identitarian vacuum also explains why the issues of Jewishness and ethnicity become such a point of contention, since they provide a major battleground in the search for alternative identities, as we have also seen in the texts of Stein and Biller. The family discussion around who is or is not a "proper" Jew is, however, dangerous and fraught with contradictions, not least because it threatens to reinstate racist thinking. At the same time, the disintegration of the family narrative uncovers a latent gender conflict between the male protagonists and the female narrator, who describes herself as "die Zuschauerin, die ich ja immer nur war, . . . alles nachgezählt und nachgeprüft, aber kein Gramm Inspiration" (V, 388)—a claim that is, of course, contradicted by her narrative.[20] The narrator's project is therefore a delicate balancing act between preserving and dismantling the family mythology, while trying to find her voice and emancipate herself from a male-dominated family tradition.

Stripped of the authority of the eyewitness generation, the familial framework can no longer hold together the multiperspectivity of personal experiences and generational, ethnic, or gendered positions. This also means that the narrative can no longer resort to the conventions of the family novel: the "Ende" chapter is followed by a section entitled "Nachruf," which is noteworthy from a narratological perspective: while most of *Vienna* is told by a third-person omniscient narrator, who manipulates the story's timeline and frequently comments on the events as they unfold, "Nachruf" features a third-person limited narrator ("personaler Erzähler") who sees the central event—the narrator's grandfather's funeral—through the eyes of various characters, most of whom are not related to the grandfather. After the breakdown of the family in the "Ende" section, the narrative thus adopts a different, multivocal perspective that is no longer held together by the framework of the family novel or a single consciousness center. This narrative arguably foreshadows the central concerns of *Quasikristalle*, which foregrounds the incongruity and multiperspectivity of personal experiences.[21] While the centrifugal forces of the diverse and oftentimes contradictory voices in *Vienna* are retained while the survivor generation is still alive, the cohesive power of the family narrative has vanished in the "Nachruf" section. The chapter adopts a different aesthetic approach that anticipates the narrative techniques applied in *Quasikristalle*.

The Poetics of (the) *Quasikristall(e)*

Although *Vienna* therefore conforms to the template of the family or multigenerational novel, it complicates intrafamilial memory and transmission as a self-reflexive example of the genre. The novel suggests that a postmemorial approach, based on transgenerational traumatization and the biological family, is no longer feasible after the end of the three-generation span. The novel ends with the complete disintegration of the family, both as a genealogical and a narrative entity. I want to argue that this decline of the family as a narrative framework is completed in *Quasikristalle*: the form of this novel no longer situates the subject within an overarching, genealogical pattern. Family or genealogical time is replaced by the time span of an individual life, which is in turn broken up into the various times of the spectators who follow, interfere with, or cross Xane's path.[22]

Quasikristalle is constructed around a multiplicity of perspectives and times, which no longer contribute to an organic whole such as the family unit or the well-rounded individual. The issue of multiperspectivity is implied in the eponymous quasicrystal that also functions as a poetological metaphor: quasicrystals were discovered in 1982 by the material scientist Dan Schechtman, who described them as a structure that is ordered but not periodic. Periodicity, the defining feature of "proper" crystals, means that the same basic structural unit recurs at regular intervals. In the case of the crystal, these units repeat themselves infinitely in all directions, filling up all of the available space. In contrast, the quasicrystal also consists of at least two basic units that repeat themselves, but the pattern is aperiodic—this means that, on a local level, identical elements might repeat themselves and form a pattern, but on a global level, this pattern does not recur at regular intervals.

As Menasse herself observed in a recent interview, this results in the fact that quasicrystals always look different, depending on the perspective: "Und genau das ist die Idee . . . dieses . . . Buchs gewesen. Wie sehe ich oder irgendeine Person aus, aus der Sicht ihres Arztes, ihres Geliebten, ihres Kindes, ihres Vaters, ihres Vermieters . . ., ihres Angestellten, ja? Immer anders. Total anders! Und das sind die Quasikristalle."[23] The extent to which this scientific metaphor adequately describes the structure of the text is debatable. As a metaphor, however, the quasicrystal accentuates the relationship between order and chaos, between the part and the whole, and between predictability and unpredictability in the text. Drawing on the quasicrystalline principle of aperiodicity, the novel presents Xane as an element that repeats itself as her story progresses in loosely chronological order. At the same time, this order is constantly broken up by the chapter structure and the changes in perspective, so that the reader recognizes certain regularities in the various descriptions of Xane but not in the form of a strict pattern. Neither the reader nor any of the characters can grasp Xane's essence, since she is "immer anders." Just like Stein, and even more so Vertlib, Menasse highlights the fluidity, mutability, and intangibility of the individual. Xane's only defining feature is the lack of defining features—the only constant in her life is the continuity of change. The way in which Xane's biography unfolds therefore remains unpredictable and—up to a point—unintelligible, since every description is necessarily subjective, partial, and limited. As Xane's son, Amos, notes toward the end of the novel, all questions relating to his mother's life are "nicht so umfassend zu beantworten, dass man am Ende zufrieden wäre" (*Q,* 425).

While the quasicrystal therefore serves as a poetological metaphor that negotiates notions of biographical writing and (female) identity, its structure also connects to the issue of Holocaust remembrance in the text. The Holocaust surfaces as part of a multifaceted—maybe even quasicrystalline—memorial assemblage that brings together familial and nonfamilial, communicative and cultural memories, different generational positions and national outlooks, which are no longer held together by the framework of the family. The Nazi period and the Holocaust feature in a variety of contexts and guises: in the form of family trauma and historiographical discourse, as a media cliché and spectacle, as a template for reading other traumas, as a moral benchmark, or as a decontextualized term of abuse when a rebellious teenager denounces a pensioner as "Nazifresse" (*Q*, 286). The extreme pluralization of Holocaust memory in *Quasikristalle* clearly supersedes and decentralizes the frame of the family narrative. What emerges instead is a metamemorial account that engages with different discursive configurations and stages of Holocaust memory in loosely chronological succession. These stages comprise personal and collective repression, oversaturation, the de- and recontextualization of Holocaust memory and, last, the eventual fading of its prevalence.

While *Quasikristalle* incorporates a multiplicity of perspectives on the Holocaust, family memory still plays a role. The novel continues *Vienna*'s legacy, however, by further challenging the dominance of the family as a narrative, biological, and commemorative framework. This destabilization of the family becomes most apparent in the text's engagement with biological definitions of the family and its reproductivity. In her thirties Xane suffers from an ectopic pregnancy, leaving her unable to conceive without the help of IVF. In chapter 5 of *Quasikristalle*, she consults Heike Guttmann, a doctor working in a fertility clinic who helps Xane to finally become pregnant. Through Guttmann's eyes, the narrator provides us with a wry account of the clinic's routine, which reduces the mythology of motherhood and parental bliss to simple biological basics: "Jeder Hunde- oder Bienenzüchter rechnet mit Erfolg oder Misserfolg, das liegt im Wesen der Zucht. Es gibt bessere und schlechtere Jahrgänge und es gibt Ausschuss. Die Natur produziert Unmengen an Ausschuss" (*Q*, 197). Guttmann's comparison to practices of animal breeding and her use of the term "Ausschuss" are problematic from a historical perspective, as I will demonstrate. The terminology of (animal) breeding and reproductive manipulation, however, stresses how the biosciences increasingly intervene in areas that for centuries have been considered "natural," such as the family, genealogy, and reproductivity. Such interventions make us question the boundary between what is and is not "natural" or "normal," along with the cultural valorization of these terms. The chapter shows how notions of naturalness and/or instinctiveness still determine heteronormative perceptions of reproduction and pregnancy, even in the age of biogenetics:

"Menschen, die sich den Zeugungsakt von Biologen entziehen lassen müssen, die des ganzen Mythos' von erfüllendem Sex und daraus folgender Frucht der Liebe bereits verlustig gegangen sind, wollen sich noch weniger krank fühlen als die meisten anderen" (*Q,* 181). Xane also falls prey to this in her irrepressible desire to have a biological child and fulfill heteronormative expectations of femininity, although she already has stepchildren from her husband's former marriage.

The collapse of the family as a stable (in the sense of "natural") narrative and biological framework also affects its role as a medium of transmission. It is only in one of the last chapters in the novel that Xane's background as the descendant of a Holocaust survivor is revealed. Xane engaged with the story of her survivor father, Kurt Molin, on a public level in her role as a "jüdische Intellektuelle" (*Q,* 360) but suffered from a complete lack of communication within the private space of the family, which is admitted by her aging father: "Zugegeben, in dieser Familie hatten sie über Unangenehmes nur gesprochen, wenn es sich gar nicht mehr vermeiden ließ" (*Q,* 334). This lack of direct interaction has led to the development of psychosomatic symptoms: Xane suffered from anxiety attacks as a young woman (*Q,* 345–46), and Kurt Molin is perplexed by the "jüdischer Selbsthass, österreichischer Selbsthass" (*Q,* 340) that plague both of his children. The reader is left guessing as to whether or not Kurt Molin ever discloses his personal trauma of having had to hide in a haystack while being hunted down by German soldiers. He cannot help but revisit the scene on the occasion of his birthday; his daughter notices his absent-mindedness and starts wondering what he is thinking about. He replies, "An etwas aus meiner Kindheit, das liegt vielleicht nahe, an so einem Tag" (*Q,* 353), but he refuses to go into any detail. In a similar vein, it remains unclear whether or not Xane passes the knowledge of her father's fate on to her sons and her grandchildren. Her decision to name her son Amos can be regarded as an endorsement of the Jewish part of her identity, but it remains unclear how (and if) this identity relates to the family trauma or to the Holocaust in general. Amos himself founds a "Nahost-Initiative" (*Q,* 424), which can be read as a commitment to his Jewishness, but one that is based on the future rather than the past. As mentioned, *Quasikristalle*'s narrative construction stresses the fluidity and changeability of personal identities and hence refutes the idea of a stable, monocausal explanation and definition of Xane's personality as the child of a survivor. Xane is a multifaceted character, and her descent from a survivor family is presented as merely one aspect of her personal history, which is revealed quite late into the novel.

In response to this destabilization of the biological family as a narrative and transmissional container, the text stresses alternative forms of affiliation that evoke yet another scientific metaphor, that of the "Wahlverwandtschaft."[24] Menasse's novel is marked by various forms of elective affinity, such as "Patenkind(er)" (*Q*, 63), surrogate and patch-work families, or "Wasserverwandte," who, according to Kurt Molin, represent "das Gegenteil von blutsverwandt" (*Q*, 351). These forms of affiliation, based on choice, appear as the privileged modes of kinship in the text, as they give rise to acts of solidarity and a sense of community that cannot be experienced within the framework of the biological family. This is the case in the relationship between the young Xane Molin and the famous resistance fighter Eli Rozmburk, who adopts Xane as "eine Art Patenkind" (*Q*, 63). While she never fully engages with her father's past and the way in which his lack of communication has left a mark on the family, she maintains quite a close, emotional relationship with Rozmburk. She even produces a documentary about his life and edits a book about him, which points to a willingness to confront, adopt, and transmit his traumatic memories and experiences in place of her father's repressed memories. Xane's indirect engagement with her father's legacy through the character of Eli shows that she steps out of the biological framework of the family but still remains indebted to the psychological dynamics associated with her birth family. Although she leaves biology behind, Xane remains attached to the logic of family and inheritance by extending the "idiom of family" to the realm of ethnicity (all characters involved are Jewish).[25]

At a later stage in her life, Xane forms a similar bond with Nelson, a foreign politician working for the International Criminal Court in The Hague, himself a survivor of a nameless civil war. It is obvious that Nelson acts as yet another incarnation of Xane's father, with whom she entertains an oedipally inflected relationship.[26] While Xane is generally attracted to older, fatherly males (Judith's father; Rozmburk; Hugo Bernays; her husband, Mor Braun; and Nelson), her links to Rozmburk and Nelson are motivated by her descent from a survivor family. *Quasikristalle* therefore explores the implications of affiliative forms of remembering against the backdrop of the breakdown of the family as a biological, narrative, and transmissional unit. Nonbiological forms of affiliation promise to secure the future of Holocaust memories and end the harmful rule of identity politics that still dominate contemporary memory discourses. Landsberg, for example, claims that "prosthetic memories are transportable and there-fore challenge more traditional forms of memory that are premised on claims of authenticity, 'heritage,' and ownership."[27] Menasse's text, how-ever, enables us to question some of the assumptions underpinning the popular notions of "affiliative" or "prosthetic" (post)memory that promise to move beyond the essentializing frameworks of the family, ethnicity, and/or the nation but ultimately extend these attachments to a larger (ethnic) group that is assumed to function *like a family* (Hirsch) or over-look the complexities involved in the production of identification and empathy (Landsberg).

Menasse's text presents acts of affiliation as neither accidental nor unconditional but as predicated on the strong bonds of ethnicity or a shared legacy of trauma. The work demonstrates that the communities Xane enters into are premised on a preexisting and very strong affinity created by her sense of Jewishness, her relationship with her father, and her status as a descendant of survivors. This contradicts Alison Landsberg, in particular, who assumes that the identification with mass-mediated depictions of trauma is automatic, unconditional, and universal. Yet Landsberg's theory fails to explain *why exactly* people should identify with an experience—or rather the artistic representation of an experience—that is in no way connected to their lives, memories, or identities.

Landsberg seems to overlook the fact that the possibility of identification and the production of empathy depend on personal disposition, but even more so on culturally and ideologically informed sensibilities. Empathy is something that needs to be learned, and as such it can be stimulated or blocked, proving itself susceptible to individual or collective manipulation. This is also the view adopted by Susan Sontag in her famous study *Regarding the Pain of Others* (2003). Sontag demonstrates that in an age of oversaturation with mediatized images, our attention and our empathy have become scarce resources. For this reason, the media—and war photography in particular—install hierarchies of suffering, often informed by Eurocentrism and racist prejudice, that guide our (in)ability to acknowledge someone else's pain and inform practices of representation: "These examples illustrate the determining influence of photographs in shaping what catastrophes and crises we pay attention to, what we care about, and ultimately what evaluations are attached to these conflicts."[28] Landsberg's theory simply ignores these multiple processes of filtering and exclusion that determine which traumas are made available for representation—and thus identification—in mainstream cinema in the first place. Even if a film is able to foster unconditional empathy, its production, execution, and dissemination employ various mechanisms of exclusion that determine the choice of traumas. Sontag furthermore helps to clarify that practices of identification do not result from acts of mass-mediated witnessing and/or affiliative memory: on the contrary, these acts of affiliation presuppose an already existing sense of belonging (which can be reinforced and consolidated by the mass media), so that we feel addressed by someone else's experience of suffering in the first place.

While thus exploring the potentials and pitfalls of "affiliative" rather than familial postmemories, *Quasikristalle* is not a truly postfamilial Holocaust text. Although the narrative of the family novel is supplanted by the poetics of the quasicrystal, enabling the exploration of alternative, nonbiological routes of transmission, these still depend on the "idiom of family" or familiarity. Xane's connection to Rozmburk and Nelson functions as an extension of the relationship she maintains with her father. The idiom of familiarity is expandable: in the case of Rozmburk this is done by way of ethnicity (they are both Jewish) and in the case of Nelson on the basis of trauma (both he and her father are survivors). Far from engendering unconditional, nonessentialist ways of relating to a history or memory that is not one's own, affiliative or "prosthetic" forms of memory, as they are presented in Menasse's text, therefore strengthen the family as a symbolic resource: the logic of the family and familiarity is transposed from the relatively small realm of the family onto the much larger domains of ethnicity and psychology.

Confronting the "Post-Auschwitz-Ethik-Schwall": Criticisms of "Travelling Trauma"

The affiliative alliances in *Quasikristalle* extend and revalidate the symbolic powers of the family at a time when Holocaust memory and its generations are facing major shifts. Despite this recourse to the family as a symbolic recourse, *Quasikristalle* is certainly not a family novel: the text focuses on the *cultural* aftereffects of the Nazi genocide and approaches the event as a depersonalized and institutionalized "Diskursfiguration."[29] The Holocaust is presented as a thoroughly mediatized and hypermobile "floating signifier"[30] that has traveled through a number of discursive and historical stages. Menasse's novel questions the mobility and omnipresence of the Holocaust icon, which increasingly affects areas that are not directly connected to the German past (such as reproductive medicine, biogenetics, and other genocides across the globe). According to Menasse, the ubiquity of the Holocaust signifier contributes to a "Post-Auschwitz-Ethik-Schwall":

> Es gibt in der deutschen Politik eine Tendenz, die ich übrigens sehr gut verstehen kann, jede große ethische und moralische Entscheidung auf Auschwitz zurückzuführen. Was kann uns Auschwitz lehren, wenn wir über Israel sprechen? Was lehrt es uns, wenn wir über Präimplantationsdiagnostik sprechen? Was lehrt es uns, wenn wir Gewalttäter frühzeitig freilassen wollen? Auschwitz ist ein Bezugspunkt in allen möglichen moralisch-ethischen Fragen. Aber das ist nicht gut und führt oft in die Irre.[31]

Menasse criticizes the universalization of the Holocaust as a common moral touchstone because it depletes the event of significance and historical specificity ("Man kann Auschwitz für fast alles vereinnahmen"),[32] which also diminishes the other instances of violence it is compared to (such as, for example, the Israeli-Palestinian conflict and the Kosovo war). *Quasikristalle* takes a critical look at these de- and recontextualizations of the Holocaust in the chapters that concern Heike Guttmann, the doctor working in a fertility clinic, and Nelson, the civil war survivor. In both cases, Menasse's text scrutinizes the consequences of these discursive cross-fertilizations in a manner that corresponds with recent shifts in the field of transnational memory studies. Scholars have started to distance themselves from the often celebratory accounts that marked early contributions to the field of transnational (Holocaust) memory, adopting a more critical and self-reflexive stance.[33] Recent contributions question the optimistic narrative of progress, reconciliation, and cosmopolitanism that underpinned early accounts of Holocaust memory in the global age,[34] and this skepticism is also detectable in *Quasikristalle*.

The omnipresence of the Holocaust signifier can furthermore provoke a feeling of oversaturation, fueled by the endless repetition and ubiquity of the same images and mantras. What Jennifer Kapczynski has recently described as a growing dissatisfaction with the current "repetitive and circular discourse"[35] had already been explored in the 1970s by Susan Sontag, who provocatively stated, "The same law holds for evil as for pornography. The shock of photographed atrocities wears off with repeated viewings, just as the surprise and bemusement felt the first time one sees a pornographic movie wear off after one sees a few more."[36] Sontag's argument on numbness and anesthetization, which she later revised in *Regarding the Pain of Others* provides the basis for my reading of the second chapter of *Quasikristalle*, which addresses the problem of representational excess and the concomitant feeling of Holocaust fatigue. Both the symbolic omnipresence of the Holocaust in the shape of a moralized and universalized memory icon and its visual overrepresentation in the media and museum culture raise the question of how (and if) we can still meaningfully relate to these events in an age of hypermediation and globalization.

"Es war das immergleiche Problem . . .": From Repression to Representational Excess and Back

The second chapter of *Quasikristalle* focuses on the encounter between Xane and Hugo Bernays, a Holocaust scholar who offers educational tours of Auschwitz. It deals with the increasing mediatization, ritualization, and commodification of Holocaust memory, which have created a climate that seems to preclude any meaningful connection with the past. The Bernays chapter demonstrates that decades of mediatization and discursivation have turned the experiences of the Holocaust into empty signifiers and congealed "icons of destruction"[37] that provoke automated responses while forestalling any meaningful narratives. This is especially vexing for the "generation after," which depends entirely on such mediatizations of the event. The impoverished state of Holocaust remembrance, in which ritualization and iconization hinder the establishment of meaningful relationships with the past, creates painful feelings of frustration that are explored in more detail in Menasse's text. In a similar vein to Stein and Vertlib, however, *Quasikristalle* also explores the realm of fiction as a potential counterspace in which a different, less automatized and formulaic approach to the issues of experience, history, and memory can be developed.

The discursivation and ritualization of Holocaust memory is at the heart of the Bernays chapter, yet it is necessary to differentiate more clearly between the various manifestations of these processes: the history professor Hugo Bernays, for example, symbolizes the incorporation of the Holocaust into historiographical discourse and *Geschichtspolitik*. During his guided tour of Auschwitz the participants are continuously confronted with the fact that all knowledge they can possibly gain is second-hand and part of various cycles of academic and political contestation as well as mediatized debate. Any statement about the events or the site as such is therefore necessarily a citation, overlaid by other intertexts. This is demonstrated by the characters' incessant references to media depictions (Alain Resnais's *Nuit et Brouillard* [1956], Spielberg's *Schindler's List*), public debates, and major historiographical studies (such as works on the David Irving trial, or Christopher Browning's seminal study *Ordinary Men* [1992]), or the works of Bernays himself. This discursivation of the Holocaust is also reflected in the emergence of certain memorial conventions and ritualized emotional responses, which Bernays pejoratively describes as "die wechselnden Moden der Gedenkpropaganda" (*Q*, 80) and "vorfabrizierte Gefühlsstürme" (*Q*, 95). One of the central problems for the participants is that they cannot find any response to Auschwitz as a site that would point beyond these predetermined frames of reference; even before they enter the former death camp, they are already worn down and paralyzed by an excess of knowledge and the proverbial weight of history. Bernays's use of the term "Gedenkpropaganda" also implies the instrumentalization of Holocaust memory, be it for political or for commercial gains. Apart from the culture of so-called *Betroffenheitstourismus*, Bernays is strongly opposed to the sensationalist exploitation of the "einzigartige . . . Sehenswürdigkeit Auschwitz" (*Q*, 93) and practices of *dark tourism*, which thrive on people's fascination with disaster. He furthermore points the finger at academia when claiming that some of his colleagues, such as his lover Pauline Sussman, deliberately choose marketable topics that are likely to cause a stir over the laborious and "wenig belohnte Grundlagenarbeit" (*Q*, 86): "Und es gab die anderen, die auf das leicht Vermarktbare setzten, Bernays nannte das 'Menscheln nach dem Spielberg-Prinzip'" (*Q*, 86).

Further, the Bernays chapter also tackles the dynamics of hypermediation. This connects Menasse's text to Benjamin Stein's novel *Die Leinwand*, which explores issues of authenticity, autobiographical writing, and appropriation in relation to the boundless transmedial travel of

Holocaust memories. Menasse's writing adds a different facet, however, by accentuating the sense of frustration and fatigue that arises from being overwhelmed by an excess of experiences, memories, and images that cannot be integrated into meaningful narratives. This excess is the result of hypermediation, which has created an impenetrable web of representations and references that encompasses documentary material, on the one hand, and Hollywood productions, on the other hand. The ubiquity of certain historical images has led to a state of extreme oversaturation, which corresponds with a feeling of overpowering numbness felt by both Xane and Bernays:

> Was kommt jetzt, fragte sie, und er sagte: Nichts, was du nicht schon gesehen hast.
> Aber will ich es noch einmal sehen?
> Wahrscheinlich nicht. Ich schau es mir nicht mehr an. Ich mach die Augen zu und konzentriere mich auf die Tonspur.
> Warum zeigen sie das überhaupt, flüsterte sie später, als die Leichen mit dem Bagger zusammengeschoben wurden.
> Weil sie glauben, dass es dazugehört. (Q, 77)

Both of them have seen the documentary images showing the liberation of the concentration camps so often that they no longer have a pedagogic (or any sort of) effect. Xane also highlights the conundrum that, by displaying these images without further comment, one eternally repeats the extreme objectification, degradation, and annihilation of the Nazi victims, which might perpetuate the perpetrator narrative: "Es sieht aus wie menschenähnlicher Müll. Eigentlich ist das Nazipropaganda" (Q, 77). The passage therefore questions the alleged power and inherent pedagogic value of displaying these images, especially when their employment is down to a sense of obligation or convention ("Warum zeigen sie das überhaupt . . . / Weil sie glauben, dass es dazu gehört" [Q, 77]). Bernays reacts to this pictorial excess by simply looking away,[38] but Xane rightly remarks that this is, of course, not a solution to the underlying problem of anesthetization.

Susan Sontag's thoughts on atrocity photographs and the issues of empathy/apathy are helpful here: Sontag famously argued that these photographs, although meant to substantiate the "realness" of horrible events and to elicit empathy, actually have the opposite effect if shown repeatedly: "An event known through photographs certainly becomes more real than it would have been if one had never seen the photographs. . . . But after repeated exposure to images it also becomes less real."[39] In *On Photography* (1978) she blames the merciless multiplication of these images in a media culture for the loss of their emotional effect:

> The vast photographic catalogue of misery and injustice throughout the world has given everyone a certain familiarity with atrocity, mak-

ing the horrible seem more ordinary—making it appear familiar, remote . . ., inevitable. At the time of the first photographs of the Nazi camps, there was nothing banal about these images. After thirty years, a saturation point may have been reached.[40]

While Sontag, in 1978, still wondered about whether a saturation point "may have been reached," this is most definitely the case from the perspective of Menasse's twenty-first-century text. Sontag's fear of abrasion and banalization seems all too justified in the light of Xane's and Bernays's exchange and experience. Images of extreme atrocities and suffering are included in the tour as a staple ingredient of a shock-based Holocaust pedagogy, and it is exactly this proliferation in all sorts of contexts—including the museum—that has made them "ordinary" or "familiar." We know these images, we expect to be confronted with them, and we are therefore no longer shocked or surprised.

Sontag later extended and revised her argument in *Regarding the Pain of Others* by clarifying that it is not repetition as such that drains images of their emotional force but rather the particular rhythm of televisual replication:

What looks like callousness has its origin in the instability of attention that television is organized to arouse and to satiate by its surfeit of images. Image-glut keeps attention light, mobile, relatively indifferent to content. Image-flow precludes a privileged image. . . . A more reflective engagement with content would require a certain intensity of awareness—just what is weakened by the expectations brought to images disseminated by the media, whose leaching out of content contributes most to the deadening of feeling.[41]

Sontag suggests that it is not so much the quantity of images but rather the lack of time we have to process and engage with them that causes "callousness." The steady flow of incentives produced by television excludes the possibility of singling out an image and contextualizing it, as it only allows for a hovering type of attention. Viewers do not have time to deepen their understanding of these images, which is why the response remains superficial. The solution to this, according to Sontag, is a different framework of reception that is contemplative and based on a "certain intensity of awareness": "But that would seem to demand the equivalent of a sacred or meditative space in which to look at them."[42] Such spaces are, however, increasingly diminished in a culture of hypermediation, speed, and immediacy. Sontag therefore advocates a withdrawal into the private sphere of reading: "Up to a point, the weight and seriousness of such photographs survive better in a book, where one can look privately, linger over the pictures, without talking."[43] Lingering implies slowness and taking one's time but also a sense of privacy and intimacy. It is here contrasted to the speed of the "image-flow" created by television as a more public or at least a collective medium.[44]

Menasse's text shows that the endless loop of images displayed in the Auschwitz visitor center has exactly the effect described by Sontag: it creates a feeling of "image-glut" that leaves no other option than to look away or keep looking but feel disgusted, as Xane does. Both variants exclude the possibility of empathy, which would require a different, more intimate, setting. The ritualization of Holocaust memory, however, which implicates the museum environment, further hinders the development of such contemplative spaces, as it points the audience's thoughts and feelings into prefabricated directions, dictated by political consensus and/or memorial conventions. Menasse's text does not feature private, intimate spaces of Holocaust memory (the family also fails, as demonstrated earlier on)—none of the characters escape hypermediation, ritualization, and commodification. Nonetheless, *Quasikristalle*, understood as the narrativization of these images and the experience of oversaturation, allows the reader to critically reflect on the current state of Holocaust anesthesia, memory, and pedagogy and escape the loop, at least to an extent. Apart from potentially fostering a different, slower or deeper, mode of attention as a literary text, as suggested by Sontag, the novel achieves this by way of multiperspectivity and metadiscursivity: the text's quasicrystalline and multiperspectival approach to Holocaust remembrance and representation arguably breaks with the monotony and uniformity of mass-mediatized images, instead highlighting the unevenness of memorial processes. Further to this, the text metamemorially depicts the memory of the event in a number of shapes and stages, thus foregrounding its historicity as well as its reach into the present and the future. This works against the naturalizing tendencies that Sontag ascribes to mass-mediated atrocity pictures, which make depictions of mass violence appear "familiar" and/or "inevitable." *Quasikristalle* thus replaces the numbing effects of the image loop and memorial routinization with the metadiscursive capabilities of the literary text. In line with Stein's and Vertlib's approaches, an ethics and aesthetics of self- and metareflexivity thus emerges as a possible response to some of the issues that arise from Holocaust hypermediation.

Whereas the documentary images in *Quasikristalle* have become "unreal" in Sontag's sense, the Hollywood depictions also gloss over the reality of events, albeit in a different manner: while documents become less and less effective, the authority of mass-mediated representations actually increases to such an extent that their visual authenticity seems greater than that of the original footage. They even have the power to supplant the historical facts, as Bernays points out:

> Die normalen Touristen . . . sahen diesen Querriegel von einem Tor, das sie längst aus Kino und Fernsehen kannten, auch wenn es dort meistens ein Nachbau war, und gruselten sich bei der Vorstellung, dass die vielen hunderttausenden Opfer erst durch dieses Tor

gefahren und dann aus den Viehwaggons herausgebrüllt worden
waren. Doch das stimmte nicht. Die längste Zeit waren sie woanders
angekommen, an der sogenannten Judenrampe, aber was machte das
schon für einen Unterschied. (Q, 93–94)

The paradoxical fact that in an age of remediation the mass-mediated
representations of an event become the yardstick for measuring its "realness" has been explored by Slavoj Žižek in his essay on 9/11,[45] and Sontag
makes similar observations in connection to the World Trade Center
attacks.[46] In relation to the issue of contemporary Holocaust memory in
Menasse's text, these findings leave us with the somewhat demoralizing
conclusion that there is, in fact, nothing (more) we can "learn" from the
image. The documentary footage has lost its emotional force owing to our
overexposure to it, while its informative or evidentiary value is diminished
by the paradoxical "authenticity effects" exerted by mass-mediated images.
The following response by one of the younger members of the tour group
reflects this problem:

> Der junge Mann, im Grunde ein halbes Kind, hatte seine Kamera auf
> die nach innen gekrümmten Zaunpfähle aus Beton gerichtet, zwis-
> chen denen sich der Stacheldraht bauschte, und dabei gemurmelt:
> Das schaut gut aus, wie die Pfosten die Köpfe hängen lassen. Und
> Xane konnte nicht anders, als ihm sarkastisch zuzustimmen: Ja, und
> ich finde, das "Arbeit macht frei" ist hier auch besonders schön
> geschmiedet. (Q, 77)

The young man appears to have replaced the urge to learn something
from the image or to convey a message with purely aesthetic concerns. He
judges the trip to Auschwitz on the basis of the visual appeal of his snap-
shots because authenticity is no longer an issue. His photographs in all
likelihood reproduce the polished aesthetics of Hollywood productions
such as *Schindler's List*, rather than the raw authenticity that we usually
expect when viewing images of extreme suffering. This approach leaves
behind (or even reverses) what Sontag identifies as a major conundrum
faced by war photographers: "For the photography of atrocity, people
want the weight of witnessing without the taint of artistry, which is
equated with insincerity or mere contrivance."[47] Artistic ambition, in the
realm of atrocity photography, traditionally provoked accusations of
manipulation or simplification. Yet from a point of view that is historically
far removed from the actual events, artistic ambition takes center stage.
The young man no longer feels personally affected by the events and can
thus reject the ethical obligation to bear witness. His attitude is unbearable
for Xane, who is still embedded in a discourse about representational
appropriateness and tied to the survivor generation by personal and familial bonds, but this is presented by the text as a generationally inflected
position. The example of the young man, which in some respects connects

to the *Yolocaust* debate mentioned in the introduction to this book, leaves the reader wondering how much longer this position will prevail and what alternative responses to the sites of suffering the future might hold.

Bernays and Xane are still participating in a discourse that clearly differentiates between "good" and "bad" (in the sense of "appropriate" and "inappropriate") representations. One of the major tasks that Bernays has set for himself consists in unsettling and shattering the conventions, prefabrications, and exploitative structures that the commodification, hypermediation, and ritualization of Holocaust memory have created. It is not clear if more appropriate responses will emerge from this, although Bernays believes that there is an instinctive (and hence "correct") reaction to a place like Auschwitz that is gradually overwritten by layers of hypermediation and ritualization (*Q*, 80). It is, of course, ironic that he sets out to perform an act of "Diskurs-Demontage,"[48] while relying on the authority that a particular discourse—that of critical pedagogy and scholarship—bestows on him. His educational program employs a mix of shock tactics, demystification, and Brechtian *Verfremdung*, understood as the strategically produced "Abweichung von unseren vorgestanzten Annahmen" (*Q*, 95). But the irony does not end here: Bernays's agenda of myth-shattering Verfremdung is itself part of a routine that he has established as an experienced tour guide: "Breitbeinig, die Daumen in den Gürtelschlaufen, stand er da und spulte seine Erzählung ab, die wie alles, was er in den kommenden Tagen sagen würde, auf das Unterhöhlen vorgefertigter Gefühle zielte" (*Q*, 70). The ironic contrast results from the clash between words that imply routine, planning, and ritualization ("abspulen," "alles, was er in den kommenden Tagen sagen würde") and Bernays's intention to actually expose the prefabricated nature of Holocaust memory and discourse. He openly admits that he is playing a part, relying on tried and tested preventive measures—such as his functional clothing, a strict timetable, and a pregiven itinerary through the concentration camp. His approach seeks to demolish the participants' ritualized patterns of perception and preconceptions, while also channeling and controlling their reactions: "Von allen wurde erwartet, dass sie den Leuten sagten, wo es langging, in jeder, auch der innerlichsten Hinsicht. Bernays's Überzeugung war: Je strenger man loslegte, desto weniger scherten sie später aus, emotional, alkoholisch. So klar geregelt wie Sadomaso" (*Q*, 69). Bernays thus replaces one form of exerting influence and control (by the media and institutionalized politics with its "Gedenkpropaganda," for example) with another, but his own influence is supposed to foster independent and critical thinking.

Quasikristalle suggests that even the most avid and self-aware critic cannot escape the entrapments of discursivity and hypermediation. Any statement about the Holocaust and Auschwitz as a site is exposed as either an intertext or a cliché, and any attempt to break out of this tangle of references is itself condemned to end in routine and ritualization. Not even the site of destruction as such can offer a sense of immediacy, as the topography of Auschwitz, the "scheinbar gut bekannte . . . Ort" (*Q*, 95), is overlaid by preexisting images and (imaginary or actually existing) directives about how to (not) feel and act in this place. This conundrum is in some ways reminiscent of *Vienna*: without the authority of the survivors, the possible perceptions, interpretations, and depictions of the event multiply uncontrollably and/or turn into empty rituals. The chapter is also marked by an unbridgeable gap between the survivors, in this case Eli Rozmburk, and those who did not experience the Holocaust personally. Bernays as well as Xane repeatedly emphasize that Rozmburk's relationship with a site like Auschwitz is not reproducible for them: "Die existenzielle Erfahrung ist nicht nur eine andere, sie hat auch andere Rechte" (*Q*, 94). This quote emphasizes that the survivor, owing to his or her discursive authority, is entitled to a different approach toward Auschwitz and the Holocaust. Bernays, for example, repeatedly points out that there are some forms of extreme black humor that can only be used by those who actually lived through the hell of the concentration camps (*Q*, 68, 76). The "generation after" is therefore doubly limited in their response to the past—there are some discursive modes they cannot resort to, while others have become completely oversaturated, empty, and meaningless. As the entrapment of the "generation after" is at center of the chapter, it is not surprising that the survivor remains silent in Menasse's text. Eli Rozmburk, the Auschwitz survivor who was supposed to guide the tour, falls ill unexpectedly and very probably dies shortly after, which is why the "Ersatzmann" (*Q*, 59) Bernays takes Eli's place. On a larger scale, Rozmburk's illness foreshadows the dying out of the survivor generation as a whole and points to the future of disembodied Holocaust memory. *Quasikristalle* demonstrates how this future will rely on the further mediatization and institutionalization of Holocaust memory, while outlining the difficulties that arise when trying to connect these free-floating memories to the lived experiences of later generations.

Faced with this impossibility of a meaningful, nonformulaic connection to the past, Menasse's text leaves Bernays—and possibly the reader—with an overarching feeling of *Holocaust fatigue*: "Er wurde müde und stumpf, wenn er nur daran dachte, an all die Querelen und Kämpfe, an die unzähligen Ausschüsse, in denen er selbst gesessen war" (*Q*, 78). This sense of frustration derives from tedium ("Vielleicht war es einfach genug"; *Q*, 89), and a sense of disgust: "Diese ekelhaften Gefühle aus zweiter Hand" (*Q*, 94).[49] In the absence of any personal connection to the event, the characters are confronted with an excess of stories, images, conventions, and debates that block access to the past. This oversaturation also hinders the expression of empathy; in Bernays's case, it is replaced by a detached sarcasm, while the other characters are so determined by their preexisting knowledge and memorial conventions that they simply do not know what to feel.

For Susan Sontag, the reception of these images and sites requires a different approach: she stresses the importance of a contemplative inwardness and a certain sense of intimacy. Sontag also observes, however, that such modes are diametrically opposed to the incessant stream of images in a hypermediated culture. The automatization and calcification caused by commemorative rules and rituals further undermine the very conditions of a more contemplative attitude, as they favor mechanical, well-rehearsed responses over more thorough engagement. While I agree with Sontag's argument, we need to keep in mind its broader political implications: if the withdrawal into the private, individualized sphere of reading or contemplation is the only response to hypermediated "image-glut" and fatigue, what does this mean for a collective culture of (Holocaust) remembrance? Is it at all possible to foster a more contemplative culture of remembrance on the collective level? Or will the future of Holocaust memory consist of ever more pluralized and individualized approaches, which practice inwardness on the smallest possible scale? There is an interesting parallel to Vladimir Vertlib's text here, which also pits the intimacy of the reader-text relationship against the unresponsiveness of broader cultural and discursive frameworks. The withdrawal into the private sphere thus emerges as a possible antidote to the problems of memorial ossification and oversaturation—but how viable is this alternative?

Uneven Memorial Development in the Global Age

It is necessary to contextualize the Bernays chapter within the broader structure of *Quasikristalle* by considering transnational or globalized Holocaust memory: the Auschwitz tour is framed by two chapters that are set in Austria, the first during Xane's adolescence and the second a few years after her meeting with Bernays. Both chapters tackle the repression of Holocaust memory and thus provide a counterpoint to the Bernays chapter. The segment dealing with Xane's teenage years tells a coming-of-age story, focusing on sexual awakening, the first confrontation with death, and, as a result, "das Ende der Kindheit" (*Q*, 48). Xane's friendship with Judith and Claudia, and the way it changes when Claudia dies unexpectedly, feature prominently. Judith's dysfunctional family relations contrast with Xane's rather carefree, petit-bourgeois upbringing. The true cause of Judith's family troubles—her father is verbally and physically abusive, and her mother, Zsuzsa, is mentally unstable—is never made explicit, but it seems to involve the issue of Jewishness. While Zsuzsa's and her daughters' ethnicity is never openly addressed, the text suggests that they are Jewish, as indicated by the children's first names: Judith and Salome. Judith's father broke free from his own Nazi parents because they rejected his wife, probably based on her ethnicity: "Weil sie Nazis gewesen waren und es dennoch wagten, seine junge Frau abzulehnen" (*Q*, 9). This suggests a connection between the family conflicts and Austria's past. Austria's private and broader political culture is obviously still marked by repression and the persistence of anti-Semitic stereotypes. The tensions between the Jewish and the Gentile parts of society are not publicly addressed and worked through, which is why they are acted out within the private space of the family. The father's aggression toward Judith may actually target her and her mother's Jewishness, which prevents them from leading a "normal" life. Judith's mother reacts to the unaddressed collective and personal aggression by escaping into mental illness, which also allows her to protect herself from her husband's bouts of violence.

It is not just the Gentile environment that rejects Zsuzsa's Jewish origins, however; she also struggles with them herself. Judith's first day at school is described as follows:

> Am ersten Schultag . . . hatte Judiths Mutter wieder einmal die Haare ihrer Tochter verleugnen wollen. Sie begann frühmorgens mit der Prozedur, die kaltes Wasser, Zitronensaft, scharfe Kämme und Brenneisen erforderte. Judith schrie und tobte, ihrer Mutter rutschte mehrmals die Hand aus, wie man die Ohrfeigen damals nannte, das Kleid wurde schmutzig, weil Judith sich zwischendurch am Boden wälzte. (*Q,* 12–13)

The violence of this interaction suggests that Zsuzsa is not merely attempting to enhance her daughter's appearance. The use of the peculiar word "verleugnen" implies that Zsuzsa is trying to disavow something that goes beyond the shape and texture of Judith's hair. The political implications of hair(styling) have been debated in the context of Afro-textured hair,[50] and I want to propose that the fight about Judith's hair—which apparently looks like "rote Zuckerwatte" (*Q,* 13)—also evokes the issue of racial/ethnic otherness. Both frizzy and red hair are part of iconographic traditions of anti-Judaism and anti-Semitism, which associated the Jew's body with what were perceived as undesirable attributes.[51] Zsuzsa's attempts to violently "verleugnen" Judith's hair thus appears as a reaction to such racial stereotyping. By trying to eradicate any visible signs of her daughter's Otherness, she is either motivated by internalized oppression or by the desire to protect her daughter from experiences of discrimination similar to her own. In any case, the first chapter of *Quasikristalle* paints a bleak picture of Austrian postwar society, in which the refusal to collectively deal with the past leads to intergenerational violence and mental illness.

Following Bernays's exploration of memorial oversaturation and Holocaust fatigue, chapter 3 of *Quasikristalle* returns to Austrian society and the issue of repression. Here we meet Ludwig Tschoch, an engineer and member of the Viennese bourgeoisie, who rents out one of his prestigious apartments in Vienna's Hietzing district to Xane in her late twenties or early thirties. Tschoch emerges as the caricature of a certain type in

Austrian society—he is an overly Catholic, crypto-fascist, homo- and xeno-phobic philistine with voyeuristic tendencies. In the course of the chapter we find out that Tschoch prefers to spend most of his time in his attic, where he keeps several ferrets as pets. The attic features as a prominent topos in recent discourse about the German and the Austrian past,[52] as a space that harbors those aspects of a personal and collective history that have been shut out, expelled, or suppressed.[53] This is no different in the case of Tschoch, whose political convictions become abundantly clear when we find out that he has secretly named one of his pets Adolf (*Q,* 129). The young Tschoch and his mother also stood idly by and witnessed the deportation of a young man during the war period. Xane, who is by now a young and rebellious documentary filmmaker with a reputation as a "Nestbeschmutzerin," uncovers this hidden history. In her opinion, Tschoch represents everything that is wrong with Austria's postwar soci-ety: "Dieses Selbstgefällige und Geschichtslose, weil sich die meisten Österreicher immer noch weigerten, sich an die Verbrechen zu erinnern, die direkt vor ihrer Haustür, ja vor ihren Augen stattgefunden hatten, stattdessen bekreuzigten sie sich und fütterten fröhlich ihre Frettchen" (*Q,* 135). The text suggests that Tschoch is not even aware of the extent of his complicity, and when the entire family supports his ignorance by denounc-ing Xane's "linken Schmafu" (*Q,* 135), any attempt at confronting the past is nipped in the bud.

The memorial excess in the Bernays chapter is thus contrasted with two different kinds of repression: one concerns Judith's Jewish-Austrian family, which tries to fit in with the mnemo-politics of the Gentile Austrian environment; the other is symptomatic of certain attitudes in postwar Austrian—and especially Viennese-bourgeois—society. The contrast between oversaturation and repression can be read in terms of a historical development when comparing the Judith and the Bernays chapters. The chapters are separated by a span of approximately fifteen years, implying that Holocaust discourse has obviously moved from one extreme (total silence) to the other (overexposure). The Bernays and Tschoch segments are, however, set at roughly the same time (probably two or three years have passed between Xane's excursion to Auschwitz and the episode in Tschoch's mansion), so that the contrast between oversaturation and repression here exposes the backwardness of Austrian society. But these clashes also point to a pluralization of Holocaust memories and the coex-istence of various stages of memorialization as part of an uneven memorial development: the Bernays chapter is set within a transnational, scholarly community, caught up in what is ultimately an elitist discourse on the Holocaust, concerned with an excess of images and knowledge. Meanwhile, the chapter focusing on Tschoch gives us an insight into the bourgeois Viennese milieu of the Hietzing district, where, several decades after the war, the unholy alliance between prescribed amnesia, Catholicism, and anti-Semitism persists. Both the Bernays and the Tschoch chapters are set in the mid-to-late 2000s, so at a time when a globalized culture of Holocaust remembrance had emerged. Yet *Quasikristalle* reveals that the transnational, hypermediated mobility of Holocaust memories is always influenced and governed by local factors, and that different or even contradictory stages of remembrance—ranging from repression to oversaturation—can indeed coexist. This points to a major problem with globalized Holocaust memory that has so far remained underexamined: namely, that the rhetoric of the "global icon" implies a temporal and memorial homogeneity that does not, in fact, exist.[54] Menasse's text furthermore highlights that the transnational mobility of Holocaust memories alone is not enough to foster new cultures of remembrance, understanding, or empathy, as suggested by Daniel Levy and Natan Sznaider. The Tschoch chapter shows that the globalization of Holocaust memory in the shape of a "floating" signifier can actually coincide with a culture of silence, repression, and continued anti-Semitism.

De- and Recontextualizations of the Holocaust Signifier

While the Bernays chapter is concerned mainly with the visual omnipresence of the Holocaust icon, *Quasikristalle* also critically examines the symbolic dominance of the Holocaust signifier, which increasingly migrates into discourses that are not directly or necessarily connected to the German past. Criticizing the "Post-Auschwitz-Ethik-Schwall," the author Menasse objects to the transformation of the Holocaust into a common moral touchstone: "Auschwitz ist ein Bezugspunkt in allen möglichen moralisch-ethischen Fragen."[55] The chapters dealing with Heike Guttmann and the politician Nelson reflect the possible consequences of this transformation. They feature a stage of Holocaust remembrance in which the personal links to the past have vanished, as the discursivation of the events has become all-encompassing. As a result, Dr. Heike Guttmann no longer sees the legacy of the Holocaust as a personal burden but as a nuisance:

> Die deutschen Gesetze! Rigide bis dort hinaus, das Embryonenschutzgesetz, man darf fast gar nichts, im internationalen Vergleich, sogar die Österreicher sind liberaler. . . . In Deutschland aber wirkt der Holocaust fort und fort, ethisch jedenfalls, jede Entscheidung wird darauf bezogen, alles Tun muss sich vom Tun der Nazis maximal unterscheiden. (*Q,* 191)

Guttmann's frustration is different from the experience Bernays and Xane undergo at Auschwitz. They are unable to empathize in a culture of mass-mediated oversaturation, and they suffer from their inability to express any feelings that go beyond the level of ritual, routine, or cliché. Guttmann, by contrast, no longer deems it necessary to feel anything about events that occurred in the distant past—it is time to move on. In her view, Germany's cultural fixation on the Holocaust hinders its future progress, especially in the realm of science and reproductive medicine. Guttmann also suggests that Germany's exaggerated concern about the past produces injustices in the present: under Germany's embryo protection law doctors are largely prohibited from selecting embryos for IVF procedures (so-called *Präimplantationsdiagnostik*). They therefore tend to implant more embryos than in other countries to increase the chances of pregnancy, a practice that often leads to "unnötig vielen Mehrlingsschwangerschaften," "wofür die deutsche Regierung folgerichtig wieder Mutterkreuze einführen sollte" (*Q*, 191), as Guttmann remarks sarcastically.

She thus echoes Menasse's personal concerns about the "Post-Auschwitz-Ethik-Schwall,"[56] which target the universalization of the Holocaust as a moral and ethical benchmark. It is, however, essential to differentiate clearly between Menasse and her fictional character Guttmann. In the above-quoted interview, Menasse is primarily concerned with the decontextualization of the Holocaust, which she fears may encourage banalization and instrumentalization ("Das ist zu einfach und banalisiert die Zusammenhänge").[57] If every political or legal decision and action is related and compared to the Holocaust, this leads to a homogenizing deflation that no longer acknowledges the historical specificities of either the Nazi period and the genocide of the Jews or the events it is compared to. Menasse's mention of the Kosovo war highlights that such Holocaust comparisons can also be used to justify politically questionable operations and aims. Lucy Bond, for example, has shown how the invocation of Holocaust analogies in the context of 9/11 was used to justify the military policies of the Bush administration, while at the same time contributing to an undifferentiated universalization of Jewish suffering.[58] She criticizes this particular comparative approach, based on analogy and aimed "towards the occlusion of difference," by "taking the specifics of one story as a blueprint for a universal experience of suffering."[59] While Levy and Sznaider use the analogy between the genocide committed during the Yugoslav wars and that of Europe's Jews to promote the ethical productivity of the Holocaust template,[60] Menasse's comments are more in line with recent critical developments in transcultural and transnational memory discourse: scholars such as Bond, Dirk Moses, and Michael Rothberg increasingly opt for a more differentiated and critical approach toward comparative and analogical practices of Holocaust memory.[61]

These are, however, not the concerns driving Guttmann, who simply wants to move on. Menasse's text criticizes this position, showing that although Guttmann denies any connection with the past, she uses extremely loaded terms such as "soziale Auslese" (*Q*, 192), "Ausschuss" (*Q*, 197), and "Aussondern" (*Q*, 202). Her choice of words evokes the register of Nazi eugenics and Social Darwinism, the latter of which shapes Guttmann's professional self-understanding and her views on reproductive medicine. She has implemented her own system of selection, based on social status and psychological fitness. She openly admits that the high costs caused by IVF treatment, half of which have to be covered by the patients, contribute to a form of "soziale Auslese," which she welcomes because this practice makes her working life easier. She also introduced a "System von Labilitätspunkten" (Q, 194–95) to minimize the drama that usually follows a failed treatment. She has divided her female patients into three groups—robust and optimistic, average, and unstable—and proceeds by notifying the "weak" ones first, "dann hat sie es hinter sich" (Q, 195). Guttmann furthermore compares her own work with practices of "Zucht," which necessarily produce "Ausschuss" (Q, 197), further suggesting a reemergence of Darwinist thinking. This does not, of course, mean that Heike Guttmann is an advocate of Nazi eugenics; rather, the text makes a subtle comment about the uncanny longevity of some aspects of Nazi ideology and the ways in which certain domains of present-day society (such as reproductive medicine) unwittingly resort to Social Darwinist terminology, although Guttmann herself is unable to spot these continuities. In her case, "the survival of the fittest" and the right to reproduce have become dependent on economic status and psychological suitability. She herself admits that these requirements favor a certain white and "biodeutsche" clientele. Guttmann's judgments are further questioned by her racist and stereotyping remarks about "Aufstiegstürken" (Q, 182), an "undeutsch temperamentvolle Ambulanzärztin" she once encountered (Q, 203), and her American dinner guests, who should be handled with care: "Manchmal sind sie Vegetarier oder Juden, aber danach kann man ja vorher schlecht fragen" (Q, 205). Evidently, the omnipresence of the Holocaust signifier has not eradicated existing mechanisms of stereotyping and racism, and this is, arguably, what Menasse's criticism of the "Post-Auschwitz-Ethik-Schwall" is aimed at: the universalization of the Holocaust as an ethical and moral benchmark neither helps to prevent future conflicts (as is shown in the Nelson chapter) nor does it contribute to a more cosmopolitan, neighborly approach toward the Other, as is demonstrated in the chapters concerning Guttmann and Tschoch. What is more, the omnipresence of Holocaust comparisons and the automatic discursive maneuvers they invoke might actually hinder "the formation of a clear view of present-day conditions" and "reflective encounter,"[62] as Jennifer Kapczynski has suggested. Menasse's assessment also points back to Vladimir Vertlib's *Das besondere Gedächtnis der Rosa Masur*, which calls into doubt the integrative potential of institutionalized Holocaust remembrance, which fulfills a redemptive function for Germany's collective psyche while leaving certain mechanisms of exclusion and Othering untouched. It might be useful here to consider Amos Goldberg's differentiation between the Holocaust as a "reaffirming memory,"[63] which essentially serves to stabilize a certain Western (European) self-image and produces its own set of exclusions and as an "ethical-political" approach "that establishes a new form of normative legitimacy according to which individuals and societies are enabled to regulate their relations in a more equitable and moral manner."[64] While both fall under the category of globalized Holocaust memory, they produce very different effects, which reaffirms my point that the one-sidedly progressive narrative behind discourses of transnational Holocaust remembrance needs to be challenged.

It is exactly this "ethical-political" approach that is under scrutiny in chapter 6 of *Quasikristalle*, which centers on the unrealized love affair between Xane and the foreign politician Nelson. At the time Xane meets him, Nelson, who lost his entire family in a nameless civil war, is an internationally renowned politician and media personality working for the International Criminal Court in The Hague. Nelson's traumatized mind keeps recalling the image of a "großen, sternförmigen Blutfleck an der Hausmauer, der wohl zum Großteil von seiner Frau und dem jüngsten Kind stammte" (*Q*, 223). This harrowing image can be read as an illustration of "multidirectional" or "palimpsestic" memory, as the star-shaped stain superimposes the violence Nelson has experienced with a key symbol of anti-Semitic oppression and persecution, the yellow star. The Nelson chapter underscores how Holocaust memory informs other discourses in a "multidirectional" fashion, particularly the public perception and collective processing of other instances of extreme violence. Holocaust memory, in the Nelson segment, is therefore present solely through its aftereffects and recontextualizations in two key areas: the iconization of the survivor figure, on the one hand, and the legal afterlives of the Nazi genocide, on the other hand.

Nelson's character is used to scrutinize the iconization of the survivor figure in the wake of Holocaust discourse. When Xane first meets Nelson, he is already an internationally renowned politician and activist, who regularly features in all the big newspapers and is a contender for the Nobel Peace Prize. Nelson is well aware of the function he fulfills in public debates and of the demands that this position places on him: "Er hatte schon früh bemerkt, dass ihn das, was geschehen war, von den anderen Menschen glatt abtrennte, nicht nur aus seiner, sondern auch aus deren Sicht. Er war der Gezeichnete, dem man aus frommen Glauben an seine bannende Wirkung zuhörte, sobald er zu sprechen begann" (*Q*, 233). Nelson is partly a living testament to the atrocities he experienced, along with the possibility of survival, and partly a totem whose magic might fight off future atrocities. Such overdetermination of the survivor figure in media culture and public debate is unthinkable without Holocaust discourse and the iconization of prominent survivor activists as Elie Wiesel.[65] Nelson's attitude toward this quasi-religious role is ambivalent: while his prominence ensures that his and other survivors' voices are heard—which was emphatically not the case in the immediate aftermath of the events—it also forces him to withhold certain aspects of his personality in public. He is famous and well respected for what he represents in public discourse—his totemic quality—and is thus under constant pressure to perform a neatly prescribed role, slipping into what he describes as his "Außenhaut" (Q, 225) whenever he is among other people. His position also means that he can show no signs of weakness in public, as this would compromise his image as a monument of resilience and survival: "Aber er selbst musste vital wirken, unverdrängbar" (Q, 220). This split between the public and the private Nelson becomes most apparent in his relationship with Xane, which is intimate, personal, and playful when they are in private but becomes formal and distanced as soon as they have an audience.[66]

The rise of the survivor figure in modern culture is, of course, aided by the mass media, which remediate and popularize certain stories to the extent that they become iconic. Nelson's relationship with the media is strained; he reproaches them for operating with sensationalist and simplifying "vorgefertigte Bezugsrahmen" (Q, 225) that do not recognize the complexities of his and other people's stories of survival. This choice of words is reminiscent of the critical tone ringing through the Bernays chapter, and a similar sense of fatigue permeates some of Nelson's observations. Shortly after he meets Xane, Nelson gets involved in a major trial at The Hague, which concerns one of the main perpetrators responsible for the war crimes that wiped out his family. While he and other survivors follow this trial with mixed feelings—they want justice, but at the same time they know that the proceedings could be potentially retraumatizing—the media simply exploit the case:

> Ihre Geschichten in den internationalen Zeitungen waren nicht zu übersehen, und nicht die blutigen Schlagzeilen, mit denen man diese Geschichten versah. Am wenigsten zu übersehen war das Foto dieses Mannes, dem Nelson nie selbst begegnet war. Es schien nur ein einziges zu geben, das klein und groß, schwarz-weiß und bunt gedruckt und gesendet wurde. Die Eintönigkeit der immergleichen Aufnahme war eine Qual für sich. (Q, 219–20)

Nelson is tired out by the ubiquity and endless repetition of the same image, which keeps confronting him with the man responsible for the crimes that killed his family. This pictorial excess weakens the indexical power of the photograph to the extent that it no longer refers to an exterior reality, creating what Sontag described as a "surfeit of images."[67] Nelson is also repelled by the sensationalism of the press, which manifests itself at various points: when, at a later stage of the trial, Nelson faints in the courtroom, the press reads this as a reaction to the "Anblick der Bestie" (Q, 225). This turns Nelson into a passive victim with no agency, while also perpetuating problematic notions of perpetration. The Nelson chapter thus critically examines the discourses and media conventions that have developed in the wake of a globalized culture of Holocaust remembrance by demonstrating how it has contributed to an extreme iconization of the survivor figure in contemporary culture. Menasse's novel questions the effects of this iconization, which favor a quasi-religious cult around the survivor figure while also highlighting the responsibility of the media and certain journalistic practices in this process, which are portrayed as reductive and sensationalist.

Menasse's text considers not only the media and cultural but also the legal aftereffects of the Holocaust, which explains the importance of the trial and the International Criminal Court in the Nelson chapter. The fact that the war crimes Nelson has experienced are subject to a legal investigation in The Hague clearly evokes the Holocaust. It is a widely held view that the moral shock caused by the Nazi persecution and extermination of the Jews gave rise to the "human rights revolution,"[68] which propelled the development and implementation of international human rights law and international criminal law.[69] What are nowadays known as war crimes, crimes against humanity, and genocide are currently all under the jurisdiction of the International Criminal Court, which plays an important role in the Nelson chapter, probably owing to its implication in the (after)history of the Holocaust. The prominence of the ICC trial in the Nelson chapter raises questions about the "legal legacies" of the Holocaust by asking whether the tools that have been installed since the Second World War really serve their main purpose—bringing justice and preventing future genocides. *Quasikristalle* arguably adopts the perspective that the legal proceedings at The Hague can only partly address the injustice at stake. The Nelson chapter shows that while the trial may well bring recognition and justice, the price the survivors pay in the judicial process is high: Nelson is completely drained by the proceedings, which attack his "letzte . . . Reserven" (*Q,* 221), and one of his best friends, who is also a survivor, ends up taking his own life because he simply cannot relive the painful past all over again. Part of the problem lies with the procedures and modes of narration that a court trial is based on. Nelson describes the time of the trial as "die zähe Zeit" (*Q,* 226), since it is based on the exact reconstruction and picking apart of every single detail in the process of uncovering reliable evidence. In the eyes of Nelson, however, this evidence is extremely difficult to obtain, owing to the nature of the crime:

> Aber diese Eruptionen soll man anschließend so detailliert untersuchen wie die vollständigen Flugbahnen aller Einzelteile einer Granate? Man bräuchte die millionenfache Zeit dafür, und selbst wenn man sie hätte, verfälschte ihr Vergehen die Wahrheit in einem tieferen Sinn. Der Scherge weiß es selbst nicht mehr, bei all dem

Adrenalin, das in ihm pochte, aber der Zeuge muss es wissen, wer zuerst umgebracht wurde, das Kleinkind oder die Großmutter. Und er muss beweisen, dass er es aus seinem Versteck so genau sehen konnte. (*Q,* 226)

The court trial requires analytical modes of narration that are predicated on cause and effect and a precise and chronological sequence of events. Nelson points out, however, that this is exactly not how the victims of mass atrocities experience the events. They perceive the killing as a murderous chaos and have probably blanked out substantial parts of it. The court is thus bound by a procedure that is completely alien to the subject it is investigating. This causes a clash between the modes of narration dictated by the framework of the trial and alternative approaches that reflect the victims' subjective experience. Nelson also remarks that the legal approach can be humiliating for the victims if they are put under more scrutiny than the perpetrators because of their inability to provide the reliable evidence that is required.

Thomas Buergenthal addresses the problem that criminal trials tend (and need to) focus on the individual perpetrator, leaving untouched those "societal forces that made crimes against humanity and genocide possible" in the first place.[70] While single perpetrators and smaller groups of instigators directly responsible for the atrocities can be put on trial and punished, the structural and systemic dimensions of genocide cannot be addressed in court. Buergenthal therefore speaks out on behalf of truth commissions, which can adopt a more comprehensive angle while also enabling different and conflicting modes of narration. Nelson himself also doubts the court's ability: "Es gibt nichts mehr zu sagen, mir fällt nichts mehr ein, sie werden ihn verurteilen, aber juristisch wird es an einem seidenen Faden hängen. . . . Ein Kompromiss. Für die einen zu viel, für die anderen zu wenig" (*Q,* 231). At the same time, Nelson acknowledges that the collective recognition of suffering via the court trial is essential for the victims and a necessary step in the process of healing.

Considering the "legal legacies" of the Holocaust and genocide, *Quasikristalle* therefore arrives at a mixed judgment. The forms of legislation and jurisdiction that have developed in the aftermath of the Holocaust have certainly not helped to prevent future genocides. The novel also questions whether they can fully address the injustices at stake, as the modes of narration dictated by the courtroom environment clash with the ways in which the events took place and were perceived by the victims. As Lawrence Langer has put it in the context of the Holocaust, the "the logic of law can never make sense to the illogic of extermination."[71] Commenting on the afterlives and commemoration of the Rwandan genocide, Karen Remmler has also made the important point that the "affective remnants of the experience of genocide" often remain unaddressed within the frameworks of state-sponsored memory templates that are often under-pinned by Western sources of funding and Western notions of "working through" traumatic pasts.[72] Echoing Langer's and Remmler's concerns, Menasse's novel also points to the need for a more comprehensive approach to transitional justice, although truth commissions, reparation programs, etc., are not mentioned in the text. The novel's stance also raises the question of whether and how the literary text might provide alternative forms of narration and commemoration that usefully complement the courtroom trial and other state-driven transitional justice measures. A work of fiction might be able to more adequately accommodate alternative, multiperspectival, and nonchronological modes of experience that reflect the network of victims, perpetrators, and bystanders involved. It might also be able to provide space for the "emotional residue" of large-scale violence,[73] which includes the traumatically repressed or the collectively forgotten. As such, fiction can accommodate conflicting perspectives, while at the same time catering to the different paces and modes of "working through" a traumatic past. The act of storytelling was a crucial part of transitional justice initiatives such as, for example, the South African Truth and Reconciliation Commission (TRC), as creating a narrative allows the victims to not only make sense of their experience but also to regain some sense of agency. These testimonies are, of course, very different from an artistic engagement with the event, but they point to a general need to supplement legal discourse with other forms of expression, as is also suggested by Menasse's text. Despite these reservations, *Quasikristalle* asserts that, for the victims, there is nothing worse than the collective misrecognition of their suffering—a flawed system of international jurisdiction is thus still better than no such system.

The Fading of Holocaust Memory?

Menasse's metamemorial novel traces and fictionalizes the development of Holocaust discourse from the extremes of oversaturation and repression to the transformation of the event into a free-floating signifier that is used as a blueprint in various cultural, political, and legal contexts. Menasse herself criticizes the emergence of the Holocaust as a "travelling trauma," and I suggest that the novel *Quasikristalle* adopts a similar perspective. While the Guttmann chapter shows that the omnipresence of the Holocaust can lead to a defensive reaction that leaves racist stereotypes untouched, the Nelson chapter explores and scrutinizes some of the aftereffects of institutionalized Holocaust discourse—such as the iconization of the survivor figure and the international persecution of genocidal crimes.

Most of the chapters considered so far—Judith, Bernays, Tschoch, Guttmann—concentrate on the (over)presence of the Holocaust signifier and/or analogy and the characters' reactions to this. This is not the case in the Nelson chapter, in which the Holocaust is no longer directly represented and remembered but is implied via its discursive and legal aftereffects. This process is taken even further in chapter 12 of *Quasikristalle*, which explores the issue of geronticide. Shanti, an investigative journalist, caused an uproar with the publication of a book that uncovered the systematic killing of older people in retirement homes, either by their relatives or by staff members. Shanti's discoveries are particularly explosive because the chapter is set in a dystopian (but possible) future in which the state-sponsored care system has broken down, making the mass murder of older people economically attractive for both private persons and institutions. Although Shanti has withdrawn from the public sphere in the wake of the scandal, she is sought out by a desperate man who is being hunted down for supposedly having killed his Aunt Mia but asserts his innocence. He partly blames Shanti for having created an "Atmosphäre von Verdacht und Denunziation" (*Q*, 389). Shanti reluctantly agrees to help him and comes across an organization advocating the right to die ("Sterbehilfeorganisation"), which is somehow connected to Aunt Mia. While she is talking to her police contact, Inspector Karimi, he uses the word "Todesengel" (*Q*, 398) to describe the head of this organization. Shanti reprimands him with the following words: "Achten Sie auf Ihre Metaphern, Herr Kommissar" (*Q*, 398), while thinking to herself, "Immer dieselben Missverständnisse und Kurzschlüsse, immer dieselben irrationalen Frontlinien" (*Q*, 398). She rejects Karimi's conflation of assisted dying, that is, the voluntary decision to end one's live with the help of others, and the forced killing of what were perceived to be inferior lives in the acts of Nazi euthanasia, as is implied in Karimi's reference to the "Todesengel" Josef Mengele. While Karimi's comparison is not historically accurate—Mengele was not involved in the euthanasia programs by the Nazis—it nevertheless demonstrates how discourses around assisted dying and euthanasia are still influenced by the Holocaust comparison. The chapter also draws a parallel between the past and the dystopian future where the Nazi concept of "lebensunwertes Leben" seems to have reemerged, although the notion of racial inferiority has been replaced with economic unproductivity. Shanti herself is convinced that the younger generations would not protect the old and the vulnerable: "Die meisten Jüngeren [würden] die Millionen Pflegebedürftigen und Dementen insgeheim am liebsten legal aus dem Weg räumen lassen" (*Q*, 389).

The Shanti chapter imagines a future in which direct and active Holocaust memory has completely vanished. "Memories" of the event have become indirect, ghostly, and completely decontextualized. The Holocaust is merely invoked on the level of metaphors and associations— as an emblem of absolute evil and inhumanity—but Karimi's inaccurate reference to Mengele demonstrates that any sound historical knowledge of the event has vanished. At the same time, *Quasikristalle* emphasizes that certain issues and patterns of thinking do actually persist. While the Nelson chapter pointed to a continuity of genocidal conflicts, the segment about Shanti demonstrates how a calculating, rationalizing approach that evaluates human life purely in terms of productivity might cause new catastrophes in the future. The chapter furthermore underlines the persistence of racist preconceptions, when Shanti is repeatedly ostracized on the basis of her "dunkle Haut" (*Q*, 401). Menasse's novel thus arrives at a skeptical verdict in relation to institutionalized Holocaust remembrance and pedagogy. The Shanti chapter warns us against using the Holocaust analogy as a knockout argument in contexts where it is not appropriate or where it is even politically dangerous. Instead, we should scrutinize the underlying structural patterns of exclusion and discrimination, which, in their persistence, link the past to the present and the future.

Conclusion: Mapping Out the Future of Holocaust Memory

Menasse's novel is prefaced by a famous quote from John Donne's 1611 poem *An Anatomy of the World*, in which the speaker mourns a world that is out of joint: "'Tis all in peeces, all cohaerence gone / All just supply, and all Relation."[74] Donne's poem presents itself as a funeral elegy mourning the death of Elizabeth Drury, who was the daughter of Donne's chief patron, Robert Drury. The poem's all-pervasive sense of melancholy and lament is seemingly caused by Elizabeth's death, which "drew the strongest vitall spirits out" and left the world in a state of sickness and decay.[75] Donne's poem is, however, also a reflection on much larger shifts in society, such as the Protestant Reformation, which majorly influenced Donne's lifetime and strongly affected the Catholic poet. Coupled with other major transformations during the so-called English Renaissance, these shifts would bring the end of the world as the speaker knows it, installing a new order. *An Anatomy of the World* can therefore be read as a skillful adaptation of the genres of the "anniversary" and the "funeral elegy" and as a poem about a time that is undergoing major transformations and is perceived as out of joint.

The paratextual reference to Donne relates to the quasicrystalline structure of Menasse's text, which is also "in pieces" and lacks the coherence of a traditional biographical narrative. Yet just as Donne's poem comments on larger cultural and social shifts of his time, the issue of incoherence also concerns the depiction and development of Holocaust remembrance in the novel. With the disappearance of the survivor generation, a certain type of coherence is irrevocably lost. This is already demonstrated in Menasse's previous novel, *Vienna*, in which the dying out of the survivor generation causes a breakdown of the family frame (and novel), giving rise to a multiperspectival final chapter of the book. This pluralization of perspectives is continued in *Quasikristalle*, in which various stages and modes of Holocaust remembrance coexist. The reader encounters the repression of memories alongside the oversaturation caused by a completely ritualized culture of Holocaust remembrance. We witness the increasing decontextualization of the Holocaust signifier and the eventual disappearance of personal and collective memories of the event. The Holocaust is portrayed as a private and familial memory, but features much more prominently in the guise of various aftereffects, which include its transformation into a ubiquitous "floating signifier" or a universal moral touchstone. Gone is not only the coherence of an era of remembrance dominated by firsthand accounts, family narratives, and clear messages such as "Never Again"—Menasse's text also stresses that the cohesive power of some of the central paradigms of Holocaust remembrance has exhausted itself: this concerns not only the family novel as a specifically artistic paradigm but also the future of Holocaust pedagogy and its reliance on shock and affect-laden approaches to the past. The Bernays chapter shows that the shock of concentration-camp images does not elicit affect but its opposite: numbness and fatigue. At the same time, Menasse's text is wary of the extreme decontextualization of the Holocaust signifier: *Quasikristalle* targets what Menasse herself describes as the "Post-Auschwitz-Ethik-Schwall," that is, the universalization of the Holocaust as a moral benchmark and ethical touchstone. Her criticism is based, at least in part, on the insight that the proliferation of Holocaust memory may actually become "a surrogate for engagement,"[76] distracting attention from ongoing instances of racist prejudice, genocidal conflicts, and the devaluation of human lives.

Quasikristalle thus explores the last thirty-five years of private and collective Holocaust discourse in a metadiscursive manner, while also considering its future. The novel at some point leaves behind the past and the present and moves into the middle of our current century—that is, the future. This future will be determined by the fading of personal and collective Holocaust memory (consider the Shanti chapter), but does this also mean that there is no future legacy of the Holocaust? While Menasse's novel challenges the usefulness of a further increase in mnemonic activity, the text does not advocate forgetting as a viable alternative. Rather, *Quasikristalle* advocates a shift in perspective toward what Michael Rothberg calls "implication" or "implicated subjects."[77] Rothberg proposes a concept of historical responsibility that responds to the increasing historical distance to events such as the Holocaust:

> I use the deliberately open-ended term "implication" in order to gather together various modes of historical relation that do not necessarily fall under the more direct forms of participation associated with

traumatic events, such as victimization and perpetration. Such "implicated" modes of relation would encompass bystanders, beneficiaries,
latecomers of the postmemory generation and others connected
"prosthetically" to pasts they did not directly experience. . . . These
subject positions move us away from overt questions of guilt and
innocence and leave us in a more complex and uncertain moral and
ethical terrain.[78]

The focus on direct, personal involvement and the victim-perpetrator
divide—categories that apply less and less to present and coming generations—is replaced with a systemic approach by Rothberg, targeting "the
conditions of possibility of violence as well as its lingering impact."[79] In
keeping with this approach, *Quasikristalle* seems to call for a transition
from memorial oversaturation and the dangers of analogous thinking to an
exploration of the "conditions of possibility of violence" that link the
Holocaust to present and future histories of violence in a manner that
"suggests new routes of opposition."[80] "Implication" is in the most literal
sense the opposite of the problematic overrepresentation of Holocaust
images and references that we find in *Quasikristalle*, as the word signals an
entanglement that is not explicit or on the surface. Rather than creating
and enforcing analogies that are oversimplified and politically charged, an
implicated approach focuses on uncovering the ways in which our present
is necessarily and inevitably connected to the past. By showing us how
certain patterns of exclusion, Othering, and rationalization—epitomized in
the novel's mention of the Israeli-Palestinian conflict, the possibility of
future genocides (Nelson), the return of eugenics (Guttmann), and organized euthanasia (Shanti)—create alarming links between the past and the
present, *Quasikristalle*'s implicated approach also (re)introduces the possibility of agency: by tackling the "conditions of possibility of violence" we
may be able to overcome the stagnation of the "Post-Auschwitz-Ethik-
Schwall" and unproductive Holocaust comparisons.

Conclusion: The Critique of the Critique of Representation— Self- and Metareflexivity in Contemporary Holocaust Fiction

THIS STUDY ANALYZED recent works of fiction by a range of contemporary German-language Jewish writers, who belong to the so-called generation after.[1] It centered on the question of how these authors depict and relate to the Nazi past and the Second World War in the face of major shifts in Holocaust memory since the turn of the millennium. The disappearance of the survivor and eyewitness generation entails the transition from firsthand memories of the war period to an increasingly mediatized and ritualized cultural memory of the events. This transformation intersects with larger changes in Holocaust memory in the last fifteen years, which have been characterized by the re- and hypermediation of Holocaust memory and the emergence of a global *Erinnerungskultur*. Memories of the Nazi past and the Holocaust are no longer discussed within an exclusively national framework but on a "transnational" or "transcultural" scale.[2] Such approaches trace the transformation of the Holocaust into a universalized memory emblem that intersects with a variety of discourses, histories, and memories.[3] Embedded in dense networks of plurimedial and transnational exchange, the Holocaust has thus emerged as a "floating signifier."[4]

The altered shape of Holocaust memory in the age of remediation necessitates new ways of relating to the event: in recent years, the notion of postmemory has established itself as the central aesthetic and theoretical category that promises to illuminate the transition toward a (hyper)mediatized memory culture. In spite of its broad applicability to family novels, a central argument of this book has been that postmemory does not adequately capture the ongoing recalibrations, renegotiations, and remediations of Holocaust memory. This is so because postmemorial discourse foregrounds the familial, biological, and psychological transmission of trauma, which is imagined as a form of contagion. I explored and problematized the genesis and implications of this contagion paradigm in Marianne Hirsch's work, tracing it back to the poststructuralist trauma theory of Cathy Caruth. I then showed that the biologizing and psychologizing concept of contagion is at odds with contemporary representations of the Holocaust, which highlight the cultural mediation of memory and trauma. It is therefore necessary to complement the notion of postmemory with alternative concepts, such as "remediation" and "travelling trauma,"[5] which contribute to a theory of cultural trauma that tackles the interplay between trauma, media, and mediatization ("remediation"), while also highlighting the (political) re- and decontextualization of traumatic memories in a global age ("travelling trauma"). I have demonstrated how this focus on the cultural mobility of trauma and the Holocaust signifier opens up new pathways in Holocaust (literature) research that go beyond the pathology of traumatic contagion or aporetic notions of unspeakability: the texts under consideration transcend the confines of the family frame and novel by focusing on cultural dynamics of memorial adoption and/or appropriation, be it via practices of intertextuality or "affiliative" postmemory. They also tackle the hypermediation of Holocaust memory by reconfiguring the notion of authenticity or by problematizing the nexus between medial oversaturation and empathy. Finally, they engage critically with the global omnipresence of the Holocaust emblem and the politics of trauma that emerge from this.

My investigations of the texts by Benjamin Stein, Maxim Biller, Vladimir Vertlib, and Eva Menasse have demonstrated the usefulness of the concept "travelling trauma" when dealing with a set of texts that, thematically and aesthetically, move away from more traditional postmemory narratives. "Travelling trauma/memory," as they are conceptualized by Astrid Erll and Terri Tomsky,[6] however, ultimately remain descriptive concepts that do not allow us to differentiate ethically productive from problematic forms of mobility. This more descriptive approach sets them apart from Hirsch's framework, and poststructuralist trauma theory more broadly, which was underpinned by a strong ethical agenda that, however, often produced certain ethical conundrums. Still, the texts under consideration here have highlighted the continued necessity of an ethics of memory, specifically in our age of re- and hypermediation. So where do we go from here? I would argue that it is precisely here that the broader theoretical frameworks applied throughout this study can benefit from a confrontation with the selected literary texts. While renegotiations of postmemory have been at the heart of this study, the recalibration of other key paradigms in recent memory and trauma studies through the lens of contemporary German-language Jewish fiction has been equally important. This has probably become most obvious in relation to discourses around transnational or cosmopolitan Holocaust memory but also appears in the context of discussions around authenticity and empathy.

I therefore want to suggest that the medium of fiction enables exactly the type of critical engagement that tends to be lacking from the more theoretical approaches, and that this is owing to the particular self- and metareflexive capabilities of the literary text. The approaches presented in the selected texts allow us to scrutinize certain manifestations of "travelling trauma," while at the same time upholding the ethical thrust behind much trauma and postmemory scholarship. While Stein's *Die Leinwand* depicts the hypermobility of the Holocaust signifier as somewhat inevitable, the text is wary of a culture that conflates the realities of trauma with its representation, so as to gain access to victimhood as a form of symbolic capital. While the mass-mediated mobility of traumas is thus not the main problem in Steins' text, his novel is critical of practices of overidentification and personification and tries to counter them via its form. In a similar vein, Biller's novella—unwittingly—demonstrates that an awareness of the transgenerational, transmedial, and transnational travel of memories, traditions, and traumas can coexist with the continuation of identity politics: *Im Kopf von Bruno Schulz* mobilizes various memories and traditions to cement a German-Jewish identity based on the "negative symbiosis."

While criticisms of "travelling trauma" are implicit in Stein's and Biller's writing, Vertlib and Menasse engage more explicitly with the phenomenon and some of the issues attached to it. Vertlib's *Das besondere Gedächtnis der Rosa Masur* shows that, contrary to the assumptions that still dominate much of transnational (memory) studies, the travel of memories across borders does not automatically produce understanding but can indeed engender and perpetuate conflict. Transnational memories can only become cosmopolitan memories if they are part of a dialogic or polyphonic exchange and memory culture. Vertlib's text furthermore shows that some memories do actually not travel so well (or at all), since they are blocked out and/or marginalized by fixed national templates. We can find the most overt criticisms of "travelling trauma" in Menasse's text, which tackles both the overrepresentation and the decontextualization of the Holocaust signifier. While the visual omnipresence of the event provokes feelings that range from fatigue to disgust, the symbolic proliferation of Holocaust analogies in all sorts of contexts can in some cases mask ongoing instances of racism and stereotyping.

In light of the analyses presented here, I want to argue that the texts featured in this study all promote an ethics and aesthetics of self- and metareflexivity in the face of and as a possible response to Holocaust hypermediation—they thus deliver not only the critique of existing representations but also "the critique of the critique of representation" that Gillian Rose called for over twenty years ago.[7] The approaches traced in this book are not uniform, however, and they encompass various components: several of the narratives presented here resort to multiperspectival strategies, often with the aim of problematizing dominant and/or monolithic memory paradigms and fostering "dialogism" in Mikhail Bakhtin's sense. This is the case in *Die Leinwand*, which uses several narrators and perspectives to illustrate the ineluctable subjectivity of our access to reality and the past. *Das besondere Gedächtnis der Rosa Masur* introduces different narrators and intratextual levels to counter monological forms of discourse, as represented by, for example, the jubilee project. And *Quasikristalle* adopts a mosaiclike aesthetic form, partially in response to the breakdown of the family frame and the pluralization of Holocaust memories, but possibly also as a reaction to "image-glut" and the uniformity of Holocaust representations in a hypermediated culture. These multiperspectival approaches are in most cases complemented by a decentering of narrative authority. Stein, Biller, and Vertlib all present us with unreliable narrators who omit and/or distort parts of their story (Bruno Schulz, Rosa) or are simply not in control of it (Wechsler). The plurality of consciousness centers in Menasse's text has a similar effect, as it makes us gradually loosen our grip on the central character of Xane rather than tighten it. Apart from questioning the reliability of memories and subjective accounts of the past, these narrative techniques, which highlight ambivalence, malleability, and plurality, are diametrically opposed to the "discursive rigidity" that dominates many present-day engagements with Holocaust memory.[8] As I have demonstrated in my Bakhtinian reading of Vertlib, the potential to accommodate and tolerate ambivalence, contradiction, and a plurality of viewpoints is a particular strength of the novelistic form, which suggests that maybe a novelization of our contemporary memory cultures is needed.

These narratological experiments necessarily make the reader aware of the materiality of these texts. This is most obviously the case with *Die Leinwand*; Katja Garloff has convincingly demonstrated how the novel's paratextual strategies foreground the book's material aspects.[9] She interprets this as a response to the discourse of personification, which, according to Amy Hungerford, seeks to obliterate the materiality of the text and/or medium.[10] *Im Kopf von Bruno Schulz*, *Quasikristalle*, and *Das besondere Gedächtnis der Rosa Masur* also bring to the fore the material dimensions of writing, be it through the mash-up of different media (*IKvBS*), the disruptions of the textual flow via a specific chapter structure (*Q*), or the use of different typographical formats (*DbG*). While all of the texts analyzed here are rich in intertextual references, this is most obvious in the case of Biller, who uses intertextual relationships to (re)negotiate contemporary Jewishness. Such self-reflexive techniques draw attention to the text's status as a mediation and representation of memories and events and to its reliance on other (inter)texts in the broadest sense. These strategies potentially counter a discourse that systematically tries to erase mediation, materiality, and textuality in the service of appropriation or identification.

Apart from these self-reflexive narrative devices, many of the texts engage humor as a central critical tool: Vertlib's *Das besondere Gedächtnis der Rosa Masur* employs irony to playfully highlight the discrepancies between expectations and reality but also to alienate us from what we perceive to be "normal," in productive ways. Irony is similarly important for Menasse's writing, particularly in *Vienna* but also in several of the chapters of *Quasikristalle* (Bernays, Tschoch, Guttmann). It here functions as a device that distances us from and makes us question the characters and their actions, motivations, and opinions. Finally, humor also plays a role in Biller's writing, mostly in the shape of the grotesque or carnivalesque. I have illustrated, however, that this is an ambivalent strategy, as the carnivalesque/grotesque reversal does not apply to all dimensions of his texts and leaves some of their problematic politics, especially in the domain of gender, untouched.

While humor thus serves as a distancing device in many of the texts, they also all adopt a metamemorial perspective that engages not only with various representations of individual and collective Holocaust memory but also with the representation of these representations via the various institutions of cultural memory (such as historiography, museums, artistic engagements, political debates, etc.). Stein's, Vertlib's, and Menasse's novels also actively contemplate the role of literary discourse in relation to these institutionalized discourses: while Vertlib's novel promotes an empathetic approach to literature as a—or maybe even the only—possible counterdiscourse to institutionalized monologism, Stein's and Menasse's stances are more subtle. *Die Leinwand* makes the case for an ethics of fictional discourse mainly via its form, as has also been illustrated by Garloff,[11] and in *Quasikristalle* we are left guessing as to whether or not literature is complicit in the hypermediated loops. Arguably, Menasse's text necessarily disrupts the stream of visual and discursive stimuli that Sontag refers to as "image-glut"[12] by virtue of its multiperspectival and fragmented form.

These considerations point us back to the question of "implication" that I raised in the Menasse chapter. I would argue that owing to their historical distance from the events, all of the texts considered here promote an "implicated" approach to an extent, in the sense that they focus on the often invisible and entangled cultural aftereffects of the events. As such, they illustrate that the past is never past but always and unavoidably entangled with the present and the future. Rather than promoting a universalizing and moralizing global Holocaust memory, which, in the words of Gavriel Rosenfeld, has turned into an "empty signifier,"[13] texts such as *Das besondere Gedächtnis der Rosa Masur* and *Quasikristalle* make the case for critically examining how certain patterns and structures of exclusion still persist in present-day societies. In this way they might also promote "futurity," to quote Amir Eshel's term,[14] in that they urge us to consider how Holocaust memories cannot only be preserved for the future but might also be developed in ways that allow us to build better futures.

These observations thus provide a possible answer to a question that was raised at the beginning of this study: namely, what Holocaust literature in the twenty-first century might look like and what sets it apart from earlier examples of the genre. I would argue that, apart from its strong focus on the transgenerational, transmedial, and transnational travels of trauma, it is also highly self- and metareflexive. While self-reflexivity can be found in the Holocaust literature of earlier generations, from Primo Levi to Ruth Klüger and Art Spiegelman, to name just a few, the metareflexive or -memorial dimension appears as a more recent development, which needs to be understood as a reaction to the increasing hypermediation and globalization of Holocaust memory. Instead of focusing on individualized processes of memory, often shaped by trauma, the novels by Stein, Biller, Vertlib, and Menasse approach the Holocaust as a culturally mediated phenomenon and focus on its discursivation. They also all actively reflect on the critical contribution and potential of literature in a climate of hypermediation, making the case for an ethics and aesthetics of self- and metareflexivity that draws on strategies and techniques such as multiperspectivity, unreliable narration, and experiments with materiality, intertextuality, and intermediality as well as humor. The fact that these aesthetic choices allow us to productively question some of the ethical implications of recent Holocaust discourse and theory highlight the continued—maybe even increased—importance of fictional engagements with the Holocaust after the end of eyewitness memory. Whether one subscribes to Vertlib's empathetic understanding of literature or instead prefers Stein's and Menasse's more subtle approaches, these texts make it irrefutably clear that literature remains a central space in which alternative—in the sense of ambivalent, implicated, ironic, and multiperspectival—versions of the past can be formulated, which are the basis for developing visions for the future.

Notes

Introduction

1 Zauzmer, "Two Thirds of US Millennials Do Not Know What Auschwitz Is."
2 See Gensing, "Wie viele Schüler wissen vom Holocaust?"; "Gravierende Wissenslücken zum Holocaust in Österreich."
3 See Claims Conference, "Holocaust Knowledge and Awareness Study."
4 Aspects of this transition, particularly pertaining to the issues of mediatization and globalization, have been debated by Assmann, "The Holocaust—a Global Memory?"; Frieden, *Neuverhandlungen*; Hartman and Assmann, *Die Zukunft der Erinnerung*; Goldberg and Hazan, eds., *Marking Evil*; Landsberg, *Prosthetic Memory*; Levy and Sznaider, *Erinnerung im globalen Zeitalter*; Rothberg, *Multidirectional Memory*.
5 Frieden, *Neuverhandlungen*, 29.
6 See USC Shoah Foundation, "Dimensions in Testimony."
7 Jones, *The Media of Testimony*, 37–40.
8 See, for example, Garde-Hansen, Hoskins and Reading, eds., *Save as . . .*; Hoskins, ed., *Digital Memory Studies*; Neiger, Meyers, and Zandberg, eds., *On Media Memory*.
9 Hoskins, "Memory Ecologies."
10 Tomlinson, *The Culture of Speed*, 91.
11 Hoskins, "Anachronisms of Media," 281.
12 Hoskins, "7/7 and Connective Memory."
13 Hoskins, "7/7 and Connective Memory," 272.
14 Hoskins, "Anachronisms of Media," 279.
15 Bolter and Grusin, *Remediation*.
16 Erll, "Literature, Film, and the Mediality of Cultural Memory," 392.
17 My understanding of "hypermediated" here is notably different from Bolter's and Grusin's notion of "hypermediacy," which I will outline toward the end of this chapter. While their idea of hypermediacy describes the opposite of immediacy and thus implies an awareness of mediation, "hypermediated," as it will be used throughout this study, means the inescapability of mediatizations which have become self-referential to a degree.
18 See, for example, Hoskins, "7/7 and Connective Memory"; Erll, "Travelling Memory"; Bond, Craps, and Vermeulen, "Introduction: Memory on the Move."

19 Hoskins, "The Restless Past," 3.
20 For an overview of the debates that shaped this phase, see Fuchs, Cosgrove, and Grote, eds., *German Memory Contests*; Niven, *Facing the Past*; Schmitz, *On Their Own Terms*; Taberner, *German Literature of the 1990s and Beyond*.
21 Cooke and Taberner, eds., *German Culture, Politics, and Literature into the Twenty-First Century*.
22 Fuchs, Cosgrove, and Grote, eds., *German Memory Contests*.
23 Garloff and Mueller, "Introduction," in *German-Jewish Literature after 1990*, 6.
24 See "Holocaust Knowledge and Awareness Study."
25 Kapczynski, "Never Over, Over and Over," 22–23.
26 Frieden, *Neuverhandlungen*, 35.
27 Funk, "Erinnern kann auch cool sein."
28 Olterman, "'Yolocaust' Artist Provokes Debate over Commemorating Germany's Past."
29 Morris, *The Translated Jew*, 69.
30 Adorno, "Kulturkritik und Gesellschaft."
31 Adorno, 29.
32 For an in-depth discussion of Adorno's famous quote, see Ryland, "Re-membering Adorno."
33 See Caruth, *Unclaimed Experience*; Felman and Laub, *Testimony*.
34 Caruth, *Unclaimed Experience*, 59.
35 Mandel, "Rethinking 'After Auschwitz,'" 204.
36 Huyssen, *Present Past*, 99.
37 On the relationship between testimony and mediation, see Jones, *The Media of Testimony*; more specifically on Holocaust testimonies, see Jones, "Mediated Immediacy."
38 On the so-called family or multigenerational novel, see Costagli and Galli, eds., *Deutsche Familienromane*; Eigler, *Gedächtnis und Geschichte*; Fuchs, *Phantoms of War*; Weigel, "Familienbande"; Weigel, *Genea-Logik*.
39 Craps, *Postcolonial Witnessing*, 75. This is, for example, the position advocated by Daniel Levy and Natan Sznaider in their seminal study *Erinnerung im globalen Zeitalter* and by Michael Rothberg in his earlier works, such as *Multidirectional Memory*.
40 Dirk Moses has emerged as a particularly vocal critic of the assumed cosmopolitanism behind globalized versions of Holocaust memory; he argues that they might actually have the opposite effect and entrench existing divisions. See Moses, "Does the Holocaust Reveal or Conceal Other Genocides?"
41 Mandel, *Against the Unspeakable*, 35.
42 Bolter and Grusin, *Remediation*, 5.
43 Bolter and Grusin, 22–23.
44 Bolter and Grusin, 6.
45 Bolter and Grusin, 5.

46 It should be noted here that the concept of authenticity has always been inextricably and inconveniently linked to issues of mediation and mediatization. Julia Straub points to this by quoting Jonathan Culler: "The paradox, the dilemma of authenticity, is that to be experienced as such it must be marked as authentic, but when it is marked as authentic it is mediated, a sign of itself, and hence lacks the authenticity of what is truly unspoiled, untouched by mediating cultural codes (Jonathan Culler, *Framing the Sign*)." See Straub, "Introduction: The Paradoxes of Authenticity," 9.

47 Meek, *Trauma and Media*; Kaplan, *Trauma Culture*; Žižek, *Welcome to the Desert of the Real*.

48 Jones, "Mediated Immediacy," 137.

49 Jones, "Testimony through Culture," 262.

50 Erll, "Remembering across Time, Space, and Cultures," 129.

51 Flanzbaum, ed., *The Americanization of the Holocaust*.

52 Examples of this "transnational" or "transcultural" shift in Holocaust (and trauma) discourse include Craps and Rothberg, "Introduction: Transcultural Negotiations of Holocaust Memory"; Craps, *Postcolonial Witnessing*; Levy and Sznaider, *Erinnerung im globalen Zeitalter*; Rothberg, *Multidirectional Memory*; Sanyal, *Memory and Complicity*; Silverman, *Palimpsestic Memory*.

53 Rothberg, *Multidirectional Memory*.

54 This is, for example, the topic of Michael Rothberg's latest project and planned book, "Citizens of Memory: Migrant Archives of Holocaust Remembrance in Contemporary Germany"; for some preliminary thoughts on the project, see Rothberg and Yildiz, "Migrant Archives."

55 This is the focus of Craps, *Postcolonial Witnessing*; Rothberg, *Multidirectional Memory*; and Silverman, *Palimpsestic Memory*.

56 Levy and Sznaider, *Erinnerung im globalen Zeitalter*.

57 More balanced and critical evaluations of the recent trend toward transnationalism and transculturalism in Holocaust discourse are provided by Moses and Rothberg, "A Dialogue on the Ethics and Politics of Transcultural Memory"; Rothberg, "From Gaza to Warsaw: Mapping Multidirectional Memory." Dirk Moses engages critically with comparative Holocaust memory in his work; see, for example, "Genocide and the Terror of History" and "Does the Holocaust Reveal or Conceal Other Genocides?"

58 McGlothlin and Kapczynski, "Introduction," in *Persistent Legacy*, 5.

59 McGlothlin and Kapczynski, 5.

60 See, for example, Herrmann, Smith-Prei, and Taberner, eds., *Transnationalism*; Taberner, *Transnationalism and German-Language Literature*.

61 Beebee, ed., *German Literature as World Literature*; Taberner, "Transnationalism and Cosmopolitanism."

62 See, for example, Garloff and Mueller, eds., *German-Jewish Literature after 1990*; Morris, *The Translated Jew*; Geller and Morris, eds., *Three-Way Street*.

63 Kilcher, "Einleitung," xiv.

64 Kilcher, xiv.
65 Davies and Hammel, eds., *New Literary and Linguistic Perspectives*; Fischer, Hammermeister, and Kramer, eds., *Der Nationalsozialismus und die Shoah*; Frieden, *Neuverhandlungen*; McGlothlin and Kapczynski, *Persistent Legacy*.
66 Yosef Yerushalmi has written more broadly about the specificities of Jewish memory and its special relation to the issues of community and survival; see his *Zakhor*.
67 Kilcher, "Exterritorialitäten."
68 Morris, *The Translated Jew*, 6.
69 Aarons and Berger, *Third-Generation Holocaust Representation*.
70 Jilovsky, Silverstein, and Slucki, eds., *In the Shadows of Memory*.
71 Efraim Sicher, "'Tancred's Wound.'"
72 McGlothlin, *Second-Generation Holocaust Literature*.
73 Aarons, ed., *Third-Generation Holocaust Narratives*.
74 Aarons and Berger, *Third-Generation Holocaust Representation*.
75 Jilovsky, *Remembering the Holocaust*.
76 Jilovsky, Silverstein, and Slucki, *In the Shadows of Memory*.
77 Fischer, Hammermeister, and Kramer, *Der Nationalsozialismus und die Shoah*.
78 McGlothlin and Kapczynski, *Persistent Legacy*.
79 Frieden, *Neuverhandlungen*.
80 Garloff and Mueller, eds., *German Jewish literature after 1990*.
81 While it is not the aim of this book to provide a comparative study of third-generation Holocaust writing across various languages and nations, it is, for example, noteworthy that German-language examples do usually not evoke traditions of folklore and magical realism, which are quite common for the third-generation Anglophone writers such as Michael Chabon, Jonathan Safran Foer, Nicole Krauss, and Nathan Englander; see also Adams, *Magic Realism in Holocaust Literature*.
82 Seminal studies and articles on the family or multigenerational novel and the concepts underlying it have been published by Costagli and Galli, eds., *Deutsche Familienromane*; Eigler, *Gedächtnis und Geschichte*; Fuchs, *Phantoms of War*; Herrmann, *Vergangenwart*; Horstkotte, *Nachbilder*; Weigel, "Familienbande"; Weigel, *Genea-Logik*.
83 This potential is particularly stressed by Eigler, *Gedächtnis und Geschichte*, and Fuchs, *Phantoms of War*.
84 Morris, *The Translated Jew*, 69.
85 This problem was addressed by the eminent critic Sigrid Loeffler in 2005 and echoed by critic Dennis Scheck in 2011. See Löffler, "Die Familie: Ein Roman"; Scheck, "Und Wieder ein Familienroman."
86 Frieden, *Neuverhandlungen*, 66.
87 This is the case for Aarons, *Third-Generation Holocaust Narratives*; Aarons and Berger, *Third-Generation Holocaust Representation*; Jilovsky,

Remembering the Holocaust; and Jilovsky, Silverstein, and Slucki, *In the Shadows of Memory*.

88 Fischer, Hammermeister, and Kramer, "Der Nationalsozialismus und die Shoah in der deutschsprachigen Literatur des ersten Jahrzehnts," 16.

89 Fischer, Hammermeister, and Kramer, 16. Their assessment is echoed by Dora Osborne, who, in connection with Katja Petrowskaja's *Vielleicht Esther*, speaks of an "archival turn" in recent memory culture, understood as a metacritical and metadiscursive investigation of the dynamics that shape private and public archives; see her "Encountering the Archive."

90 Hirsch's output on the issue of postmemory is considerable and spans a period of almost fifteen years; some of her most important works include *Family Frames*; "Surviving Images"; "The Generation of Postmemory"; and *The Generation of Postmemory*.

91 Hirsch, *Family Frames*, 22.

92 Hirsch, 22.

93 Freud, "Jenseits des Lustprinzips."

94 Leys, *Trauma*, 252; see Felman and Laub, *Testimony*.

95 Leys, *Trauma*, 269.

96 Caruth, *Unclaimed Experience*, 8.

97 For criticisms of poststructuralist trauma theory as well as the unspeakability paradigm, see Crownshaw, "The Limits of Transference"; Hungerford, "Memorizing Memory"; Hungerford, *The Holocaust of Texts*; LaCapra, *Writing History, Writing Trauma*; Leys, *Trauma*; Mandel, "Rethinking 'After Auschwitz'"; Mandel, *Against the Unspeakable*; Radstone, "Trauma Theory."

98 Meek, *Trauma and Media*, 195.

99 Leys, *Trauma*, 249.

100 Hirsch, *The Generation of Postmemory*, 38.

101 Hirsch, 62.

102 Hirsch, 122.

103 This has, for example, been demonstrated in Judith Butler's influential study *Frames of War*, which illuminates that and how some lives and forms of suffering are constructed and framed as more or less "grievable" than others. A precursor to such considerations is, of course, Susan Sontag's work on the ethics of (war) photography, *On Photography*.

104 For a criticism of this universalization see LaCapra, *Writing History, Writing Trauma*.

105 Hirsch, *The Generation of Postmemory*, 48.

106 Crownshaw, "The Limits of Transference," 73.

107 Hirsch, *The Generation of Postmemory*, 120.

108 Crownshaw, "The Limits of Transference," 88.

109 Craps, "Beyond Eurocentrism," 50. One example of this is Robert Eaglestone's book *The Holocaust and the Postmodern*, in which the author defines certain characteristics of "trauma fiction" that are all centered on fragmentariness, openness, and anti-identificatory textual strategies.

110 Craps, "Beyond Eurocentrism"; for a more in-depth critique of the Eurocentric bias that shapes trauma theory as a whole, see also Craps, *Postcolonial Witnessing*.
111 Jones, "Testimony through Culture," 263.
112 Hirsch, *The Generation of Postmemory*, 5.
113 Hirsch, 221.
114 Caruth, *Unclaimed Experience*, 8.
115 Caruth, 34.
116 Hirsch, "The Generation of Postmemory," 114–15.
117 Hirsch, 159.
118 Hirsch, 158–59.
119 Hirsch, 159.
120 One could argue that as a Jewish artist, Novak is somehow scarred by the fate of the Jewish community. I, however, find this universalization of trauma and victimhood problematic. I am not denying that Lorie Novak, as a present-day Jew, may still be deeply affected by the Holocaust and its aftereffects, but I object to the use of the vocabulary of (transgenerational) traumatization in this context.
121 See Alexander et al., eds., *Cultural Trauma;* see also Alexander, *Trauma*.
122 Alexander, *Trauma*, 13.
123 Alexander, 14.
124 The distinction between "collective" and "cultural" trauma suggested here functions in analogy to the theory of "collective" and "cultural" memory, as it was first introduced by Jan Assmann. Whereas collective memory, broadly speaking, encompasses the ways in which memories are socially mediated and transferred within groups, "cultural" memory looks at their transmission and institutionalization in various media and across large temporal distances; see Assmann, *Das kulturelle Gedächtnis*.
125 Tomsky, "From Sarajevo to 9/11."
126 The term "floating signifier" is used by Andreas Huyssen in his seminal study on the interplay between cityscapes, monumentalization, and historical traumas (specifically the Holocaust); see his *Present Pasts*, 99.
127 Tomsky, "From Sarajevo to 9/11," 50.
128 Erll, "Travelling Memory."
129 Tomsky, "From Sarajevo to 9/11," 49.
130 Tomsky, 49.
131 Tomsky, 53.
132 Huyssen, *Present Pasts*, 99.
133 Mandel, *Against the Unspeakable*, 35.
134 See, for example, Erll, "Travelling Memory"; Erll and Rigney, *Mediation, Remediation, and the Dynamics of Cultural Memory;* Bond, Craps, and Vermeulen, "Introduction: Memory on the Move."
135 McGlothlin and Kapczynski, "Introduction," in *Persistent Memory*, 6.
136 Rose, "Beginnings of the Day," 41.

137 Rose, 41.

138 Rose, 62.

139 The term "Holocaust etiquette" has been coined by Des Pres, "Holocaust Laughter?," 217.

140 Jones, "Testimony through Culture," 274.

141 Fischer, Hammermeister, and Kramer, "Der Nationalsozialismus und die Shoah," 16.

142 Luhmann, "Weltkunst."

143 Rose, "Beginnings of the Day," 62.

144 Erll, "Literatur als Medium des kollektiven Gedächtnisses," 265.

145 Weissman, *Fantasies of Witnessing*, 5.

146 Fischer, Hammermeister, and Kramer, "Der Nationalsozialismus und die Shoah," 22.

147 Bloom, *The Anxiety of Influence*.

148 See Bakhtin, *Problems of Dostoevsky's Poetics*, "Epic and Novel," and "Discourse in the Novel."

Chapter One

1 Henceforth cited in the text as *DL*.

2 Most research on *Die Leinwand* concentrates on the prominent issues of autobiographical memory and (Jewish) identity in the text, while somewhat bypassing the novel's engagement with the re- and hypermediation of Holocaust memory. Silke Horstkotte, however, examines the novel's take on the issues of authenticity and witnessing and the broader implications for Holocaust discourse in the new millennium. See Horstkotte, "'Ich bin, woran ich mich erinnere'"; see also Garloff, "The Power of Paratext." Other contributions include Costazza, "Benjamin Steins *Die Leinwand*"; Langenhorst, "'Die erzählte Geschichte ist, was am Ende zählt'"; Schuchmann, "'Unser Gedächtnis ist der wahre Sitz unseres Ichs.'"

3 Stier, *Committed to Memory*, 120.

4 Henceforth cited in the text as *BS*.

5 This is asserted by Stefan Maechler, who conducted extensive historical research on the case, which provides the basis for my short account of the affair; see his *The Wilkomirski Affair*.

6 Quoted from Maechler, 129.

7 Jones, "Testimony through Culture," 263.

8 Quoted from Oels, "'A Real-Life Grimm's Fairy Tale,'" 381.

9 This has also been noted by Kathrin Schuchmann: "Im Sinne einer 'Rhetorik des Traumas' simuliert das Erzählen in *Bruchstücke* Authentizität durch den Rekurs auf vorgeprägte Topoi"; Schuchmann, "'Unser Gedächtnis ist der wahre Sitz unseres Ichs,'" 206.

10 Rowland, "The Future of Testimony: Introduction," 114.

11 For a discussion of the relationship between fact and fiction in the genre of autobiography, see Schabacher, *Topik der Referenz*; for a discussion of these issues in relation to the Holocaust memoir, see Düwell, *"Fiktion aus dem Wirklichen."*

12 Whitehead, "Telling Tales," 122.

13 Düwell, *"Fiktion aus dem Wirklichen,"* 13–14.

14 Hungerford, "Memorizing Memory"; Whitehead, "Telling Tales"; and Oels, "'A Real-Life Grimm's Fairy Tale.'"

15 Hungerford, "Memorizing Memory," 68.

16 Assmann, "Canon and Archive," 99.

17 This has also been noted by Gabriele Schabacher: "So gesehen beruhen Skandal und Empörung, die der Fall Wilkomirski impliziert, vor allem darin, die grundlegenden Zuschreibungsmechanismen sichtbar werden zu lassen, derer sich ein diskursives System bedient"; Schabacher, *Topik der Referenz*, 178. On a more fundamental level, Sara Jones has demonstrated that testimony is an inherently mediated genre that unfolds within various discursive frameworks; see her *The Media of Testimony* and "Mediated Immediacy."

18 Schaff, "Der Autor als Simulant authentischer Erfahrung," 438.

19 For a detailed account of the reception of Wilkomirski's *Bruchstücke*, see Maechler, *The Wilkomirski Affair*.

20 Funk, Gross, and Huber, "Exploring the Empty Plinth," 10. Julia Straub rightly remarks, however, that the idea of authenticity as performance is not limited to the postmodern age: "It is the double bind of the authentic—that it sends off signals both of immediacy and mediation, genuineness and performance, spontaneity and staging"; Straub, "Introduction: The Paradoxes of Authenticity," 10.

21 Jones, "Testimony through Culture," 264.

22 It should be noted here that the "authenticity effect" is something that takes place on the level of textual production and reception and does not concern the ontological status—that is, the reality—of the events in question. By saying that authenticity should be approached as inextricably tied to practices of mediation, I am denying neither historical realities nor the fact that such a thing as historical facts can be established. What I am questioning, rather, is whether this historical reality can ever be authentically—in the sense of accurately, purely, transparently—accessed and expressed. Concurrently, I have tried to show that the illusion of transparency can, paradoxically, be manufactured through the recourse to certain aesthetic strategies and tropes.

23 Jones, "Mediated Immediacy," 137.

24 Oels, "'A Real-Life Grimm's Fairy Tale,'" 373–74. Reto Sorg and Michael Angele also point out that the afterword "garantiert die autobiographische Lesart des Textes"; Sorg and Angele, "Selbsterfindung und Autobiographie," 328–29.

25 Maechler, *The Wilkomirski Affair*, 131.

26 Barthes, "The Reality Effect," 148.

27 Barthes, 148.
28 Reto Sorg and Michael Angele therefore speak of a "Rhetorik der Anti-Rhetorik" or "Sprache der Wahrhaftigkeit," both of which are necessary to generate the "referential illusion"; Sorg and Angele, "Selbsterfindung und Autobiographie," 331.
29 Amy Hungerford therefore reads *Bruchstücke* as "the epitome of the very assumptions that underline trauma theory's analytic discourse"; Hungerford, "Memorizing Memory," 69.
30 Caruth, *Unclaimed Experience*, 59.
31 Bolter and Grusin, *Remediation*, 21.
32 I am following the paging style suggested by the novel, which uses a *W.* to indicate the pages in the Wechsler narration and a *Z.* to mark those in the Zichroni plotline.
33 The glossary that comes with *Die Leinwand* gives the following definition: "*Tikkun* (*hebr.*) Verbesserung, Reparieren; häufig mit Bezug auf Tikkun Olam, als die 'Verbesserung der Welt' durch Menschenhand, ein Konzept, das in der Kabbala eine zentrale Rolle spielt" (*DL*, G.8).
34 For details on the role Bernstein played during the affair, see Maechler, *The Wilkomirski Affair*.
35 The structure of Stein's book is reminiscent of David Lynch's movie *Mulholland Drive* (2001). It might be worth considering whether Stein's book is also structured like a Möbius strip, which is how the narrative construction of Lynch's film has been described by, for example, Hudson, "'No Hay Banda, and Yet We Hear a Band'" 18.
36 The issues raised here extend to my own interpretation of the text, of course, as my decision on how to read Stein's *Die Leinwand* has also colored my interpretation of it.
37 Norbert Otto Eke has coined the term "Diskursfiguration" to describe this phenomenon in "'Was wollen sie?,'" 90.
38 Actually, Wechsler meets Minsky twice, but he can only remember the second encounter, which takes place long after the affair. The first time they meet is in 1995, during a joint reading at the Leipziger Buchmesse. Both Wechsler's own and Zichroni's narrations hint at the fact that Wechsler was envious of Minsky's success and that this was the primary motive for his involvement in the case.
39 Jones, "Mediated Immediacy," 136.
40 The whole matter becomes even more complicated when the reader finds out that the biography that might or might not have been stolen from Wechsler belongs to the author Benjamin Stein, who then fictionalized it in his first novel, *Das Alphabet des Juda Liva* (1998).
41 This is, in fact, a fairly accurate description of the actual Wilkomirski readings, with the difference that the real Wilkomirski played the clarinet, not the violin; see Maechler, *The Wilkomirski Affair*, 116.
42 This point is also stressed by Costazza, "Benjamin Steins *Die Leinwand*."
43 Horstkotte, "'Ich bin, woran ich mich erinnere,'" 130.

44 We find out that Wechsler has a family history that involves the Holocaust (that applies to both his identities—the real as well as the appropriated one), which he uncovers during a trip to the registration office. Instead of digging deeper into this history, however, as would probably be the case in the genre of the conventional family novel, he remains focused on his adopted identity.

45 Horstkotte, "'Ich bin, woran ich mich erinnere,'" 131.

46 Kunisch, "Fernduell."

47 Stier, *Committed to Memory*, 18.

48 See Garloff, "The Power of Paratext."

49 See Luhmann, "Weltkunst."

50 Garloff, "The Power of Paratext," 143.

51 Barthes, *S/Z*.

52 Barthes, 4.

53 Garloff, "The Power of the Paratext," 147.

54 Landsberg, *Prosthetic Memory*.

55 Landsberg, 18.

56 Landsberg, 2.

57 Landsberg, 2.

58 Landsberg, 141.

59 Landsberg, 28.

60 Crownshaw, "The Future of Memory: Introduction," 7.

61 Landsberg, *Prosthetic Memory*, 9.

62 Landsberg, 45.

63 Tomsky, "From Sarajevo to 9/11."

64 Freud, "Über Deckerinnerungen," 548.

65 Freud, 553.

66 Freud, 552.

67 Although Zichroni's and Freud's assessments are thus remarkably similar, there is one crucial difference: Zichroni conceptualizes memory as a palimpsestic accumulation of several layers that could theoretically be peeled off to reach "das Ursprüngliche." This logic is also implied in the metaphor of the canvas and the various coatings of paint that need to be removed by Minsky. By contrast, Freud's screen memory and the logic of *Nachträglichkeit* call into question this archaeological trajectory: "Zu diesen Zeiten der Erweckung sind die Kindheitserinnerungen nicht, wie man zu sagen gewohnt ist, *aufgetaucht*, sondern sie sind damals *gebildet* worden [italics in the original]." For Freud, there is no "Ursprung," as the notion of the origin always implies retroactive construction; Freud, "Über Deckerinnerungen," 553–54.

68 Costazza, "Benjamin Steins *Die Leinwand*," 313–14.

69 In his blog, Stein has published two articles that deal with his own biography, which is similar to Wechsler's: "Der Autor als Seelenstripper" and "Familiengeschichte"

70   The issue of "personification" marks a broad range of texts in postwar American culture, as Hungerford shows in her more extensive study, *The Holocaust of Texts.*

71   Hungerford, "Memorizing Memory," 88.

72   Hungerford, 79.

73   Hungerford, 88.

74   Bolter and Grusin, *Remediation,* 55.

75   Garloff, "The Power of the Paratext," 153.

76   Mangold, "Religion ist kein Wunschkonzert."

77   This has also been noted by Kathrin Schuchmann: "Die komplementären Erzählungen zeigen, dass sich jüdische Identität in *Die Leinwand* nicht ex negativo, sondern durch den Bezug auf religiöse Traditionen konstituiert. Das Trauma der Shoah, das in den vermeintlichen Erinnerungen von Minsky bzw. Wilkomirski als der realhistorischen Folie für den fiktiven Skandal ins Zentrum rückt, wird in den Ich-Erzählungen der Figuren Wechsler und Zichroni an die Peripherie gedrängt. Der Fall eines pathologisch angeeigneten Judentums bildet im Roman *Die Leinwand* den Erzählanlass, um die Ich-Erzähler mit ihrer problematisch gewordenen Identität zu konfrontieren"; Schuchmann, "'Unser Gedächtnis ist der wahre Sitz unseres Ichs,'" 219. Similar points are made by Katja Garloff, "The Power of Paratext."

78   Garloff, "The Power of Paratext," 141.

79   See, for example, this quote by Stein in the interview: "Wenn sich jemand an mich wendet, weil er seine jüdische Identität sucht, dann sage ich ihm: 'Versuche doch mal, Schabbes-Kerzen anzuzünden, und schau, was das mit dir macht.'" Mangold, "Religion ist kein Wunschkonzert."

80   Although parts of the novel are set in three additional countries—reunified Germany, Switzerland, and the United States—I would argue that only the GDR and Israel play a major role for the characters' development and Jewish self-understanding.

81   The breach in tradition after the Holocaust is stressed by Thomas Nolden in his attempt to define contemporary German-Jewish literature, *Junge jüdische Literatur.*

82   For a detailed comparison of FRG and GDR memory politics, see Herf, *Divided Memory.*

83   Garloff, "The Power of Paratext," 142.

84   Garloff, 145.

85   The issue of the glossary is also discussed in Stein's blog—apparently, the author himself was against the idea of a glossary, and it was the publisher's idea to include one. Stein, however—and some of his readers—reject the glossary mainly because it disrupts the reading experience; see Stein, "Glossar."

86   Geertz, "Thick Description," 27.

87   Geertz, 16.

88   Geertz, 14.

89   Geertz, 13.

90   Geertz, 29.

91   This is how Stein's book is still being advertised on the website of the C. H. Beck Verlag, its German publisher: https://www.beck-shop.de/stein-leinwand/product/29815; accessed September 30, 2019.

92   Zipes, "The Contemporary German Fascination for Things Jewish," 15.

93   Jonathan Safran Foer's critically acclaimed debut novel, *Everything Is Illuminated*, tells the story of a third-generation American Jewish writer who travels to the shtetl where his grandfather grew up to recover a lost history; the travel narrative is interwoven with a fantastical account of life in the shtetl before the destruction of the Holocaust. Foer's book experiment *Tree of Codes* is a cut-and-paste rearrangement of Schulz's *The Street of Crocodiles*. Krauss's novel *The History of Love* is also partly set in a prewar shtetl and alludes to Schulzian traditions of surrealism. On the popularity of Schulz among contemporary Jewish writers, see Goldfarb, "Appropriations of Bruno Schulz."

94   See *New American Haggadah*.

Chapter Two

1   Krüger, "In jeder Ecke ein dicker Klumpen Angst"; Mangold, "Grotesk wie der Tod."

2   Biller, "Letzte Ausfahrt Uckermark."

3   Biller's long and profound engagement with Reich-Ranicki as a literary father figure is one of the central topics in his "Selbstporträt" *Der gebrauchte Jude*, henceforth cited in the text as *DgJ*.

4   Codrai, "Lost in Third Space?," 130.

5   Henceforth cited in the text as *IKvBS*.

6   My analysis of the intertextual relationships in Biller's work draws on Gérard Genette's definition of intertextuality "as a relationship of copresence between two texts or among several texts: that is to say, eidetically and typically as the actual presence of one text within another." See Genette, *Palimpsests*, 1–2. While intertextuality in this sense captures Biller's textual relationship with Bruno Schulz's *Die Zimtläden* (1934; translated as *The Street of Crocodiles*, 1963), the term *intermediality* refers to Biller's engagement with Schulz's graphic oeuvre. Biller's intermediality involves the insertion of Schulz's drawing into the novella *Im Kopf von Bruno Schulz*, alongside the translation of the visual medium into textual form by way of ekphrasis. The term *remediation* will be used to describe Biller's repurposing of entire writing traditions (such as "ghetto writing") or specific literary configurations (such as the artistic representations of sadomasochism), which assemble various literary texts and media formats. Both intertextuality and intermediality can be understood as subcategories of remediation, which is a term that I have used in the preceding chapters. Broadly speaking, remediation includes any form of media recycling, repurposing, or revision. Such an inflationary use of

the term *remediation*, however, entails the risk of hollowing it out, which is why it seems advisable to stick to the media-specific and well-established terminology when dealing with concrete cases of intertextuality/intermediality.

7   Biller, *Im Land der Väter und Verräter.*
8   Gwyer, "'You Think Your Writing Belongs to You?'"
9   Gwyer.
10 Gwyer.
11 Bloom, *The Anxiety of Influence*, 5.
12 Bloom, 30.
13 Bloom, 19.
14 Bloom, 96.
15 It is therefore not only the father who creates the son, but "the father will not be born until he finds his own central ephebe"; Bloom, *The Anxiety of Influence*, 61.
16 Bloom, 94.
17 Bloom explains each of these ratios in great detail and offers a "synopsis" at the beginning of his study, 14–16.
18 Begley, "Colossus among Critics: Harold Bloom."
19 Gilbert and Gubar, *The Madwoman in the Attic*, 47.
20 Gilbert and Gubar, 6.
21 Gilbert and Gubar, 49.
22 Manuel Gogos also applies a Bloomian framework to his analysis of Biller's writing in his *Philip Roth & Söhne.*
23 Bloom, *The Anxiety of Influence*, 95.
24 Similarly, Manuel Gogos speaks of a "versuchten *Vatermord* [italics in the original]" in the relationship between Biller and Philip Roth; *Philip Roth & Söhne*, 23.
25 Ijoma Mangold, for example, speaks of a "Kaddisch"; Mangold, "Grotesk wie der Tod."
26 The connection between elegy and anxiety is also noted by Bloom: "The great pastoral elegies, indeed all major elegies for poets, do not express grief but center upon their composer's own creative anxieties"; *The Anxiety of Influence*, 151.
27 Gilbert and Gubar, *The Madwoman in the Attic*, 48.
28 Henceforth cited in the text as *HH.*
29 Beßlich, "Unzuverlässiges Erzählen im Dienst der Erinnerung," 43.
30 On the commodification and hypermediation of Holocaust memory in *Harlem Holocaust*, see Chase, "Shoah Business."
31 Eke, "'Was wollen sie?,'" 90.
32 Eke, 96.
33 Gogos, *Philip Roth & Söhne*, 45.
34 It is stressed throughout the novella that Rosenhain suffers from repeated bouts of dizziness and has a propensity for hallucinations and wild fantasies: "Dabei machte das mir ja auch Spaß, es war eine verzweifelte Spielerei, die

mich mitunter dazu antrieb, mir mein Leben anders und besser vorzustellen, was immer funktionierte und manchmal sogar so weit ging, dass ich mir, zum Zeitvertreib nur, etwa auf der Straße die Gesichter der Passanten in surrealistischer Manier zurechtbog" (*HH*, 10).

35 Diner, "Negative Symbiose," 185.

36 Seibt, "Der letzte Augenblick der Unschuld," 65.

37 According to Schulz's German translator, Doreen Daume, the actual Bruno Schulz did really write a letter to Thomas Mann, which also contained a copy of Schulz's first German-language text, *Die Heimkehr*. Both the letter and the manuscript have been lost, which makes it impossible to verify this claim; see Daume's "Afterword," 189, in Schulz, *Die Zimtläden*, henceforth cited in the text as *DZ*.

38 For a concise introduction to the literary genre of the apocalypse, see Torrey, "Apocalypse."

39 Monstrous, reptilelike birds are also mentioned briefly in *Die Zimtläden*: "Unmöglich, in diesen Monstern mit ihren riesigen phantastischen Schnäbeln, die sie gleich nach ihrer Geburt, gefräßig aus dem Schlund ihrer Kehlen zischend, weit aufsperrten, in diesen Echsen mit ihren schwächlichen nackten, buckligen Körpern künftige Pfauen, Fasane, Auerhähne und Kondore zu erkennen. In Körben auf Watte lagernd, hoben diese drachenhaften Subjekte auf ihren dürren Hälsen die blinden, mit trüber Haut überzogenen Köpfe und quakten lautlos aus stummen Rachen" (36).

40 In fact, the Hebrew "churban," which refers to the destruction of the Second Temple, is used as an alternative term for the Holocaust. For pointing this out to me I thank Hanna Schumacher, who in this context made me aware of the Yiddish "khurbn-literatur." On the topic of "khurbn-literatur," see Roskies and Diamant, *Holocaust Literature*, 105–8.

41 On the topic of "ghetto writing," see Fuchs and Krobb, eds., *Ghetto Writing*, and Glasenapp, "Deutsch-jüdische Ghettoliteratur."

42 On the theme of sadomasochism in Schulz's work, see Chrostowska, "'Masochistic Art of Fantasy.'"

43 See *Bruno Schulz: Das graphische Werk*. I thank Ulrike Henneke from Kiepenheuer & Witsch for her generous help with tracking down this source.

44 Fuchs and Krobb, "Writing the Ghetto," 3.

45 Krobb, "Reclaiming the Location," 51.

46 Krobb, 53.

47 Fuchs and Krobb, "Writing the Ghetto," 5.

48 Krobb, "Reclaiming the Location," 46.

49 See Fuchs and Krobb, "Writing the Ghetto."

50 See *Bruno Schulz: Das graphische Werk*, 69–76.

51 Fuchs and Krobb, "Writing the Ghetto," 5.

52 Boym, *The Future of Nostalgia*, 3.

53 Krobb, "Reclaiming the Location," 49.

54 Hartley, *The Go-Between*, 5.

55 Another genealogical line actually connects Kafka and Sacher-Masoch, not only via the identical names of their protagonists (Gregor) but also via a newspaper clipping of a woman dressed in furs gracing the wall of Gregor Samsa's room. Holger Rudloff has interestingly also brought Mann into this equation; see his *Gregor Samsa und seine Brüder*.

56 Gilbert and Gubar, *The Madwoman in the Attic*, 6.

57 On this and other dichotomies in Schulz's text, see Janicka, "Mapping the Father."

58 The subversive potential of Adela's actions is also stressed by Chrostowska, along with the irony resulting from the role reversal she provokes—the formless, passive female ultimately dominates the active, male (wannabe) demiurge; see Chrostowska, "'Masochistic Art of Fantasy.'"

59 See Sacher-Masoch, *Venus im Pelz*. E. L. James's *Fifty Shades of Grey* is a hugely successful erotic novel that uses sadomasochistic imagery to depict what has been widely criticized as an abusive relationship between a woman and an older man.

60 Deleuze, *Masochism*.

61 Chrostowska, "'Masochistic Art of Fantasy,'" 497n13.

62 The fact that the fake Mann is described as an "Abbild," which acts "steif und hochmütig" (*IKvBS*, 33), also points to his alignment with Sacher-Masoch's Venus in furs, who is, after all, a living marble statue whose stiffness and coldness is repeatedly stressed in the text.

63 The feminizing of Thomas Mann is also noted by Gwyer, "'You Think Your Writing Belongs to You?'"

64 Schulz, *Bruno Schultz: Das graphische Werk*, 61.

65 Schulz, 63.

66 Erll, "Travelling Memory."

67 Chrostowska also points to "misogynistic impulses" in Schulz's writing. Moreover, visual references to the topos of the femme fatale can be frequently found in Schulz's graphic works; see Chrostowska, "'Masochistic Art of Fantasy,'" 489.

68 Interestingly, the real Mann's silence reproduces the coldness and cruelty of the female in the sadomasochistic constellation; this would support the interpretation that Schulz's imaginary sadomasochistic relationship with the fake Mann is an expression of his actual relationship with the real Mann.

69 It should be noted that *Der gebrauchte Jude* is a heavily fictionalized autobiography, in which the narrator repeatedly stresses the unreliability and fragmentariness of his account. The reader is thus urged not to take the text at face value, which gives rise to the question of whether or not Biller's hateful relationship with Thomas Mann should be taken seriously. I would argue that while some of the encounters Biller describes in his "Selbstporträt" are heavily edited—including those with Reich-Ranicki—the issues that are being negotiated via the triangle Biller-Mann-Reich-Ranicki remain unaffected by the ontological status of these events. The question of whether or not Biller

"really" hates Mann is not as important as the ways in which Biller uses Thomas Mann to express an extremely negative view on the issue of pre- and post-Holocaust German-Jewish symbiosis.

70 Biller's negative obsession with Mann has unfolded across various genres: apart from prose (*Im Kopf von Bruno Schulz*) and autofiction (*Der gebrauchte Jude*), he also voiced his hatred in several interviews, see Posener, "Maxim Biller will Thomas Mann zerstören"; Käppeler, "'Mit Angst kenne ich mich aus.'"

71 This has also been noted by some of the more critical reviews of the novella; see especially Granzin, "Janusköpfiger Kollege aus Deutschland"; Hartz, "Im Kopf von Maxim Biller."

72 Bloom, *The Anxiety of Influence*, 141.

73 Bloom, 141.

74 The feminization of the (fake) Mann could allude to a number of things: it may serve as a rather crude reference to Mann's alleged homosexuality, while also alluding to Gustav von Aschenbach's character in *Der Tod in Venedig* (1912) and thus being yet another allusion to Mann's alleged homosexuality. The fact that the fake Mann is described as wearing make-up (*IKvBS*, 50) supports this reading. Finally, it could also be read as an ironic reversal of the stereotype of the effeminate Jew, which would feed into a broader carnivalization of German-Jewish relations in the novella.

75 For a deeper engagement with the misogyny in Schulz's writing, see Chrostowska, "'Masochistic Art of Fantasy.'" I thank Christine Achinger for pointing out that some of the misogynistic tropes present in Schulz's and Biller's writing resonate with the descriptions of woman in Otto Weininger's *Geschlecht und Charakter* (1903); there might thus be yet another Jewish intertextual genealogy, linking Biller to Schulz and Weininger. On conceptions of femininity in Weininger, see Achinger, "Allegories of Destruction."

76 The fake Mann is not only connected to the femme fatale. By continually stressing his fakeness and status of a mere "Abbild" (*IKvBS*, 33), he is also cast as a "false idol" and thus connected to the practice of idolatry, one of the worst transgressions in Judaism.

77 I am referring to the iconic stanza from Celan's "Todesfuge": "Schwarze Milch der Frühe wir trinken dich nachts/wir trinken dich mittags der Tod ist ein Meister aus / Deutschland/wir trinken dich abends und morgens wir trinken und trinken / der Tod ist ein Meister aus Deutschland sein Auge ist blau / er trifft dich mit bleierner Kugel er trifft dich genau/ein Mann wohnt im Haus dein goldenes Haar Margarete/er hetzt seine Rüden auf uns er schenkt uns ein Grab in der / Luft/er spielt mit den Schlangen und träumet der Tod ist ein / Meister aus Deutschland," see Celan, "Todesfuge," 18–19.

78 Bakhtin, *Rabelais and His World*, 11.

79 Bakhtin, 13.

80 See Bakhtin, *Rabelais and His World*.

81 Richter 9:16–20 (*Luther-Bibel*).

82   Richter 9:56–57.
83   Gilbert and Gubar, *The Madwoman in the Attic*, 51.
84   Gilbert and Gubar, 51.
85   Gwyer, "'You Think Your Writing Belongs to You?'"
86   Garloff and Mueller, "Introduction," in *German-Jewish Literature after* 1990, 7–8.
87   Gwyer, "'You Think Your Writing Belongs to You?'"
88   Gwyer.

Chapter Three

1   Arguably, the "transnational turn" can be seen as part of a broader rise of the prefix "trans-" in the humanities. The *Freie Universität Berlin* recently hosted a summer school entitled "Becoming TransGerman: Transnational, Transdisciplinary, Transgender, Transhuman," which was indicative of this larger trend. This also raises the question whether "trans-" might have replaced "post-" as the defining prefix of an entire age; see H-German, "CFP: 5th Berlin Program Summer Workshop."

2   Some of the most recent and important contributions to the field of "transnational/transcultural memory studies" include Brunow, *Remediating Transcultural Memory*; Bond and Rapson, eds., *The Transcultural Turn*; De Cesari and Rigney, eds., *Transnational Memory*; Crownshaw, ed., *Transcultural Memory*, which is based on a 2011 edition of the journal *Parallax*. A pioneer in the field of transcultural studies is Welsch, "Transculturality."

3   Moses and Rothberg, "A Dialogue on the Ethics and Politics of Transcultural Memory," 32.

4   Rigney, "The Dynamics of Remembrance." Lucy Bond, Stef Craps, and Pieter Vermeulen have dedicated an entire volume, *Memory Unbound*, to the recent dynamization of memory studies, examining memory's transnational, transgenerational, transmedial and transdisciplinary movements.

5   Hoskins, "7/7 and Connective Memory."

6   The term "methodological nationalism" is used by de Cesari and Rigney, "Introduction," in *Transnational Memory*, 1. Astrid Erll uses the term "methodological culturalism" in a recent article; see Erll, "Transcultural Memory."

7   Erll, "Travelling Memory," 7. Erll derives this idea of cultures as "containers" from Wolfgang Welsch's essay on "transculturality," who in turn traces it back to Johann Gottfried Herder, see Welsch, "Transculturality."

8   Bond and Rapson, "Introduction," 19.

9   Assmann, "Transnational Memories," 546–47. It is important to note, however, that this utopian impetus is not shared by all scholars working on the "transcultural," as Astrid Erll points out: "In addition to accentuating a specific optics and approach of memory research, the term 'transcultural' is also often deployed to highlight what is seen as 'productive' mnemonic processes.

This is where the distinction between normative and descriptive, 'hot' and 'cold,' empathic/activist and analytic research on transcultural memory comes into play"; Erll, "Transcultural Memory." Her own concept of "travelling memory" is clearly on the descriptive and analytic side. See also her "Travelling Memory."

10   Craps and Rothberg, "Introduction: Transcultural Negotiations of Holocaust Memory," 518.

11   Rothberg, "From Gaza to Warsaw."

12   Erll, "Travelling Memory," 12.

13   Astrid Erll remarks elsewhere that she considers the term "transcultural memory" to be tautological, since all memory is fundamentally in motion and crossing cultural borders. She therefore argues that "transcultural memory" might best be "replaced by (a reflected version of) the term 'memory,'" see Erll, "Transcultural Memory."

14   Erll, "Transcultural Memory."

15   Brunow, *Remediating Transcultural Memory*, 28.

16   Vertovec, *Transnationalism*; de Cesari and Rigney, "Introduction," in *Transnational Memory*.

17   De Cesari and Rigney, "Introduction," in *Transnational Memory*, 4.

18   This is an observation shared by Stef Craps in a recent interview: "I'm under the impression that memory scholars who favor the term 'transnational' generally have a background in the social sciences and are concerned with the obstacles that prevent memory from circulating freely across boundaries. By contrast, people who prefer the term "transcultural" tend to have a literary or cultural studies background and focus primarily on processes of border-crossing without paying as much attention to such impediments." See Roca Lizarazu and Vince, "Memory Studies Goes Planetary."

19   De Cesari and Rigney, "Introduction," in *Transnational Memory*, 4–5. A recent volume on transnationalism in German-language literature stresses the dialectical dimension of the "transnational" which takes into account flows and stagnations, allowing us "to conceptualize the continued importance of the nation as the organizing unit of global affairs and the continued significance—indeed increased significance—of borders in a world in which the ease, or difficulty, of border crossing defines not only products but also people," Herrmann, Smith-Prei, and Taberner, "Introduction: Contemporary German-Language Literature and Transnationalism," 5.

20   This is also the thrust of a 2013 volume, *Memory and Theory in Eastern Europe*, edited by Uilleam Blacker, Alexander Etkind, and Julie Fedor, which sets out to "examine how the theoretical approaches and academic practices of Memory Studies can be applied and transformed in this region (i.e., Eastern Europe)"; see "Introduction," 2.

21   There are, however, attempts to read the (post-)Soviet states in post-colonial terms; this is for example the case for the editors of the above-mentioned volume, who claim that "Eastern Europe can be broadly characterized as

"postsocialist, postcatastrophic, and, as some of the chapters in this volume argue, postcolonial," see Blacker and Etkind, "Introduction," 2.

22 De Cesari and Rigney, "Introduction," in *Transnational Memory*, 4.

23 Welsch, "Transculturality," 208n26.

24 Brunow, *Remediating Transcultural Memory*, 26.

25 Bond and Rapson, "Introduction," 9.

26 De Cesari and Rigney, "Introduction"; the importance of locatedness is also stressed by Radstone, "What Place Is This?"

27 On the issue of "scales of memory" and multi-scalarity see also Kennedy and Nugent, "Scales of Memory."

28 I follow Bakhtin's understanding of the novel as a quintessentially dialogic genre that is furthermore able to incorporate other literary forms and modes of discourse. I will come back to Bakhtin's theory of the novel in my conclusion, see Bakhtin, *Problems of Dostoevsky's Poetics*; Bakhtin, "Epic and Novel"; Bakhtin, "Discourse in the Novel."

29 Erll, "Transcultural Memory."

30 Levy and Sznaider, *Erinnerung im globalen Zeitalter*, 235.

31 See for example Craps and Rothberg, "Introduction: Transcultural Negotiations of Holocaust Memory"; Craps, *Postcolonial Witnessing*; Rothberg, *Multidirectional Memory*; Silverman, *Palimpsestic Memory*; Sanyal, *Memory and Complicity*.

32 Rothberg, "From Gaza to Warsaw," 524.

33 Natan Sznaider has, however, recently published a co-written book in which he critically examines the usefulness of the slogan "Never Again" in various non-Western contexts, among them Eastern Europe, see Baer and Sznaider, *Memory and Forgetting in the Post-Holocaust Era*.

34 Blacker and Etkind, "Introduction," in *Memory and Theory in Eastern Europe*, 5.

35 Haines, "Introduction: The Eastern European Turn in Contemporary German-language Literature."

36 For a more detailed discussion of some of these authors and the recent increase of Russian voices in German Jewish discourse see Garloff and Mueller, eds., *German Jewish Literature after 1990*.

37 Bakhtin, "Epic and Novel," 12.

38 Bakhtin, *Problems of Dostoevsky's Poetics*, 32.

39 Tomsky, "From Sarajevo to 9/11," 49.

40 "The title of the volume in which Gigricht immigrants" stories are to be published, *Fremde Heimat. Heimat in der Fremde*, while professing inclusivity, actually preserves the binary divide between those who belong in the town, and those who do not," see Haines, "Poetics of the 'Gruppenbild,'" 238.

41 For an introduction to the issue of unreliability in narration see Shen, "Unreliability."

42 For an in-depth exploration of autobiographical memory see Markowitsch and Welzer, *Das autobiographische Gedächtnis*.

43 Brigid Haines is therefore correct in pointing out that "the deceptively conventional formal composition" of this and other Vertlib novel(s) usually conceals a multifaceted and highly ambiguous narrative, see Haines, "Poetics of the 'Gruppenbild,'" 234. This point is also stressed by Dieter Neidlinger und Silke Pasewalk in their exploration of Vertlib's poetics: "Ja, es ist ein Grundzug von Vertlibs Erzählen, dass Eindeutigkeiten und eigene Vorstellungsmuster evoziert und sogleich ihrer Absurdität überführt werden, um Ambivalenz und Ambiguität der Wirklichkeit in den Geschichten (Situationen und Perspektiven) zur Sprache zu bringen," see Neidlinger and Pasewalk, "Die Redlichkeit des Betrugs," 484–85.

44 "Der bewußte Akt des Aussprechens wird zwar als schmerzhaft dargestellt, wirkt aber für Rosa befreiend, weil sie damit das internalisierte Trauma . . . wiederholen muß, in eine narrative Forms bringt und damit externalisiert. Das Trauma . . . wird von Rosa durch das Erzählen kathartisch überwunden." I also take issue with the evidence that Wogenstein cites for his hypothesis, since it is based on a misreading. Wogenstein interprets Rosa's dead friend Mascha, who talks to her from beyond the grave, as a symptom of Rosa's trauma; according to Wogenstein, the fact that Mascha falls silent toward the end of the narrative symbolizes Rosa's mastery of this trauma. What Wogenstein reads as Mascha's lapse into silence on page 414 of the novel is, however, only a temporary suspension of their conversation, which is revived on page 428. See Wogenstein, "Topographie des Dazwischen," 77.

45 Wogenstein, 78.

46 Tomsky, "From Sarajevo to 9/11," 49.

47 Jessica Ortner makes a similar argument about a de-centring of the Holocaust in Vertlib's writing. She reads this as the precondition for a more "multidirectional" approach to what she terms the "current memory conflict between Western and Eastern Europe." I, however, will stress the clash—rather than the multidirectional interaction—between various memory templates in the text. See Ortner, "The German Jewish Migrant Novel after 1990," 95.

48 Stuart Taberner arrives at a similar evaluation when he stresses that Rosa's "persecution as a Jew" is "emphatically not the only" element that constitutes her personal history. See Taberner, "Vladimir Vertlib," 39.

49 De Cesari and Rigney, "Introduction," in *Transnational Memory*, 5.

50 De Cesari and Rigney, 5.

51 Haines, "Poetics of the 'Gruppenbild,'" 237.

52 The status of Leningrad within the broader framework of Hitler's destruction campaign has been hotly debated among German historians, as the following article demonstrates: Hass, "Die deutsche Historiografie und die Belagerung Leningrads (1941–1944)." A growing awareness of the genocidal strategy driving the siege has trickled down from the realm of academia into the broader cultural arena, as is shown by two articles in major German newspapers: Ganzenmüller, "Ein stiller Genozid"; Das Gupta, "Als die Menschen Leim und Ratten aßen."

53 See Wertsch, "Collective Memory and Narrative Templates," 142–43.

54 Assmann, "Europe's Divided Memory," 33.

55 This point is also stressed by Wertsch, who states that narrative templates "operate at a level that can be called 'deep collective memory'" and are thus not easily accessible on a conscious level and are usually resistant to change; see Wertsch, "Collective Memory," 130; see also Wertsch, "Deep Memory and Narrative Templates."

56 For a concise introduction to Holocaust memory and historiography in the (post-)Soviet context see Klier, "The Holocaust and the Soviet Union" and Fox, "The Holocaust under Communism."

57 See Taberner, "Vladimir Vertlib," 35.

58 This tension is also highlighted by Stuart Taberner and Sebastian Wogenstein: see Taberner, "Vladimir Vertlib," and Wogenstein, "Topographie des Dazwischen."

59 For an in-depth discussion of the term "intersectionality" see Chepp and Hill Collins, "Intersectionality."

60 Bakhtin, "Epic and Novel," 37. The concept of "unfinalizability" is another central component of Bakhtin's analysis of Dostoevsky's work; see Bakhtin, *Problems of Dostoevsky's Poetics*.

61 I thank Dr. Christine Achinger for pointing this out to me.

62 Zipes, "The Contemporary German Fascination for Things Jewish," 15.

63 On traditions of "ghetto writing," see Fuchs and Krobb, eds., *Ghetto Writing*.

64 The issue of essentialism is also addressed in Sebastian Wogenstein's analysis of the novel, "Topographie des Dazwischen."

65 Rothberg, "Multidirectional Memory and the Implicated Subject," 42.

66 Rothberg, 43.

67 Rothberg, 51.

68 Silverman, *Palimpsestic Memory*, 28–29.

69 In his recent study *Cosmopolitan Parables*, David Kim criticizes Rothberg for not properly considering the aesthetics of multidirectional memory and makes efforts to define in more detail what such an aesthetics might look like. He, however, also remains unclear as to how what he calls a "cosmopolitan aesthetics" is different from literariness as such. Another problem with Kim's approach, which also applies to Rothberg and Silverman (at least to an extent), is that he automatically assumes literature to have an enabling, politically progressive function when it might just as well yield the opposite effect. This might be owing to the fact that all three theorists ultimately subscribe to an avant-garde inspired and partially elitist notion of what (aesthetically and morally "good") literature is.

70 Teufel and Schmitz, "Wahrheit und 'subversives Gedächtnis,'" 248.

71 Brigid Haines also stresses the "dialogism" of Vertlib's works and poetics; she also briefly mentions Bakhtin's concept of polyphony but does not go into any further detail. See Haines, "Poetics of the 'Gruppenbild.'"

72 Bakhtin, *Problems of Dostoevsky's Poetics*, 17.

73 Bakhtin, 6.

74 Bakhtin, 8.

75 Bakhtin, "Discourse in the Novel," 272.

76 Bakhtin, "Epic and Novel," 12. Bakhtin's concept of "interillumination" is surprisingly similar to Michael Rothberg's idea of "multidirectionality"; in fact, Bakhtin's entire theory of dialogism is in many respects a theory of "multidirectionality" avant la lettre. See Rothberg, *Multidirectional Memory*.

77 Ortner, "The German Jewish Migrant Novel after 1990," 95.

78 Assmann, "Europe's Divided Memory," 33. This point is also stressed by Ortner, "The German Jewish Migrant Novel after 1990."

79 Bakhtin, *Problems of Dostoevsky's Poetics*, 28.

80 Sebastian Wogenstein arrives at a similar assessment: "Indem er das Scheitern der institutionalisierten Historiographie darstellt, inszeniert der Roman den Triumph des besonderen, narrativen Gedächtnisses"; Wogenstein, "Topographie des Dazwischen," 79.

81 Bakhtin repeatedly stresses the difference between dialectics and dialogism; while dialogism promotes coexistence and diversity, dialectics aims for evolution and unity. This is also why dialogism is a spatial (or spatiotemporal) rather than a temporal concept. *Problems of Dostoevsky's Poetics*, 31.

82 Bakhtin, "Discourse in the Novel," 320–21.

83 Bakhtin, "Epic and Novel," 5.

84 Bakhtin, 35.

85 Tomsky, "From Sarajevo to 9/11."

86 This difference is also stressed by Wogenstein in connection to Vertlib: "Vertlibs Roman ist eine Antwort auf essentialistische Vorstellungen, nicht jedoch, indem er ihnen mit einem aufklärerisch-instruktiven Gestus begegnet, sondern indem er sie viel mehr ironisch dekonstruiert"; Wogenstein, "Topographie des Dazwischen," 76.

87 Taberner, "Transnationalism and Cosmopolitanism," 57.

88 Vertlib, *Spiegel im fremden Wort*, 25.

89 Bakhtin, *Problems of Dostoevsky's Poetics*, 68.

90 Vertlib, *Spiegel im fremden Wort*, 26.

91 The letter is, of course, also written with a particular addressee in mind and therefore shaped by expectations and a certain performance element. This mediation, however, comes from Rosa and thus from the inside and not from an external third-person party who filters the contents, as is the case with the narrator.

92 See, for example, Neidlinger and Pasewalk, "Die Redlichkeit des Betrugs"; Teufel and Schmitz, "Wahrheit und 'subversives Gedächtnis.'"

93 Aleida Assmann differentiates between active "working memory" and passive "reference memory"; as a mere transcript, Rosa's story would be *passively stored away*; it is only through the act of reading that it is *actively re-stored* by the reader. Assmann, "Canon and Archive," 99.

94 "Rosa Masur hätte beinahe vergebens erzählt—wäre da nicht der Erzähler von Vertlibs Roman. Ohne diesen Erzähler, der von der Erzählerin Rosa erzählt, wäre auch ihre Geschichte verloren." Teufel and Schmitz, "Wahrheit und 'subversives Gedächtnis,'" 248.

95 Bakhtin, *Problems of Dostoevsky's Poetics*, 18.

Chapter Four

1 See, for example, Eigler, *Gedächtnis und Geschichte*; Fuchs, *Phantoms of War*.

2 See Costagli and Galli, eds., *Deutsche Familienromane*; Eigler, *Gedächtnis und Geschichte*; Fuchs, *Phantoms of War*; Herrmann, *Vergangenwart*; Horstkotte, *Nachbilder*; Jahn, "Familienkonstruktionen 2005"; Weigel, "Familienbande"; Weigel, *Genea-Logik*; as well as a recent special collection of *Modern Languages Open*, Souchuk and Gruber, eds., "Reading between the Bloodlines: Reflections on the German-Language Family Story."

3 Fischer, Hammermeister, and Kramer, "Der Nationalsozialismus und die Shoah," 17.

4 Frieden, *Neuverhandlungen des Holocaust*, 40.

5 Frieden, 17.

6 Frieden, 24.

7 Frieden, 66.

8 Hirsch, *Family Frames*.

9 On the affirmation and partial transcendence of the family paradigm in Petrowskaja's writing, see two of my own recent contributions: "Liaisons Dangereuses" and "The Family Tree, the Web, and the Palimpsest."

10 On the family novel as a critical resource for processes of Vergangenheitsbewältigung, see Fuchs, *Phantoms of War*; Eigler, *Gedächtnis und Geschichte*; Horstkotte, *Nachbilder*.

11 Frieden, *Neuverhandlungen des Holocaust*, 69–70.

12 Henceforth cited in the text as *V*.

13 For a brief introduction to Austria's history of Vergangenheitsbewältigung, see Bailer-Galanda, "Vergangenheitspolitik in Österreich"; Botz, "Die Waldheim-Affäre und ihre Folgen"; Stuhlpfarrer, "Österreich."

14 A similar interpretation has been put forward by Seemann, "The Re-Construction and Deconstruction of a Family Narrative."

15 Hirsch, *Family Frames*, 22.

16 Seemann, "Re-Construction and Deconstruction," 43.

17 The performativity of family memory in *Vienna* is also stressed by Gruber, "Performing Family Identity, Memory and Hybridity"; Müllender, "Generationenkonzepte in zeitgenössischen österreichisch-jüdischen Romanen"; Hakkarainen, "Melange of Memories"; Jahn, "Familienkonstruktionen 2005."

18 It should be noted that the portrayal of the narrator's brother in *Vienna* is inspired by Menasse's real-life half brother Robert Menasse, whose critical voice has shaped Austrian public discourse about the past since the mid-1980s. An even closer resemblance exists between the narrator's father and Menasse's real-life father, Hans, who is indeed a Kindertransport survivor and former member of Austria's national football team. Menasse reflects on the relationship between the factual and the fictional elements of her text in an interview by Matthias Prangel, "Normale Familie."

19 This point is stressed by Daphne Seemann, who claims that the new family narrative that emerges after the death of the survivor generation "relies on its distinct dissociation from the traumatic frame of the preceding narrative": see Seemann, "Moving beyond Post-Traumatic Memory Narratives," 171.

20 This gendered conflict is also stressed by Seemann in "The Re-Construction and Deconstruction of a Family Narrative."

21 Menasse's work is characterized by a long-standing engagement with the issue of multiperspectivity, which brings together her early short-story anthology *Lässliche Todsünden* (2009) with the novels *Vienna* and *Quasikristalle* and, most recently, her short-story collection *Tiere für Fortgeschrittene* (2017); these lines of continuity are also noted by Weber, "'Jedes einzelne Bild nur ein Mosaikstück?'"

22 Literary critic Ijoma Mangold has furthermore identified "das Vergehen der Zeit selbst" as one of the central topics in *Quasikristalle*. This would imply that time has an agency in the text that goes beyond that of the human—it stubbornly moves on whether we like it to or not. In contrast, time in the family only exists to the extent that it can be linked back to the human and the genealogical chain. See Mangold, "Alles ist eitel."

23 "Literaturpreis Alpha 2014—Gewinnerin Eva Menasse," 2:28–2:45.

24 Interestingly enough, Menasse herself mentions the concept of the "Wahlverwandtschaft" and Johann Wolfgang Goethe's seminal text in "Auschwitz ist zu oft Bezugspunkt," an interview with Ulrich Wickert. She thereby situates her own reference to scientific metaphors in a wider tradition, although the parallels between her work and Goethe's arguably end there.

25 Hirsch, *The Generation of Postmemory*, 39.

26 There is one episode in particular that implies an oedipal tension between daughter and father. Kurt Molin treats "sein kleines Mäderl" (*Q*, 347) to a new watch and flirts with her: "Nachher legte er ihr auf der Straße den Arm um die Schultern, schaute sie verliebt an und machte den alten, hundertfach gebrauchten Witz: Das raffinierte Luder . . . hat sich den Millionär geangelt, ergänzte Xane" (*Q*, 347).

27 Landsberg, *Prosthetic Memory*, 3.

28 Sontag, *Regarding the Pain of Others*, 93.

29 Eke, "'Was wollen sie? Die Absolution?,'" 90.

30 Huyssen, *Present Pasts*, 99.

31 Wickert, "Auschwitz ist zu oft Bezugspunkt."

32 Wickert.

33 This is very much the case for two recent volumes on the topic: Lucy Bond and Jessica Rapson, eds., *The Transcultural Turn*; and Chiara de Cesari and Ann Rigney, eds., *Transnational Memory*.

34 Dirk Moses and Michael Rothberg, for example, advocate for an "ethics of transcultural memory" that differentiates more clearly between the various purposes that comparative and analogical approaches to the Holocaust and other memories serve; see their "A Dialogue on the Ethics and Politics of Transcultural Memory." Moses in particular is extremely critical of the assumed cosmopolitanism behind globalized versions of Holocaust memory; he argues that they might actually have the opposite effect and entrench existing divisions. See his "Genocide and the Terror of History" and "Does the Holocaust Reveal or Conceal Other Genocides?"

35 Kapczynski, "Never Over, Over and Over," 25.

36 Sontag, *On Photography*, 20.

37 Young, *Writing and Rewriting the Holocaust*, 174.

38 It is noteworthy, however, that Bernays concentrates on the acoustic dimension of the videos, which might point to a different approach. While the images, owing to their repetitive nature, do not allow for a deeper engagement, the "Tonspur" might allow for some form of focus, as is implied by the word "konzentrieren" (*Q*, 77), which, in the context of the Auschwitz museum, of course has a very specific ring to it.

39 Sontag, *On Photography*, 20.

40 Sontag, 21.

41 Sontag, *Regarding the Pain of Others*, 94–95.

42 Sontag, 107.

43 Sontag, 109.

44 One can certainly challenge Sontag's conviction that such alternative modes of attention can only flourish during the act of reading. In his book *On Slowness*, Lutz Koepnick shows how the "mode of slowness" (4)—an idea that is very similar to Sontag's concept of contemplation—can be developed and employed in relation to a range of media and artistic forms. Koepnick's focus on visual media, such as photography, films, video art, and multimedia installation art, complicates Sontag's assumption that image-driven forms of representation tend to simplify and produce "image-glut." One should note, though, that Sontag's criticism of visual media mainly targets their mass-mediated manifestations (war photography, print journalism, news channels); she does not consider the realm of avant-garde-inspired contemporary art, which is at the center of Koepnick's study.

45 Žižek, *Welcome to the Desert of the Real*.

46 Sontag, *Regarding the Pain of Others*, 19.

47 Sontag, 23.

48 Frieden, *Neuverhandlungen*, 70.

49 It might be fruitful to read the Bernays chapter in conjunction with Iris Hanika's *Das Eigentliche* (2010), which addresses problems of memorial routinization and commodification in Holocaust discourse via a recourse to traditions and tropes of melancholy, sloth, and boredom, as Mary Cosgrove has shown. These sentiments seem to resonate with the sense of tedium, frustration, and fatigue experienced by Bernays. See Cosgrove, *Born under Auschwitz*, 185–200.

50 Byrd and Tharps, *Hair Story*.

51 Martin Gubser, for example, points out that the Jew in nineteenth-century German literature often possessed "rotes, auf jeden Fall aber struppiges Haar," making him/her the "exakte . . . Gegenteil des in den gleichen Werken gezeichneten nichtjüdischen Schönheitsideals"; *Literarischer Antisemitismus*, 128. Andrew Colin Gow traces the negative association of Jews with the color red back to be Middle Ages in *The Red Jews*, 66–69.

52 Most notably in Arno Geiger's *Es geht uns gut* (2005), which centers on a grandchild trying to clear his grandparents' attic in a mansion which is also located Vienna's Hietzing district.

53 The basement fulfills a similar function in memory discourse, as can be seen in Ulrich Seidl's 2014 documentary *Im Keller*. Seidl's film portrays various individuals whose basements harbor repressed stories, desires, or convictions, among them one full of Nazi memorabilia.

54 The term "global icon" is borrowed from Assmann, "The Holocaust—a Global Memory?," 109. In a recent publication Amos Goldberg and Haim Hazan elaborate further on the problem that the "global" in recent Holocaust discourse often means "'Western' or perhaps even 'American'"; see Goldberg and Hazan, *Marking Evil*, xi.

55 Wickert, "Auschwitz ist zu oft Bezugspunkt."

56 Wickert.

57 Wickert.

58 Bond, "Types of Transculturality," 61–80.

59 Bond, 66.

60 Levy and Sznaider, *Erinnerung im globalen Zeitalter*, 194–211.

61 See, for example, Bond, "Types of Transculturality"; Moses and Rothberg, "A Dialogue on the Ethics and Politics of Transcultural Memory"; Moses, "Does the Holocaust Reveal or Conceal Other Genocides?"

62 Kapczynski, "Never Over, Over and Over," 25 and 23.

63 Goldberg, "Ethics, Identity and Antifundamental Fundamentalism," 15.

64 Goldberg, 5.

65 A recent international conference was dedicated to this rise of the "survivor" in contemporary discourse: see Kalkbrenner, Review of *Survivors: Politics and Semantics of a Concept*. In connection with this, see also Martin Sabrow and Norbert Frei's volume on the rise of the eyewitness in postwar discourse, *Die Geburt des Zeitzeugen*.

66 This split is also obvious for the reader, who has access to Nelson's thoughts and feelings, which reveal a side of him that is usually hidden. Menasse's

novel, or novelistic discourse more generally, is therefore established as a more intimate counterdiscourse to the public, highly mediatized discourse that normally surrounds Nelson.

67 Sontag, *Regarding the Pain of Others*, 94.
68 This is a term coined by Thomas Buergenthal, "International Law and the Holocaust."
69 The legal history of the concept of genocide is explored by Schabas in "The Law and Genocide."
70 Buergenthal, "International Law and the Holocaust," 18.
71 Langer, *Admitting the Holocaust*, 171.
72 Remmler, "Remembering Genocide in the Digital Age," 274.
73 Remmler, 85.
74 This and the following quotes from Donne's poem are taken from "An Anatomie of the World." For a short introduction to the genre of the "anniversary" see Roebuck, "The Anniversary Poem."
75 Donne, "An Anatomie of the World."
76 Kapczynski, "Never Over, Over and Over," 23.
77 This is the topic of Rothberg's most recent book, *The Implicated Subject: Beyond Victims and Perpetrators*. Previously, Rothberg published an article and a blog entry on the issue of implication: "Multidirectional Memory and the Implicated Subject" and "Trauma Theory, Implicated Subjects, and the Question of Israel/Palestine."
78 Rothberg, "Multidirectional Memory and the Implicated Subject," 40.
79 Rothberg, "Trauma Theory, Implicated Subjects and the Question of Israel/Palestine."
80 Rothberg.

Conclusion

1 Sicher, "'Tancred's Wound.'"
2 See, for example, Craps and Rothberg, "Introduction: Transcultural Negotiations of Holocaust Memory"; Craps, *Postcolonial Witnessing*; Rothberg, *Multidirectional Memory*; Silverman, *Palimpsestic Memory*; Levy and Sznaider, *Erinnerung im globalen Zeitalter*.
3 This is the focus of Craps, *Postcolonial Witnessing*; Rothberg, *Multidirectional Memory*; and Silverman, *Palimpsestic Memory*.
4 Huyssen, *Present Pasts*, 99.
5 See Erll and Rigney, eds., *Mediation, Remediation, and the Dynamics of Cultural Memory*; Tomsky, "From Sarajevo to 9/11."
6 Erll, "Travelling Memory"; Tomsky, "From Sarajevo to 9/11."
7 Rose, "Remains of the Day," 157.
8 Kapczynski, "Never Over, Over and Over," 23.
9 Garloff, "The Power of Paratext."

10 Hungerford, "Memorizing Memory"; Hungerford, *The Holocaust of Texts*.
11 Garloff, "The Power of Paratext."
12 Sontag, *Regarding the Pain of Others*, 94.
13 Rosenfeld, *Hi Hitler!*, 341.
14 Eshel, *Futurity*.

Bibliography

Aarons, Victoria, ed. *Third-Generation Holocaust Narratives: Memory in Memoir and Fiction*. Lanham, MD: Lexington Books, 2016.

Aarons, Victoria, and Alan L. Berger. *Third-Generation Holocaust Representation: Trauma, History, and Memory*. Evanston, IL: Northwestern University Press, 2017.

Achinger, Christine. "Allegories of Destruction: 'The Woman' and 'the Jew' in Otto Weininger's *Geschlecht und Charakter*." *Germanic Review* 88, no. 2 (June 2013): 121–49.

Adams, Jenni. *Magic Realism in Holocaust Literature: Troping the Traumatic Real*. Houndmills, Basingstoke, UK: Palgrave Macmillan, 2011.

Adorno, Theodor W. "Kulturkritik und Gesellschaft." In *Kulturkritik und Gesellschaft I: Prismen; Ohne Leitbild*, edited by Rolf Tiedemann et al., 11–30. Vol. 10.1. of *Theodor W. Adorno: Gesammelte Schriften*. Frankfurt am Main: Suhrkamp, 1977.

Alexander, Jeffrey. *Trauma: A Social Theory*. Cambridge, MA: Polity Press, 2012.

Alexander, Jeffrey, et al., eds. *Cultural Trauma and Collective Identity*. Berkeley: University of California Press, 2004.

Assmann, Aleida. "Canon and Archive." In *A Companion to Cultural Memory Studies*, edited by Astrid Erll and Ansgar Nünning, 97–108. Berlin: De Gruyter, 2010.

———. "Europe's Divided Memory." In Blacker, Etkind, and Fedor, *Memory and Theory in Eastern Europe*, 25–41.

———. "The Holocaust—a Global Memory? Extensions and Limits of a New Memory Community." In *Memory in a Global Age: Discourses, Practices, Trajectories*, edited by Aleida Assmann and Sebastian Conrad, 97–117. Houndmills, Basingstoke, UK: Palgrave Macmillan, 2010.

———. "Transnational Memories." *European Review* 22, no. 4 (October 2014): 546–56.

Assmann, Jan. *Das kulturelle Gedächtnis: Schrift, Erinnerung und politische Identität in frühen Hochkulturen*. 7th ed. Munich: C. H. Beck, 2013.

Baer, Alejandro, and Natan Sznaider. *Memory and Forgetting in the Post-Holocaust Era: The Ethics of Never Again*. London: Routledge, 2017.

Bailer-Galanda, Brigitte. "Vergangenheitspolitik in Österreich." In *Vergangenheitsbewältigung in Europa im 20. Jahrhundert*, vol. 1, edited by Heiner Timmermann, 63–74. Berlin: LIT Verlag, 2010.

Bakhtin, Mikhail. *The Dialogic Imagination: Four Essays*, edited by Michael Holquist; translated by Caryl Emerson and Michael Holquist. Austin: University of Texas Press, 1981.

———. "Discourse in the Novel." In *The Dialogic Imagination*, 259–422.

———. "Epic and Novel: Toward a Methodology for the Study of the Novel." In *The Dialogic Imagination*, 3–40.

———. *Problems of Dostoevsky's Poetics*. Edited and translated by Caryl Emerson. Manchester: Manchester University Press, 1984.

———. *Rabelais and His World*. Translated by Hélène Iswolsky. Bloomington: Indiana University Press, 1984.

Barthes, Roland. "The Reality Effect." In *The Rustle of Language*. Translated by Richard Howards, 141–48. Oxford: Basil Blackwell, 1986.

———. *S/Z: An Essay*. Translated by Richard Miller. New York: Hill and Wang, 1987.

Beck Shop. "Die Leinwand." Accessed August 1, 2019, https://www.beck-shode/stein-leinwand/product/29815?product=29815.

Beebee, Thomas Oliver, ed. *German Literature as World Literature*. New York: Bloomsbury, 2015.

Begley, Adam. "Colossus among Critics: Harold Bloom." *New York Times*, September 24, 1994. http://www.nytimes.com/books/98/11/01/specials/bloom-colossus.html.

Beßlich, Barbara. "Unzuverlässiges Erzählen im Dienst der Erinnerung: Perspektiven auf den Nationalsozialismus bei Maxim Biller, Marcel Beyer und Martin Walser." In *Wende des Erinnerns? Geschichtskonstruktionen in der deutschen Literatur nach 1989*, edited by Barbara Beßlich, Katharina Grätz, and Olaf Hildebrand, 35–52. Berlin: Erich Schmidt Verlag, 2006.

Biller, Maxim. *Biografie*. Cologne: Kiepenheuer & Witsch, 2016.

———. *Der gebrauchte Jude*. Frankfurt am Main: Fischer, 2009.

———. *Harlem Holocaust*. Afterword by Gustav Seibt. Cologne: Kiepenheuer & Witsch, 1998.

———. *Im Kopf von Bruno Schulz*. Cologne: Kiepenheuer & Witsch, 2013. Translated by Anthea Bell as *Inside the Head of Bruno Schulz*. London: Pushkin Press, 2015.

———. *Im Land der Väter und Verräter*. Frankfurt am Main: Fischer, 2010.

———. "Letzte Ausfahrt Uckermark." *Die Zeit Online*, February 20, 2014, http://www.zeit.de/2014/09/deutsche-gegenwartsliteratur-maxim-biller.

Blacker, Uilleam, Alexander Etkind, and Julie Fedor, eds. *Memory and Theory in Eastern Europe*. New York: Palgrave Macmillan, 2013.

Bloom, Harold. *The Anxiety of Influence: A Theory of Poetry*. New York: Oxford University Press, 1973.

Bolter, Jay David, and Richard Grusin. *Remediation: Understanding New Media*. Cambridge, MA: MIT Press, 2000.

Bond, Lucy. "Types of Transculturality: Narrative Frameworks and the Commemoration of 9/11." In Bond and Rapson, *The Transcultural Turn*, 61–80.

Bond, Lucy, and Jessica Rapson. "Introduction." In *The Transcultural Turn*, 1–26.

———, eds. *The Transcultural Turn: Interrogating Memory between and beyond Borders*. Berlin: De Gruyter, 2014.

Bond, Lucy, Stef Craps, and Pieter Vermeulen. "Introduction: Memory on the Move." In *Memory Unbound: Tracing the Dynamics of Memory Studies*, edited by Lucy Bond, Stef Craps, and Pieter Vermeulen, 1–26. New York: Berghahn, 2017.

Botz, Gerhard. "Die Waldheim-Affäre und ihre Folgen: Der Wandel von Österreichs kollektiven Erinnerungen (1986–2006)." In *Vergangenheitsbewältigung in Europa im 20. Jahrhundert*, vol. 1, edited by Heiner Timmermann, 75–92. Berlin: LIT Verlag, 2010.

Boym, Svetlana. *The Future of Nostalgia*. New York: Basic Books, 2001.

Brunow, Dagmar. *Remediating Transcultural Memory: Documentary Filmmaking as Archival Intervention*. Berlin: De Gruyter, 2015.

"Buch der Richter." In *Luther-Bibel: 1984 Edition*. Accessed September 15, 2019. https://www.die-bibel.de/online-bibeln/luther-bibel-1984/bibeltext/.

Buergenthal, Thomas. "International Law and the Holocaust." *Joseph and Rebecca Meyerhoff Annual Lecture*. United States Holocaust Memorial Museum, Washington, DC, October 28, 2003. https://www.ushmm.org/m/ pdfs/20050428-buergenthal.pdf.

Butler, Judith. *Frames of War: When Is Life Grievable?* New York: Verso, 2009.

Byrd, Ayana D., and Lori L. Tharp. *Hair Story: Untangling the Roots of Black Hair in America*. Revised and updated. New York: St. Martin's, 2014.

Caruth, Cathy. *Unclaimed Experience: Trauma, Narrative and History*. Baltimore: Johns Hopkins University Press, 1996.

Celan, Paul. "Todesfuge." In *Ausgewählte Gedichte: Zwei Reden*, 2nd ed., 18–19. Frankfurt am Main: Suhrkamp, 1969.

Chase, Jefferson. "Shoah Business: Maxim Biller and the Problem of Contemporary German-Jewish Literature." *German Quarterly* 74, no. 2 (Spring 2001): 111–31.

Chepp, Valerie, and Patricia Hill Collins. "Intersectionality." In *The Oxford Handbook of Gender and Politics*, edited by Georgina Waylen, Karen Celis,

Johanna Kantola, and S. Laurel Weldon, 57–87. Oxford: Oxford University Press, 2013.

Chrostowska, S. D. "'Masochistic Art of Fantasy': The Literary Works of Bruno Schulz in the Context of Modern Masochism." *Russian Literature* 55 (2004): 469–501.

Claims Conference. "Holocaust Knowledge and Awareness Study," accessed June 24, 2019, http://www.claimscon.org/wp-content/uploads/2018/04/Holocaust-Knowledge-and-Awareness-Study-%E2%80%93-Topline-Results-1-1.pdf.

Codrai, Bettina A. "Lost in Third Space? Narrating German-Jewish Identity in Maxim Biller's Autobiography *Der gebrauchte Jude* (2009)." *Jewish Culture and History* 14, nos. 2–3 (July–November 2013): 126–39.

Cooke, Paul, and Stuart Taberner, eds. *German Culture, Politics, and Literature into the Twenty-First Century: Beyond Normalization*. Rochester, NY: Camden House, 2006.

Cosgrove, Mary. *Born under Auschwitz: Melancholy Traditions in Postwar German Literature*. Rochester, NY: Camden House, 2014.

Costagli, Simone, and Matteo Galli, eds. *Deutsche Familienromane: Literarische Genealogien und internationaler Kontext*. Munich: Wilhelm Fink, 2010.

Costazza, Alessandro. "Benjamin Steins *Die Leinwand* oder über die (Un-) Möglichkeit (auto-)biographischen Schreibens." In *Logik der Prosa: Zur Poetizität ungebundener Rede*, edited by Astrid Arndt, Christoph Deupmann, and Lars Korten, 301–32. Göttingen: V&R unipress, 2012.

Craps, Stef. "Beyond Eurocentrism: Trauma Theory in the Global Age." In *The Future of Trauma Theory: Contemporary Literary and Cultural Criticism*, edited by Gert Buelens, Sam Durrant, and Robert Eaglestone, 45–61. London: Routledge, 2014.

———. *Postcolonial Witnessing: Trauma out of Bounds*. New York: Palgrave Macmillan, 2013.

Craps, Stef, and Michael Rothberg. "Introduction: Transcultural Negotiations of Holocaust Memory." *Criticism* 53, no. 4 (Fall 2011): 517–21.

Crownshaw, Rick. "The Future of Memory: Introduction." In *The Future of Memory*, edited by Rick Crownshaw, Jane Kilby, and Anthony Rowland, 3–15. New York: Berghahn, 2010.

———. "The Limits of Transference. Theories of Memory and Photography in W. G. Sebald's *Austerlitz*." In Erll and Rigney, *Mediation, Remediation, and the Dynamics of Cultural Memory*, 67–90.

———, ed. *Transcultural Memory*. London: Routledge, 2014.

Das Gupta, Oliver. "Als die Menschen Leim und Ratten aßen." *Süddeutsche Zeitung Online*, January 24, 2014, http://www.sueddeutsche.de/politik/blockade-von-leningrad-im-zweiten-weltkrieg-als-die-menschen-leim-und-ratten-assen-1.1872865.

Davies, Peter, and Andrea Hammel, eds. *New Literary and Linguistic Perspectives on the German Language, National Socialism, and the Shoah.* Rochester, NY: Camden House, 2014.

De Cesari, Chiara, and Ann Rigney, eds. *Transnational Memory: Circulation, Articulation, Scales.* Berlin: De Gruyter, 2014.

Deleuze, Gilles, and Leopold von Sacher-Masoch. *Masochism: Coldness and Cruelty & Venus in Furs.* Translated by Jean McNeil. New York: Zone Books, 1991.

Des Pres, Terrence. "Holocaust Laughter?" In *Writing and the Holocaust,* edited by Berel Lang, 216–33. New York: Holmes & Meier, 1988.

Diner, Dan. "Negative Symbiose: Deutsche und Juden nach Auschwitz." In *Ist der Nationalsozialismus Geschichte? Zu Historisierung und Historikerstreit,* edited by Dan Diner, 185–97. Frankfurt am Main: Fischer, 1987.

Donne, John. *An Anatomy of the World.* London: Printed for Samuel Macham, 1611. Republished as "An Anatomie of the World: The First Anniversary." In *The Poems of John Donne,* vol. 1: *The Text of the Poems with Appendixes,* edited by Herbert J. C. Grierson. Oxford Scholarly Editions Online, September 6, 2012. http://www.oxfordscholarlyeditions.com/view/10.1093/actrade/97 80199692378.book.1/actrade-9780199692378-div1-14.

Düwell, Susanne. *"Fiktion aus dem Wirklichen": Strategien autobiographischen Erzählens im Kontext der Shoah.* Bielefeld: Aisthesis, 2004.

Eaglestone, Robert. *The Holocaust and the Postmodern.* Oxford: Oxford University Press, 2004.

Eigler, Friederike. *Gedächtnis und Geschichte in Generationenromanen seit der Wende.* Berlin: Erich Schmidt, 2005.

Eke, Norbert Otto. "'Was wollen sie? Die Absolution?' Opfer- und Täterprojektionen bei Maxim Biller." In *Deutsch-jüdische Literatur der neunziger Jahre: Die Generation nach der Shoah,* edited by Sander L. Gilman and Hartmut Steinecke, 89–107. Berlin: Erich Schmidt, 2002.

Erll, Astrid. "Literatur als Medium des kollektiven Gedächtnisses." In *Gedächtniskonzepte der Literaturwissenschaft: Theoretische Grundlegung und Anwendungsperspektiven,* edited by Astrid Erll and Ansgar Nünning, 249–76. Berlin: De Gruyter, 2005.

———. "Literature, Film, and the Mediality of Cultural Memory." In Erll and Nünning, *A Companion to Cultural Memory Studies,* 389–98.

———. "Remembering across Time, Space, and Cultures: Premediation, Remediation and the 'Indian Mutiny.'" In Erll and Rigney, *Mediation, Remediation, and the Dynamics of Cultural Memory,* 109–38.

———. "Transcultural Memory." In *Encyclopédie critique du témoignage et de la mémoire,* April 21, 2014, http://memories-testimony.com/en/notice/transcultural-memory/.

———. "Travelling Memory." *Parallax* 17, no. 4 (October 2011): 4–18.

Erll, Astrid, and Ansgar Nünnin, eds. *A Companion to Cultural Memory Studies*. Berlin: De Gruyter, 2010.

Erll, Astrid, and Ann Rigney, eds. *Mediation, Remediation, and the Dynamics of Cultural Memory*. Berlin: De Gruyter, 2009.

Eshel, Amir. *Futurity: Contemporary Literature and the Quest for the Past*. Chicago: University of Chicago Press, 2012.

Felman, Shoshana, and Dori Laub. *Testimony: Crises of Witnessing in Literature, Psychoanalysis, and History*. London: Routledge, 1992.

Fischer, Torben, Philipp Hammermeister, and Sven Kramer, eds. *Der Nationalsozialismus und die Shoah in der deutschsprachigen Gegenwartsliteratur*. Amsterdam: Rodopi, 2014.

———. "Der Nationalsozialismus und die Shoah in der deutschsprachigen Literatur des ersten Jahrzehnts. Zur Einführung." In Torben, Hammermeister, and Kramer, *Der Nationalsozialismus und die Shoah*, 9–25.

Flanzbaum, Hilene, ed. *The Americanization of the Holocaust*. Baltimore: Johns Hopkins University Press, 1999.

Foer, Jonathan Safran. *Everything Is Illuminated*. London: Penguin, 2002.

———. *Tree of Codes*. London: Visual Editions, 2010.

Fox, Thomas C. "The Holocaust under Communism." In Stone, *Historiography of the Holocaust*, 420–39.

Frei, Norbert, and Volkhard Knigge, eds. *Verbrechen Erinnern: Die Auseinandersetzung mit Holocaust und Völkermord*. Munich: C. H. Beck, 2002.

Freud, Sigmund. "Jenseits des Lustprinzips." In *Sigmund Freud: Gesammelte Werke*, vol. 12: *Werke aus den Jahren 1920–1924*, edited by Anna Freud et al., 3–69. Frankfurt am Main: Fischer, 1999.

———. "Über Deckerinnerungen." In *Sigmund Freud: Gesammelte Werke*, vol. 1: *Werke aus den Jahren 1892–1899*, edited by Anna Freud et al., 531–54. Frankfurt am Main: Fischer, 1999.

Frieden, Kirstin. *Neuverhandlungen des Holocaust: Mediale Transformationen des Gedächtnisparadigmas*. Bielefeld: transcript, 2014.

Frisch, Max. *Mein Name sei Gantenbein*. Frankfurt am Main: Suhrkamp, 1964.

Fuchs, Anne. *Phantoms of War in Contemporary German Literature, Films and Discourse: The Politics of Memory*. Houndmills, Basingstoke, UK: Palgrave Macmillan, 2008.

Fuchs, Anne, Mary Cosgrove, and George Grote, eds. *Memory Contests: The Quest for Identity in Literature, Film and Discourse since 1990*. Rochester, NY: Camden House, 2006.

Fuchs, Anne, and Florian Krobb, eds. *Ghetto Writing: Traditional and Eastern Jewry in German-Jewish Literature from Heine to Hilsenrath*. Rochester, NY: Camden House, 1999.

———. "Writing the Ghetto—An Introduction." In Fuchs and Krobb, *Ghetto Writing*, 1–8.

Funk, Mirna. "Erinnern kann auch cool sein." *Die Zeit Online*, January 26, 2018, https://www.zeit.de/freitext/2018/01/26/holocaust-ns-zeit-erinnerungskultur/.

———. "Leichenberge, bäm!" *Die Zeit Online*, January 21, 2017, http://www.zeit.de/freitext/2017/01/21/yolocaust-shahak-shapira-erinnerungs kultur/.

Funk, Wolfgang, Florian Gross, and Irmtraud Huber. "Exploring the Empty Plinth: The Aesthetics of Authenticity." In *The Aesthetics of Authenticity: Medial Constructions of the Real*, edited by Wolfgang Funk, Florian Gross, and Irmtraud Huber, 9–21. Bielefeld: transcript, 2012.

Ganzenmüller, Jörg. "Ein stiller Genozid." *Die Zeit Online*, January 15, 2004, http://www.zeit.de/2004/04/A-Belagerung_L.

Ganzfried, Daniel. *. . . alias Wilkomirski—Die Holocaust-Travestie: Enthüllung und Dokumentation eines literarischen Skandals*, edited by Sebastian Hefti. Berlin: Jüdische Verlagsanstalt, 2002.

Garde-Hansen, Joanne, Andrew Hoskins, and Anna Reading, eds. *Save as . . . Digital Memories*. Houndmills, Basingstoke, UK: Palgrave Macmillan, 2009.

Garloff, Katja. "The Power of Paratext: Jewish Authorship and Testimonial Authority in Benjamin Stein's *Die Leinwand*." In McGlothlin and Kapczynski, *Persistent Legacy*, 141–55.

Garloff, Katja, and Agnes Mueller, eds. *German-Jewish Literature after 1990*. Rochester, NY: Camden House, 2018.

Geertz, Clifford. "Thick Description: Toward an Interpretive Theory of Culture." In *The Interpretation of Cultures*, 3–30. London: Fontana Press, 1993.

Geiger, Arno. *Es geht uns gut*. Munich: Hanser, 2005.

Geller, Jay Howard, and Leslie Morris, eds. *Three-Way Street: Jews, Germans, and the Transnational*. Ann Arbor: University of Michigan Press, 2016.

Genette, Gérard. *Palimpsests: Literature in the Second Degree*. Lincoln: University of Nebraska Press, 1997.

Gensing, Patrick. "Wie viele Schüler wissen vom Holocaust?" *Tagesschau*, January 31, 2019, https://www.tagesschau.de/faktenfinder/inland/holo caust-113.html.

Gilbert, Sandra M., and Susan Gubar. *The Madwoman in the Attic: The Woman Writer and the Nineteenth-Century Literary Imagination*. 2nd ed. New Haven, CT: Yale University Press, 2000.

Glasenapp, Gabriele von. "Deutsch-jüdische Ghettoliteratur." In *Handbuch der deutsch-jüdischen Literatur*, edited by Hans-Otto Horch, 407–21. Berlin: De Gruyter, 2015.

Gogos, Manuel. *Philip Roth & Söhne: Zum jüdischen Familienroman.* Hamburg: Philo, 2005.

Goldberg, Amos. "Ethics, Identity and Antifundamental Fundamentalism: Holocaust Memory in the Global Age." In *Marking Evil: Holocaust Memory in the Global Age*, edited by Amos Goldberg and Haim Hazan, 3–29. New York: Berghahn Books, 2015.

Goldfarb, David. "Appropriations of Bruno Schulz." *Jewish Quarterly*, June 16, 2011, http://jewishquarterly.org/2011/06/appropriations-of-bruno-schulz/.

Gow, Andrew Colin. *The Red Jews: Antisemitism in an Apocalyptic Age 1200–1600.* Leiden: E. J. Brill, 1995.

Granzin, Katharina. "Janusköpfiger Kollege aus Deutschland." *die tageszeitung*, December 21, 2013, http://www.taz.de/!418016/.

"Gravierende Wissenslücken zum Holocaust in Österreich," *DerStandard*, May 2, 2019, https://derstandard.at/2000102362845/Gravierende-Wissensluecken-ueber-den-Holocaust-in-Oesterreich.

Gruber, Julia. "Performing Family Identity, Memory and Hybridity in the Works of Eva Menasse." *Modern Languages Open*, December 5, 2017, https://www.modernlanguagesopen.org/articles/10.3828/mlo.v0i0.184/.

Gubser, Martin. *Literarischer Antisemitismus: Untersuchungen zu Gustav Freytag und anderen bürgerlichen Schriftstellern des 19. Jahrhunderts.* Göttingen: Wallstein, 1998.

Gwyer, Kirstin. "'You Think Your Writing Belongs to You?': Intertextuality in Contemporary Jewish Post-Holocaust Literature." *Humanities*, March 1, 2018, https://www.mdpi.com/2076-0787/7/1/20/htm.

Haines, Brigid. "Introduction: The Eastern European Turn in Contemporary German-Language Literature." *German Life and Letters* 68, no. 2 (April 2015): 145–53.

———. "Poetics of the 'Gruppenbild': The Fictions of Vladimir Vertlib." *German Life and Letters* 62, no. 2 (April 2009): 233–43.

Hakkarainen, Marja-Leena. "Melange of Memories: Negotiating Transcultural Identities in Eva Menasse's *Vienna*." *Orbis Litterarum* 66, no. 6 (December 2011): 468–86.

Hanika, Iris. *Das Eigentliche: Roman.* Munich: btb, 2010.

Hartley, L. *The Go-Between.* London: Penguin, 2004.

Hartman, Geoffrey, and Aleida Assmann. *Die Zukunft der Erinnerung und der Holocaust.* Konstanz: Konstanz University Press, 2012.

Hartz, Bettina. "Im Kopf von Maxim Biller." *Fixpoetry.com*, December 12, 2013, http://www.fixpoetry.com/feuilleton/kritiken/maxim-biller/im-kopf-von-bruno-schulz.

Hass, Gerhart. "Die deutsche Historiografie und die Belagerung Leningrads (1941–1944)." *Zeitschrift für Geschichtswissenschaft* 54, no. 2 (February 2006): 139–62.

Herf, Jeffrey. *Divided Memory: The Nazi Past in the Two Germanys.* Cambridge, MA: Harvard University Press, 1997.

Herrmann, Elisabeth, Carrie Smith-Prei, and Stuart Taberner, eds. *Transnationalism in Contemporary German-Language Literature.* Rochester, NY: Camden House, 2015.

Herrmann, Meike. *Vergangenwart: Erzählen vom Nationalsozialismus in der deutschen Literatur seit den neunziger Jahren.* Würzburg: Könighausen & Neumann, 2010.

H-German. "CFP: 5th Berlin Program Summer Workshop (Due February 2016)," February 11, 2016, https://networks.h-net.org/node/35008/discussions/111744/cfp-5th-berlin-program-summer-workshop-due-february-2016.

Hirsch, Marianne. *Family Frames: Photography, Narrative, and Postmemory.* Cambridge, MA: Harvard University Press, 1997.

———. "The Generation of Postmemory." *Poetics Today* 29, no. 1 (Spring 2008): 103–28.

———. *The Generation of Postmemory: Writing and Visual Culture after the Holocaust.* New York: Columbia University Press, 2012.

———. "Surviving Images: Holocaust Photographs and the Work of Postmemory." *Yale Journal of Criticism* 14, no. 1 (Spring 2001): 5–37.

Horstkotte, Silke. "'Ich bin, woran ich mich erinnere': Benjamin Steins *Die Leinwand* und der Fall Wilkomirski." In Fischer, Hammermeister, and Kramer, *Der Nationalsozialismus und die Shoah,* 115–32.

———. *Nachbilder: Fotografie und Gedächtnis in der deutschen Gegenwartsliteratur.* Cologne: Böhlau, 2009.

Hoskins, Andrew. "Anachronisms of Media, Anachronisms of Memory: From Collective Memory to a New Memory Ecology." In *On Media Memory: Collective Memory in a New Media Age,* edited by Motti Neiger, Oren Meyers, and Eyal Zandberg, 278–88. Houndmills, Basingstoke, UK: Palgrave Macmillan, 2011.

———. "Memory Ecologies." *Memory Studies* 9, no. 3 (July 2016): 348–57.

———. "The Restless Past: An Introduction to Digital Memory and Media." In *Digital Memory Studies: Media Pasts in Transition,* edited by Andrew Hoskins, 1–24. New York: Routledge, 2017.

———. "7/7 and Connective Memory: Interactional Trajectories of Remembering in Post-Scarcity Culture." *Memory Studies* 4, no. 3 (July 2011): 269–80.

Hudson, Jennifer A. "'No Hay Banda, and Yet We Hear a Band': David Lynch's Reversal of Coherence in *Mulholland Drive.*" *Journal of Film and Video* 56, no. 1 (Spring 2004): 17–24.

Hungerford, Amy. *The Holocaust of Texts: Genocide, Literature, and Personification.* Chicago: University of Chicago Press, 2003.

———. "Memorizing Memory." *Yale Journal of Criticism* 14, no. 1 (Spring 2001): 67–92.

Huyssen, Andreas. *Present Pasts: Urban Palimpsests and the Politics of Memory.* Stanford, CA: Stanford University Press, 2003.

Jahn, Bernhard. "Familienkonstruktionen 2005: Zum Problem des Zusammenhangs der Generationen im aktuellen Familienroman." *Zeitschrift für Germanistik* 16, no. 3 (2006): 581–96.

James, E. L. *Fifty Shades of Grey.* London: Arrow Books, 2012.

Janicka, Iwona. "Mapping the Father: The Application of Greimassian Semiotics to Bruno Schulz's *Sklepy Cynamonowe.*" *Welt der Slaven: Internationale Halbjahresschrift für Slavistik* 55 (2010): 45–66.

Jilovsky, Esther. *Remembering the Holocaust: Generations, Witnessing and Place.* London: Bloomsbury Academic, 2015.

Jilovsky, Esther, Jordana Silverstein, and David Slucki, eds. *In the Shadows of Memory: The Holocaust and the Third Generation.* London: Vallentine Mitchell, 2016.

Jones, Sara. *The Media of Testimony: Remembering the East German Stasi in the Berlin Republic.* New York: Palgrave Macmillan, 2014.

———. "Mediated Immediacy: Constructing Authentic Testimony in Audio-visual Media." *Rethinking History* 21, no. 1 (April 2017): 135–53.

———. "Testimony through Culture: Towards a Theoretical Framework." *Rethinking History* 23, no. 3 (June 2019): 257–78.

Kafka, Franz. *Die Verwandlung.* Edited by Ralf Kellermann. Stuttgart: Reclam, 2013.

Kalkbrenner, Anke. Review of *Survivors. Politics and Semantics of a Concept. H-Soz-u-Kult,* June 2015, https://www.h-net.org/reviews/showpdf. php?id=44591.

Kapczynski, Jennifer M. "Never Over, Over and Over." In McGlothlin and Kapczynski, *Persistent Legacy,* 19–32.

Kaplan, Ann E. *Trauma Culture: The Politics of Terror and Loss in Media and Literature.* New Brunswick, NJ: Rutgers University Press, 2005.

Käppeler, Christine. "'Mit Angst kenne ich mich aus.'" *Der Freitag,* November 11, 2013, https://www.freitag.de/autoren/christine-kaeppeler/mit-angst-kenne-ich-mich-aus.

Kennedy, Rosanne, and Maria Nugent. "Scales of Memory: Reflections on an Emerging Concept." *Australian Humanities Review* 59, April and May

2016, http://australianhumanitiesreview.org/2016/08/29/scales-of-memory-reflections-on-an-emerging-concept/.

Kilcher, Andreas B. "Einleitung." In *Metzler Lexikon der deutsch-jüdischen Literatur: Jüdische Autorinnen und Autoren deutscher Sprache von der Aufklärung bis zur Gegenwart*, edited by Andreas B. Kilcher, v–xx. Stuttgart: Metzler, 2000.

———. "Exterritorialitäten: Zur kulturellen Selbstreflexion der aktuellen deutsch-jüdischen Literatur." In *Deutsch-jüdische Literatur der neunziger Jahre: Die Generation nach der Shoah*, edited by Sander L. Gilman and Hartmut Steinecke, 131–46. Berlin: Erich Schmidt, 2002.

Kim, David D. *Cosmopolitan Parables: Trauma and Responsibility in Contemporary Germany*. Evanston, IL: Northwestern University Press, 2017.

Klier, John. "The Holocaust and the Soviet Union." In Stone, *The Historiography of the Holocaust*, 276–95.

Koepnick, Lutz. *On Slowness: Toward an Aesthetic of the Contemporary*. New York: Columbia University Press, 2014.

Krauss, Nicole. *The History of Love*. London: Penguin, 2006.

Krobb, Florian. "Reclaiming the Location: Leopold Kompert's Ghetto Fiction in Post-Colonial Perspective." In Fuchs and Krobb, *Ghetto Writing*, 41–53.

Krüger, Michael. "In jeder Ecke ein dicker Klumpen Angst." *Frankfurter Allgemeine Zeitung*, November 8, 2013, http://www.faz.net/aktuell/feuilleton/buecher/rezensionen/belletristik/maxim-biller-im-kopf-von-bruno-schulz-in-jeder-ecke-ein-dicker-klumpen-angst-12651360.html.

Kunisch, Hans-Peter. "Fernduell." *Die Weltwoche* 11, 2010, http://www.weltwoche.ch/ausgaben/2010-11/artikel-2010-11-literatur-fernduell.html.

LaCapra, Dominick. *Writing History, Writing Trauma*. Baltimore: Johns Hopkins University Press, 2001.

Landsberg, Alison. *Prosthetic Memory: The Transformation of American Remembrance in the Age of Mass Culture*. New York: Columbia University Press, 2004.

Langenhorst, Georg. "'Die erzählte Geschichte ist, was am Ende zählt': Postmoderne Spiegelungen jüdischen Lebens im literarischen Werk Benjamin Steins." *Communicatio Socialis* 46, no. 2 (2013): 164–82.

Langer, Lawrence L. *Admitting the Holocaust: Collected Essays*. New York: Oxford University Press, 1995.

Leo, Per. *Flut und Boden: Roman einer Familie*. Stuttgart: Klett-Cotta, 2014.

Levy, Daniel, and Natan Sznaider. *Erinnerung im globalen Zeitalter: Der Holocaust*. Frankfurt am Main: Suhrkamp, 2001.

Leys, Ruth. *Trauma: A Genealogy*. Chicago: University of Chicago Press, 2000.

"Literaturpreis Alpha 2014—Gewinnerin Eva Menasse." YouTube, November 11, 2014, online video recording, 3:02, https://www.youtube.com/watch?v=PMOF1M4EIVU.

Löffler, Sigrid. "Die Familie: Ein Roman, geschrumpft und gestückelt, aber heilig." *Literaturen* 6 (2005): 18–16.

Long, Jonathan. "Monika Maron's *Pawels Briefe*: Photography, Narrative, and the Claims of Postmemory." In *German Memory Contests: The Quest for Identity in Literature, Film, and Discourse since 1990*, edited by Anne Fuchs, Mary Cosgrove, and Georg Grote, 147–65. Rochester, NY: Camden House, 2006.

Luhmann, Niklas. "Weltkunst." In *Unbeobachtbare Welt: Über Kunst und Architektur*, edited by Niklas Luhmann, Frederick D. Bunsen, and Dirk Baecker, 7–45. Bielefeld: Haux, 1990.

Maechler, Stefan. *The Wilkomirski Affair: A Study in Biographical Truth*. New York: Schocken Books, 2001.

Mandel, Naomi. *Against the Unspeakable: Complicity, the Holocaust and Slavery in America*. Charlottesville: University of Virginia Press, 2006.

———. "Rethinking 'After Auschwitz': Against a Rhetoric of the Unspeakable in Holocaust Writing." *boundary 2* 28, no. 2 (Summer 2001): 203–28.

Mangold, Ijoma. "Alles ist eitel." *Die Zeit Online*, February 14, 2012, http://www.zeit.de/2013/08/Eva-Menasse-Quasikristalle.

———. "Grotesk wie der Tod." *Die Zeit Online*, November 16, 2013, http://www.zeit.de/2013/46/maxim-biller-im-kopf-von-bruno-schulz.

———. "Religion ist kein Wunschkonzert." *Die Zeit Online*, April 6, 2010, https://www.zeit.de/2010/15/Schriftsteller-Benjamin-Stein.

Mann, Thomas. *Der Tod in Venedig*. Frankfurt am Main: Fischer, 1992.

Markowitsch, Hans Jürgen, and Harald Welzer. *Das autobiographische Gedächtnis: Hirnorganische Grundlagen und biosoziale Entwicklung*. Stuttgart: Klett-Cotta, 2005.

McGlothlin, Erin. *Second-Generation Holocaust Literature: Legacies of Survival and Perpetration*. Rochester, NY: Camden House, 2006.

McGlothlin, Erin, and Jennifer M. Kapczynski, eds. *Persistent Legacy: The Holocaust and German Studies*. Rochester, NY: Camden House, 2016.

Meek, Allen. *Trauma and Media: Theories, Histories, and Images*. New York: Routledge, 2010.

Menasse, Eva. *Lässliche Todsünden*. Cologne: Kiepenheuer & Witsch, 2009.

———. *Quasikristalle*. Cologne: Kiepenheuer & Witsch, 2013.

———. *Tiere für Fortgeschrittene*. Cologne: Kiepenheuer & Witsch, 2017.

———. *Vienna*. Munich: btb, 2007. Translated by Anthea Bell as *Vienna*. London: Phoenix, 2007.

Morris, Leslie. *The Translated Jew: German Jewish Culture outside the Margins.* Evanston, IL: Northwestern University Press, 2018.

Moses, Dirk. "Does the Holocaust Reveal or Conceal Other Genocides? The Canadian Museum for Human Rights and Grievable Suffering." In *Hidden Genocides: Power, Knowledge, Memory,* edited by Alexander Laban Hinton, Thomas La Pointe, and Douglas Irvin-Erickson, 21–51. New Brunswick, NJ: Rutgers University Press, 2014.

———. "Genocide and the Terror of History." *Parallax* 17, no. 4 (October 2011): 90–108.

Moses, Dirk, and Michael Rothberg. "A Dialogue on the Ethics and Politics of Transcultural Memory." In Bond and Rapson, *The Transcultural Turn,* 29–38.

Müllender, Yannick. "Generationenkonzepte in zeitgenössischen österreichisch-jüdischen Romanen." *Journal of Austrian Studies* 46, no. 2 (Summer 2013): 23–47.

Neidlinger, Dieter, and Silke Pasewalk. "Die Redlichkeit des Betrugs—Literarische Erinnerung und Totalitarismus bei Herta Müller und Vladimir Vertlib." *Interlitteraria* 18, no. 2 (February 2013): 476–92.

Neiger, Motti, Oren Meyers, and Eyal Zandberg, eds. *On Media Memory: Collective Memory in a New Media Age.* Houndmills, Basingstoke, UK: Palgrave Macmillan, 2011.

New American Haggadah. Edited by Jonathan Safran Foer. Translated by Nathan Englander. New York: Little, Brown, 2012.

Niven, Bill. *Facing the Past: United Germany and the Legacy of the Third Reich.* London: Routledge, 2002.

Nolden, Thomas. *Junge jüdische Literatur: Konzentrisches Schreiben in der Gegenwart.* Würzburg: Könighausen & Neumann, 1999.

Oels, David. "'A Real-Life Grimm's Fairy Tale': Korrekturen, Nachträge, Ergänzungen zum Fall Wilkomirski." *Zeitschrift für Germanistik* 14, no. 2 (2004): 373–90.

Olterman, Philip. "'Yolocaust' Artist Provokes Debate over Commemorating Germany's Past." *Guardian,* January 19, 2017, https://www.theguardian.com/ world/2017/jan/19/yolocaust-artist-shahak-shapira-provokes-debate-over-commemorating-germanys-past.

Ortner, Jessica. "The German Jewish Migrant Novel after 1990: Politics of Memory and Multidirectional Writing." In Garloff and Mueller, *German-Jewish Literature after 1990,* 83–101.

Osborne, Dora. "Encountering the Archive in Katja Petrowskaja's *Vielleicht Esther.*" *Seminar* 52, no. 3 (September 2016): 255–72.

Perz, Bertrand. "Österreich." In Frei and Knigge, *Verbrechen Erinnern,* 150–62.

Petrowskaja, Katja. *Vielleicht Esther.* Frankfurt am Main: Suhrkamp, 2014.

Posener, Alan. "Maxim Biller will Thomas Mann zerstören." *Die Welt*, September 28, 2009, https://www.welt.de/kultur/article4654102/Maxim-Biller-will-Thomas-Mann-zerstoeren.html.

Prangel, Matthias. "Normale Familie: Ein Gespräch mit Eva Menasse." *literaturkritik.de*, May 21, 2008, http://literaturkritik.de/public/rezension.php?rez_id =11706.

Radstone, Susannah. "Trauma Theory: Contexts, Ethics, Politics." *Paragraph* 30, no. 1 (March 2007): 9–29.

———. "What Place Is This? Transcultural Memory and the Locations of Memory Studies." *Parallax* 17, no. 4 (October 2011): 109–23.

Remmler, Karen. "Remembering Genocide in the Digital Age: The Afterlife of the Holocaust in Ruanda." In McGlothlin and Kapczynski, *Persistent Legacy*, 271–89.

Rigney, Ann. "The Dynamics of Remembrance: Texts between Monumentality and Morphing." In Erll and Nünning, *Cultural Memory Studies*, 345–53.

Roca Lizarazu, Maria. "Liaisons Dangereuses—Nachbarn, (Mit-)Täter und 'implicated subjects' in Katja Petrowskajas *Vielleicht Esther*." In *Opfernarrative in transnationalen Kontexten/Victim Narratives in Transnational Contexts*, edited by Eva Binder, Christof Diem, Miriam Finkelstein, Sieglinde Klettenhammer, Birgit Mertz-Baumgartner, Marijana Milošević, and Julia Pröll. Berlin: De Gruyter, forthcoming.

———. "The Web, the Tree, the Palimpsest: Figures of Postmemory in Katja Petrowskaja's *Vielleicht Esther*." *Modern Language Review* 113, no. 1 (January 2018): 169–89.

Roca Lizarazu, Maria, and Rebekah Vince. "Memory Studies Goes Planetary: An Interview with Stef Craps." *Exchanges: The Interdisciplinary Research Journal* 5, no. 2 (Spring 2018): 1–15.

Roebuck, Graham. "The Anniversary Poem." In *The Oxford Handbook of John Donne*, edited by Jeanne Shami, Dennis Flynn, and M. Thomas Hester, 273–95. Oxford: Oxford University Press, 2011.

Rose, Gillian. "Beginnings of the Day—Fascism and Representation." In *Mourning Becomes the Law: Philosophy and Representation*, 41–62. Cambridge: Cambridge University Press, 1996.

Rosenfeld, Gavriel D. *Hi Hitler! How the Nazi Past Is Being Normalized in Contemporary Culture*. Cambridge: Cambridge University Press, 2015.

Roskies, David, and Naomi Diamant. *Holocaust Literature: A History and a Guide*. Waltham, MA: Brandeis University Press, 2012.

Rothberg, Michael. "From Gaza to Warsaw: Mapping Multidirectional Memory." *Criticism* 53, no. 4 (Fall 2011): 523–48.

———. *The Implicated Subject: Beyond Victims and Perpetrators*. Stanford, CA: Stanford University Press, 2019.

———. "Multidirectional Memory and the Implicated Subject: On Sebald and Kentridge." In *Performing Memory in Art and Popular Culture*, edited by Liedeke Plate and Anneke Smelik, 39–58. New York: Routledge, 2013.

———. *Multidirectional Memory: Remembering the Holocaust in the Age of Decolonization*. Stanford, CA: Stanford University Press, 2009.

———. "Trauma Theory, Implicated Subjects, and the Question of Israel/Palestine." *Profession*, May 2, 2014, https://profession.commons.mla.org/2014/05/02/trauma-theory-implicated-subjects-and-the-question-of-israelpalestine/.

Rothberg, Michael, and Yasemin Yildiz. "Memory Citizenship: Migrant Archives of Holocaust Remembrance in Contemporary Germany." *Parallax* 17, no. 4 (October 2011): 32–48.

Rowland, Anthony. "The Future of Testimony: Introduction." In *The Future of Memory*, edited by Rick Crownshaw, Jane Kilby, and Anthony Rowland, 113–21. New York: Berghahn, 2010.

Rudloff, Holger. *Gregor Samsa und seine Brüder: Kafka—Sacher-Masoch—Thomas Mann*. Würzburg: Könighausen & Neumann, 1997.

Ryland, Charlotte. "Re-Membering Adorno: Political and Cultural Agendas in the Debate about Post-Holocaust Art." *German Life and Letters* 62, no. 2 (April 2009): 140–56.

Sabrow, Martin, and Norbert Frei, eds. *Die Geburt des Zeitzeugen nach 1945*. Göttingen: Wallstein, 2012.

Sacher-Masoch, Leopold von. *Venus im Pelz*. Frankfurt am Main: Fischer, 2013.

Salzmann, Sasha Marianna. *Außer Sich*. Frankfurt am Main: Suhrkamp, 2017.

Sanyal, Debarati. *Memory and Complicity: Migrations of Holocaust Remembrance*. New York: Fordham University Press, 2015.

Schabacher, Gabriele. *Topik der Referenz: Theorie der Autobiographie, die Funktion "Gattung" und Roland Barthes' "Über Mich Selbst."* Würzburg: Könighausen & Neumann, 2007.

Schabas, William A. "The Law and Genocide." In *The Oxford Handbook of Genocide Studies*, edited by Donald Bloxham and A. Dirk Moses, 123–14. Oxford: Oxford University Press, 2010.

Schaff, Barbara. "Der Autor als Simulant authentischer Erfahrung: Vier Fallbeispiele fingierter Autorschaft." In *Autorschaft: Positionen und Revisionen*, edited by Heinrich Detering, 426–43. Stuttgart: Metzler, 2002.

Scheck, Denis. "Und Wieder ein Familienroman: Literaturkenner Denis Scheck über die Gewinner des Deutschen Buchpreises 2011." *Deutschlandfunk*, October 11, 2011. https://www.deutschlandfunk.de/und-wieder-ein-familienroman.691.de.html?dram:article_id=56148.

Schmitz, Helmut. *On Their Own Terms: The Legacy of National Socialism in Post-1990 German Fiction*. Birmingham: University of Birmingham Press, 2004.

Schuchmann, Kathrin. "'Unser Gedächtnis ist der wahre Sitz unseres Ichs': Erinnerung und Geschichte(n) in Benjamin Steins *Die Leinwand*." *Zagreber Germanistische Beiträge* 21 (2012): 201–20.

Schulz, Bruno. *Bruno Schulz: Das graphische Werk 1892–1942*. Munich: dtv, 2000.

———. *Die Zimtläden*. Translated into German, with an afterword, by Doreen Daume. 4th ed. Munich: Deutscher Taschenbuch Verlag, 2014. Translated into English by Celina Wieniewska as *Cinnamon Shops, and Other Stories*. London: MacGibbon & Kee, 1963. English translation also published as *The Street of Crocodiles*. New York: Walker, 1963. Originally published as *Sklepy cynamonowe*. Warsaw: Towarzystwo wydawnicze "Rój," 1934.

Seemann, Daphne. "Moving beyond Post-Traumatic Memory Narratives: Generation, Memory and Identity in Doron Rabinovici, Robert Menasse and Eva Menasse." *Austrian Studies* 19 (2011): 157–72.

———. "The Re-Construction and Deconstruction of a Family Narrative: Eva Menasse's *Vienna*." In *Transitions: Emerging Women Writers in German-Language Literature*, edited by Valerie Heffernan and Gillian Pye, 35–51. Amsterdam: Rodopi, 2013.

Shen, Dan. "Unreliability." In *The Living Handbook of Narratology*, June 27, 2011, http://www.lhn uni-hamburg.de/article/unreliability.

Sicher, Efraim. "'Tancred's Wound': From Repression to Symbolization of the Holocaust in Second-Generation Narratives." *Journal of Modern Jewish Studies* 5, no. 2 (January 2006): 189–201.

Silverman, Max. *Palimpsestic Memory: The Holocaust and Colonialism in French and Francophone Fiction and Film*. New York: Berghahn, 2013.

Sontag, Susan. *On Photography*. New York: Farrar, Straus and Giroux, 1978.

———. *Regarding the Pain of Others*. London: Penguin, 2003.

Sorg, Reto, and Michael Angele. "Selbsterfindung und Autobiographie: Über Wahrheit und Lüge im außermoralischen Sinne am Beispiel von Binjamin Wilkomirskis *Bruchstücke: Aus einer Kindheit 1939–1948*." In *Lese-Zeichen: Semiotik und Hermeneutik in Raum und Zeit; Festschrift für Peter Rusterholz*, edited by Henriette Herwig, Irmgard Wirtz, and Stefan B. Würffel, 325–45. Tübingen: Francke, 1999.

Souchuk, Anna, and Julia Gruber, eds. "Reading between the Bloodlines: Reflections on the German-Language Family Story." *Modern Languages Open*, 2017, https://www.modernlanguagesopen.org/collections/special/german-special-collection-2017/.

Stein, Benjamin. *Das Alphabet des Juda Liva*. Munich: dtv, 1998.

———. "Der Autor als Seelenstripper." *Turmsegler* (blog), posted June 3, 2010, http://turmsegler.net/20100603/der-autor-als-seelenstripper/.

———. "Familiengeschichte." *Turmsegler* (blog), posted June 14, 2010, http://turmsegler.net/20100614/familiengeschichte/.

———. "Glossar." *Turmsegler* (blog), posted July 15, 2009, http://turmseg ler.net/ 20090715/glossar/.

———. *Die Leinwand.* Munich: C. H. Beck, 2010. Translated by Brian Zumhagen as *The Canvas.* Rochester, NY: Open Letter, 2012.

Stier, Oren Baruch. *Committed to Memory: Cultural Mediations of the Holocaust.* Amherst: University of Massachusetts Press, 2009.

Stone, Dan, ed. *The Historiography of the Holocaust.* Houndmills, Basingstoke, UK: Palgrave Macmillan, 2004.

Straub, Julia. "Introduction: The Paradoxes of Authenticity." In *Paradoxes of Authenticity: Studies on a Critical Concept,* edited by Julia Straub, 9–29. Bielefeld: transcript, 2012.

Stuhlpfarrer, Karl. "Österreich." In Frei and Knigge, *Verbrechen Erinnern,* 233–52.

Taberner, Stuart. *German Literature of the 1990s and Beyond: Normalization and the Berlin Republic.* Rochester, NY: Camden House, 2005.

———. "Transnationalism and Cosmopolitanism: Literary World-Building in the Twenty-First Century." In Herrmann, Smith-Prei, and Taberner, *Transnationalism in Contemporary German-Language Literature,* 43–64.

———. *Transnationalism and German-Language Literature in the Twenty-First Century.* London: Palgrave, 2017.

———. "Vladimir Vertlib, *Das besondere Gedächtnis der Rosa Masur*: Performing Jewishness in the New Germany." In *Emerging German-Language Novelists of the Twenty-First Century,* edited by Stuart Taberner and Lyn Marven, 32–45. Rochester, NY: Camden House, 2011.

Teufel, Annette, and Walter Schmitz. "Wahrheit und 'subversives Gedächtnis': Die Geschichte(n) von Vladimir Vertlib." In Vladimir Vertlib, *Spiegel im fremden Wort: Die Erfindung des Lebens als Literatur; Dresdner Chamisso Poetikvorlesungen 2006,* 201–53. Dresden: Thelem, 2007.

Tomlinson, John. *The Culture of Speed: The Coming of Immediacy.* Los Angeles: SAGE Publications, 2007.

Tomsky, Terri. "From Sarajevo to 9/11: Travelling Memory and the Trauma Economy." *Parallax* 17, no. 4 (2011): 49–60.

Torrey, Charles C. "Apocalypse." In *Jewish Encyclopedia,* accessed September 16, 2019, http://www.jewish encyclopedia.com/articles/1642-apocalypse.

USC Shoah Foundation. "Dimensions in Testimony," accessed June 26, 2019, https://sfi.usc.edu/dit.

Vertlib, Vladimir. *Das besondere Gedächtnis der Rosa Masur* (2001). 3rd ed. Munich: dtv, 2007.

————. *Spiegel im fremden Wort: Die Erfindung des Lebens als Literatur; Dresdner Chamisso Poetikvorlesungen 2006.* Dresden: Thelem, 2007.

Vertovec, Steven. *Transnationalism.* New York: Routledge, 2010.

Weber, Armin. "'Jedes einzelne Bild nur ein Mosaikstück?' Zur Funktion des Erzählens in Eva Menasses Werken." *Weimarer Beiträge* 61, no. 1 (2015): 46–62.

Weigel, Sigrid. "Familienbande, Phantome und die Vergangenheitspolitik des Generationendiskurses: Abwehr von und Sehnsucht nach Herkunft." In *Generationen: Zur Relevanz eines wissenschaftlichen Grundbegriffs,* edited by Ulrike Jureit and Michael Wildt, 108–26. Hamburg: Hamburger Edition, 2005.

————. *Genea-Logik: Generation, Tradition und Evolution zwischen Kultur- und Naturwissenschaften.* Munich: Wilhelm Fink, 2006.

Weissman, Gary. *Fantasies of Witnessing: Postwar Efforts to Experience the Holocaust.* Ithaca, NY: Cornell University Press, 2004.

Welsch, Wolfgang. "Transculturality: The Puzzling Form of Cultures Today." In *Spaces of Culture: City, Nation, World,* edited by Mike Featherstone and Scott Lash, 194–213. London: SAGE Publications, 1999.

Wertsch, James V. "Collective Memory." In *Memory in Mind and Culture,* edited by James V. Wertsch and Pascal Boyer, 117–37. Cambridge: Cambridge University Press, 2009.

————. "Collective Memory and Narrative Templates." *Social Research: An International Quarterly* 75, no. 1 (Spring 2008): 133–56.

————. "Deep Memory and Narrative Templates: Conservative Forces and Collective Memory." In *Memory and Political Change,* edited by Aleida Assmann and Linda Shortt, 173–85. Houndmills, Basingstoke, UK: Palgrave Macmillan, 2012.

Whitehead, Anne. "Telling Tales: Trauma and Testimony in Binjamin Wilkomirski's *Fragments.*" *Discourse* 25, nos.1–2 (Winter–Spring 2003): 119–37.

Wickert, Ulrich. "Auschwitz ist zu oft Bezugspunkt." *Die Welt,* February 9, 2012, http://www.welt.de/print/die_welt/literatur/article113501207/Auschwitz-ist-zu-oft-Bezugspunkt.html.

Wilkomirski, Binjamin. *Bruchstücke: Aus einer Kindheit 1939–1948.* Frankfurt am Main: Suhrkamp, 1997. Translated by Carol Brown Janeway as *Fragments: Memories of a Wartime Childhood.* New York: Schocken Books, 1995.

Wogenstein, Sebastian. "Topographie des Dazwischen: Vladimir Vertlibs *Das besondere Gedächtnis der Rosa Masur,* Maxim Billers *Esra* und Thomas Meineckes *Hellblau.*" *Gegenwartsliteratur: Ein germanistisches Jahrbuch* 3 (2004): 71–96.

Yerushalmi, Yosef H. *Zakhor: Jewish History and Jewish Memory*. Seattle: University of Washington Press, 1982.

Young, James E. *Writing and Rewriting the Holocaust: Narrative and the Consequence of Interpretation*. Bloomington: Indiana University Press, 1988.

Zauzmer, Julie. "Two Thirds of US Millennials Do Not Know What Auschwitz Is." *Independent*, April 13, 2018, https://www.independent.co.uk/news/ world/americas/auschwitz-us-millennials-not-know-nazi-concentration-camp-a8302476.html.

Zipes, Jack. "The Contemporary German Fascination for Things Jewish: Toward a Minor Jewish Culture." In *Reemerging Jewish Culture in Germany: Life and Literature since 1989*, edited by Sander L. Gilman and Karen Remmler, 15–45. New York: NYU Press, 1994.

Žižek, Slavoj. *Welcome to the Desert of the Real*. London: Verso, 2002.

Films Mentioned

Fiddler on the Roof. Directed by Norman Jewison. United Artists, 1971.

Holocaust. Directed by Marvin J. Chomsky. Television miniseries, 4 episodes. NBC, 1978.

Im Keller. Directed by Ulrich Seidl. Neue Visionen Filmverleih, 2014.

Mulholland Drive. Directed by David Lynch. Universal Pictures, 2001.

Nuit et Brouillard. Directed by Alain Resnais. Argos Films, 1956.

Schindler's List. Directed by Steven Spielberg. Universal Pictures, 1993.

Shoah. Directed by Claude Lanzmann. Les Films Aleph, 1985.

Yentl. Directed by Barbra Streisand. Metro-Goldwyn-Mayer, 1983.

Index